Re-Appropriating
"Marvelous Fables"

12-25-2013

Heather & Jim,

I hope you guys enjoy the book. Merry Christmas and a Happy New Year!

Blessings,

Neil

Re-Appropriating "Marvelous Fables"

Justin Martyr's Strategic Retrieval of Myth in *1 Apology*

NOËL WAYNE PRETILA

Foreword by
Fr. David Vincent Meconi, S.J.

PICKWICK *Publications* · Eugene, Oregon

RE-APPROPRIATING "MARVELOUS FABLES"
Justin Martyr's Strategic Retrieval of Myth in *1 Apology*

Pickwick Publications
An Imprint of Wipf and Stock Publishers
199 W. 8th Ave., Suite 3
Eugene, OR 97401

www.wipfandstock.com

ISBN 13: 978–1–62564–095–6

Cataloging-in-Publication data:

Pretila, Noël Wayne

Re-appropriating "marvelous fables" : Justin Martyr's strategic retrieval of myth in 1 Apology / Noël Wayne Pretila

xviii + 166 p. ; 23 cm. —Includes bibliographical references.

ISBN 13: 978–1–62564–095–6

1. Justin, Martyr, Saint. 2. Christian literature, early—History and criticism. 3. Myth. I. Title.

BR1720 J8 P75 2014

Manufactured in the U.S.A.

This book is dedicated in part to the late David Phillips whose untimely passing over seven years ago has been a constant reminder to me of how fragile life is. I will always be grateful for how much he influenced the trajectory of my life by introducing me to the wonderful world of theology. In many ways, I consider this book an extension of the fruit of his labor. But above all, I dedicate this work to my incredible wife, Jennifer, who has demonstrated extraordinary patience, love, and support throughout the entire crafting of this monograph. Words really cannot express how much I appreciate the sacrifices she has made along the way in order for me to pursue a career in theology. It is my hope that I can somehow adequately return the favor in this lifetime.

Contents

Tables

Figures

Foreword

THERE IS NO POSITIVE usage of the term *mythos* in the New Testament. The first followers of Jesus were clearly mistrustful about the use of stories and characters that were not grounded in historical realities of God's chosen people. The New Testament authors thus came to contrast perni-cious *mythos* with life-giving *logos* or *aletheia*, the truth which alone could set one free (cf. 1 Tim 4:4–7; 2 Tim 4:4; Tit 1:14; 2 Pet 1:16). Centuries later, we still hear Origen warn his readers that only those who seek truth above all are given the grace to flee from myth and its many entanglements (cf. *Contra Celsum* 8.66). Bishop Augustine even went so far as to draw from his own experience as a student in pagan schools to caution against the use of Roman myth. These stories deform the passions of the young (cf. *Confessions* 1.16.25), and prove to be nothing more than machinations of the fallen demons who try to allure the unsuspecting with fanciful tales and elaborate word play (cf. *City of God* 18.13). The lines had become clearly set: the Christian Church proclaimed one narrative, a life-giving account of the power of Jesus, and the pagans had their stories, moribund tales of deceit and destruction.

As Noël Pretila sets out to show in the following pages, however, envi-sioning the early Christians' understanding of myth in this way now seems overly-facile and misleading. While such binary accounts, a clear "us" ver-sus "them," may make teaching the history of ideas a bit easier, it is rarely without serious scholarly shortcomings. For against this standard explana-tion of the use of myth in late antiquity, Pretila places Justin, the second century philosopher from Flavia Neopolis.

A hybrid between the pagan learning he acquired throughout his youth and the Christianity he later came to embrace, Justin saw in the governing stories of Hellenism, powerful apologetic possibilities. With great schol-arly delicacy and an appreciation for the Greek nuance, Pretila deftly slices between Justin's synchronic incorporation and exclusion of non-Christian myth. Pretila thus shows exactly how and where Justin uses these "marvelous fables" of Athens as an invitation for others to see the universal and timeless power of Christ to attract through stories that catch the human heart's desire for new life and beatitude. But then Dr. Pretila just as skillfully shows where Justin distances himself from Hellenic epics, arguing how demons use such fables to win innocent seekers over to their own prideful malevolence. As such, Pretila's great contribution is to show us modern readers how a second century Christian philosopher espied in the cultural milieu of his day the exact struggle which marks the church's very life in any culture—namely, how to encounter the divine in the world without ever being subsumed into the world.

With an intellect more spacious than any maltreatment or attack against him and his Church, Justin could write during the height of persecution that anyone who lived in accord with logos was already a Christian. This was true of Heraclitus, true of Socrates. In his subversive reading of Greek culture, Justin thereby appropriated all truth for Jesus Christ, arguing that the stories upon which Graeco-Roman culture had been built, can be read as refractions of the one and only true God. As Pretila deftly shows, Justin detects hints of the paschal mystery in the Greek poets' stories of death and resurrection. Like a skilled Greek wrestler, Justin uses the very literary moves which might otherwise cause harm against the faith in service of the faith, twisting and turning, reinterpreting and rereading, all traces of truth as instances of Christ's universal power.

Yet in this world-friendly approach to pre-Christian culture, Justin is as equally insistent (if not more so) that myth can also be a very powerful tool of Christ's enemies. Pretila therefore shows why a majority of the *First Apology* (§30–53) is dedicated to weaning the Greeks off their own poets and epics and inviting them to see in Moses and Prophets the true precursors to God's incarnation in this world. Here is the new chosen race, the Jewish people to whom God first comes. Pretila illumines this move by showing how Justin employs the same typological reading to both Hellenic as well as Hebraic literature: while Moses and the Prophets may be more trustworthy than the poets of Athens, in varying degrees and with varying levels of insight, all authors of truth are in some way serving Christ by preparing his way. In such a welcomed reading of Justin, Pretila carefully shows the means by which Justin judges some non-Christian stories worthy of appropriation and why others must be shunned as too insidious to entertain. In this diverse use of myth, Pretila is also able to answer questions of Justin's intent, audience, and pedagogy.

Justin Martyr inaugurated a glorious legacy of Christian apologetic. He did this neither by naively believing his culture's defining stories, nor by simply shunning them outright (as his disciple Tatian would do). Instead, Justin simultaneously displays a prudence which weaves what it can for Christ, as well as a courage which forbids what is dangerous into his church's story. As such, the pages that follow collect and commemorate beautifully the opening chapter of Christian philosophy and the church's post- apostolic engagement with culture.

Fr. David Vincent Meconi, S.J.

Preface

1 APOLOGY HAS BEEN understood by traditional scholarship as written by Justin Martyr to an external audience consisting of educated pagans and/or the emperor himself. With this as an assumption, Justin's mythical allusions have been viewed as nothing more than volleys aimed at undercutting paganism. But the paradigm has changed of late with now an internal audience (i.e., Christians) in view as the recipients of 1 Apology. If this is the case, why these allusions to pagan narrative when his audience has already abandoned the ancestral religion for Christianity?

To answer this question, I am arguing that Justin is actually leveraging these once revered pagan religious narratives of his now Christian audience for the purpose of either strengthening their current faith and/or providing them direction on how to use this form of religious discourse (i.e., myth) in their discussions to those outside of Christianity. I have identified three particular strategies Justin employs in appropriating myth in this fashion.

First, Justin takes advantage of his reader's simultaneous suspicion and reverence of myth. I assert that Justin was merely tapping into an established pagan hermeneutic of ancient poetry which is best exemplified in Hesiod's *Theogony* where the Muses boast about the whimsical nature in which they would inspire him as a poet, "We know how to say many lies that are similar to the true things, and we know how to speak true things, when we wish." In light of this love/hate approach to myth Justin's audience would have been most certainly trained, this study seeks to transform the traditional categorization of "positive" and "negative" use of myth attributed to Justin and instead replace it with more dynamic categories of "incorporation of myth" and "separation of myth."

Second, Justin employs a *guarded* typological framework as it relates to myth discussing how much of the details surrounding the story of Christ resonated with those of the stories of the sons of Zeus (*ad similia*). But he establishes such a relationship with the ultimate end of demonstrating how the aspects of Christ's story surpass those of his pagan counterparts both in quality and in greatness (*a fortiori*). In fact, I will argue in this paper that this typological framework encompasses the whole of *1 Apology*—providing the modern reader a coherent flow and rhythm to a text that has been often been scrutinized by scholarship as being "disorganized."

Finally, Justin's mythical allusions are characteristically short yet the entire story behind the brief mentioning would have brought the entire story to the forefront of his ancient reader's memory—something missed by most modern readers. This work goes about reconstructing those silent elements that Justin's ancient reader would have included in the typology. In order to provide substantiation to the selection of these elements, I will be employing what I call "a typology trajectory"—a safeguard which serves to limit the number of parallels a modern reader can propose. That is, one can only make connections based upon the biblical testimony of the life and ministry of Jesus that Justin provides us in *1 Apology*.

Acknowledgments

THIS WORK WAS MADE possible through the support and guidance of Professors Kenneth Steinhauser, David Meconi, and Peter Martens; I learned so much from them throughout this entire process—from discussing with them at the very beginning nothing more than a handful of curious ideas to now the crafting of this fully completed study. The lessons I learned from these gentlemen through each successive stage of the project—I will carry with me for the rest of my life.

I would like to thank many of my academic colleagues within the Saint Louis University Department of Theological Studies who were always willing to allow me to wrestle through my thoughts via the many impromptu conversations we had over meal and/or merriment. This collegiality was characteristic of this department and perhaps the most gratifying aspect of my doctoral experience. I would especially like to single out fellow PhD colleague Rob Rexroat for not only taking special interest in my project but his willingness to comb through my manuscript and provide insightful feedback.

I would also like to convey my special appreciation to Aaron Atsma the developer of the online mythological database known as www.theoi.com. This robust, well-organized database proved to be perhaps my most invaluable resource allowing me to fluidly interact with the sea of primary source material in this ancient literary genre.

1

Introduction

JUSTIN MARTYR'S VARIED USE of Greco-Roman myth within his writings has led to conflicting opinions regarding the apologist's overall attitude to these primeval stories. As such, scholars have had difficulty reconciling how Justin could allude to these "marvelous fables" in a positive light when throughout his writings he categorically denounced them on the grounds of their diabolical origin and purpose.[1] The solutions that have been proffered to resolve this dilemma range from viewing these troublesome allusions as only ostensibly positive in nature to declaring that the contradiction in his approach to myth is the unfortunate result of Justin's rambling prose.

THESIS AND PROBLEM

Unlike previous scholarly assessments of Justin Martyr's use of Greco-Roman mythology, I will contend that his varied use of myth as seen in *1 Apology* reveals a form of pedagogy in which the apologist intentionally incorporated certain aspects of these popular religious narratives and yet was able to declare Christianity's separation from the ancient tradition. Although Justin perceived in these mythical pre-figurations a wealthy resource of images that could serve the purpose of illuminating Christian dogma in the minds of recent converts still feeling out their newfound faith, his critical assessment of these myths (e.g., that a majority were demonically

---

1. In their critical edition of *1 Apology*, Minns and Parvis translate τερατολογίαν as "marvelous fables" (*1 Apol.* 54.2)—a colorful way in which Justin described the nature of the μυθοποιηθέντα or "myths invented by the poets" (*Justin, Philosopher and Martyr*, 218–19).

1

inspired) begged of his audience to hasten their abandonment of these corrupted pre-figurations in favor of the pure, unadulterated ones found within Moses and the Prophets.

This dynamic form of pedagogy is confirmed by the structural flow of *1 Apology* (Table 1.1) itself where Justin's first sustained treatment of myth (§21–22) is primarily in the vein of *ad similia* with the apologist's incorporating myth to illuminate his description of Christ. This is then followed by a section (§23–29) where Justin focused solely upon separation from myth so to signal his readers that they must transfer their trust from the narratives of the ancestral religion to Moses and the Prophets—even if elements within these myths hinted at the eventual arrival of the Logos. This shift begins in chapter 30 where Justin devoted a massive block of material (§30–53) to demonstrate how the anticipation of Christ's incarnation was most visibly apparent within the writings of Moses and the Prophets. Although mythical allusions are altogether sparse within this section, it is my contention that there exists a typological interaction between the pagan foreshadowings that Justin previously established in the first section (§21–22) with this section (§30–53) thereby demonstrating a subtle form of incorporation of myth at work. Finally, Justin concluded his strategy by employing a decisive separation from myth altogether in chapters 54 through 66. In this last movement, Justin repeated the montage of mythical analogies he established in chapters 21 and 22 but this time went at great lengths to expose the diabolical origin behind these Greco-Roman religious narratives.[2]

Table 1.1
Flow of Myth Related to Christology in 1 Apology

chapters	flow of myth
§ 1- 20	NONE
§ 21- 22	Incorporation & Partial Separation
§ 23- 29	Full Separation
§ 30- 53	Incorporation & Partial Separation
§ 54- 66	Full Separation

2. Prigent, *Justin et l'Ancien Testamente*, 160: "Dans le chapitre 21 Justin veut montrer que les grandes affirmations de la foi chrétienne (la naissance virginale du Christ, se crucifixion, sa mort, se résurection et son ascension) ne demandent aux païens aucun sacrificium intellectus: leurs dieux ne connaissent-ils pas des destinées souvent comparables? Par exemple : 1)Hermès; 2) Asclépios; 3) Dionysos; 4) Héraclès; 5) Les Dioscures; 6) Persée; 7) Bellérophon . . . Les mêmes matériaux sont encore repris ultérieurement dans la première Apologie (chapitre 54), mais Justin leur fait server une intention différente: Il s'agit cette fois de montrer que les mythes grecs sont les imitations, diaboliques et falslifées, des prophéties christologiques."

Furthermore, in order to show how Justin's diverse use of myth reveals a pattern of pedagogy, I am departing from the traditional historiography that assumes Justin wrote *1 Apology* for an external pagan audience either pleading for benevolence on behalf of Christians or making a case for educated pagans to convert to Christianity.[3] Rather, I am adopting the newer theory that Justin wrote *1 Apology* for the purpose of educating an internal Christian audience.[4] In this framework, Justin strategically utilized myth as a form of *paidea* to strengthen the nascent faith of his once mythologizing students so as to arm them with arguments they could then utilize later when confronted by their pagan detractors.[5] Although the fully developed theory that *1 Apology* was a document primarily meant for internal Christian consumption has been around for more than a decade now, there has been no work to date that explores the didactic possibilities of Justin's usage of myth when this newly proposed audience is taken into account.

Utilizing myth as a form of *paidea* was not unique to Justin. His Christian predecessors provided a model to incorporate mythical allusions

3. In terms of the time period this project is covering, I am aware that the use of the word *pagan* (from Latin *paganus*, meaning "country dweller") is anachronistic, as it was a pejorative term coined much later during the reign of Christendom to call superstitious those who continued to hold on to the practices of the ancient, Greco-Roman polytheistic religion. I am, therefore, using the term "pagan" as a convenient adjective to describe followers of the ancient polytheistic religion during Justin's time that certainly were considered within the norm of society.

4. What gives this theory even greater support is that scholars like Tcherikover have argued that the apologies of ancient Jewish thinkers like Artapanus, Aristobulus, and Philo (which came to strongly influence later Christian apologists) should not be understood as propaganda aimed at Greeks and Romans but rather texts that were meant to be posed to Alexandrian Jews thinking about leaving their ancient faith: "This tendency to extol Judaism resulted from an inner need so characteristic of educated Jewish circles in Egypt. Those Jews who approached Hellenistic civilization by all possible ways and were influenced by it in their way of life and thought, found it easier to cling to Judaism as long as they knew that Judaism stood on an equal level with Hellenism" ("Jewish Apologetic Literature," 180).

5. In Andresen's groundbreaking work, *Logos und Nomos,* he argues that the entirety of Celsus famous diatribe, *The True Logos,* was a direct response to Justin's *Apologies* although Celsus never mentions the apologist by name. Andresen argues that Celsus not mentioning Justin's name was an intentional move on the part of the pagan critic meant to insult the memory of the Christian apologist as a form of *damnatio memoriae;* that is, Justin's arguments were so ridiculous to Celsus that his name was not even worthy of being mentioned (q.v., *Logos und Nomos,* 363). On the other hand, Osborn argues that Justin's arguments rapidly became "the common property of all Christians through whom it would be disseminated far and wide" and were so popular by the time they reached Celsus that they had most likely lost their attribution (*Justin Martyr,* 170). It is interesting to note that Osborn's theory fits well with the premise that *1 Apology* was intended for an internal audience who then in turn freely promulgated their master's arguments in their own encounters with educated pagans.

for the purpose of strengthening the faith of new believers. For instance, Mark Edwards argues that Luke deliberately brought up Paul's numerous encounters with paganism in *Acts of the Apostles* (e.g., being mistaken as Zeus in Lystra [Acts 14], his preaching in the Aeropagus [Acts 17]) for the purpose of assuaging the anxiety recent converts naturally began to experience because they had left the ancient religion. By orienting the Pauline theme of Christian supercession as it relates to paganism, Luke exemplified to his internal audience how Christian belief was superior to belief in the pagan gods.[6] I will demonstrate in this study that Justin's use of myth in *1 Apology* was driven by a similar impulse to that of the apostolic writer, Luke: to prevent recent Christian converts from reverting back to the ancient religion. He would do so in a much more advanced manner than his predecessor through his extensive as well as dynamic interaction with the wealthy resource of mythical symbols replete in the collective memory of his followers.[7]

By virtue of reinforcing his new converts of the supremacy of Christian belief over and against the ancient religion they had just freshly renounced, Justin would also go on to surpass Luke's use of these pagan narratives by laying down a model to his students of how to share their newfound faith in the language and symbols of ancient myth in which their culture was immersed.

Regarding the intent behind the creation of these myths, Justin Martyr's candor in declaring their demonic origin and purpose cannot be denied. At least once in each of his three extant treatises, Justin explicitly reckoned them as pernicious inventions of demons meant to lead humankind astray from the eventual incarnation of the Logos.[8] The following, for example, serves as a worthy representative of such an assessment:

6. Edwards, "Introduction: Apologetics," 5–6: "[A]s writers of texts intended for insiders inevitably have to wrestle with doubts and uncertainties felt by members, simply because they too reflect the values and assumptions of society at large."

7. While there were Christian thinkers who preceded Justin in mentioning myth within their works (e.g., Luke [Paul's sermon at the Areopagus], Clement of Rome [the Phoenix], and Aristides the Apologist), he was the first Christian writer who displayed the willingness to name the poet (i.e., Homer) to which a myth belonged, "so führen uns nun die Werke Justins erneut um einen erheblichen Schritt weiter: Zum ersten Mal in der christlichen Literatur begegnen hier sowohl der Name des Dichters als auch Zitate aus seiner Dichtung" (Glockmann, *Homer in der frühchristlichen Literatur*, 115). The passages in Justin's works that mention Homer are *1 Apol.* 18.5 and *2 Apol.* 10.6.

8. This assessment is found in *2 Apology* 4.5–6, where Justin connects the proliferation of pagan myth to the Jewish Enochic tradition surrounding Genesis 6: "Hence it is that poets and storytellers, not knowing that the things which they have recorded were done to men and women and cities and nations by the angels and the demons they begot, attributed these things to the god himself and to the sons who were begotten

> For when [the demons] heard through the prophets that the
> future coming of Christ was proclaimed and that the impious
> among human beings were going to be punished by fire, they
> threw many so-called sons of Zeus into the discussion, consider-
> ing that they would be able to bring it about that human beings
> would consider the things said about Christ to be a marvelous
> fable, and similar to the things said by the poets.[9]

Refrains similar to the example cited here appear on six different occasions in the *1 Apology* alone. Hence, Justin's constant repetition of the harmful function behind the myths in his initial apology has played no small
part in having convinced scholars such as Henry Chadwick to conclude that
Justin possessed a "sharply negative" attitude towards Greco-Roman myth.[10]

Yet in contrasting fashion, we also see instances where the apologist
seemed to place myth in a positive light. A textbook example of this is seen
in chapters 21 and 22 of *1 Apology* where Justin brings to the reader's attention characteristics the so-called sons of Zeus shared with that of Christ:
extraordinary births, the rendering of benevolent service towards humanity,
dying, and eventually rising to the heavens.

Scholars have sought to explain such variability in Justin's overall approach to myth. Carlos Contreras asserts that the apologist was just being
"flagrantly inconsistent" in his overall stance towards myth—clearly violat-
ing his own explicit disavowal of mythology.[11] Therefore, Contreras dismisses this phenomenon as simply the unfortunate byproduct of a disorganized
writing style that has been characteristic of Justin's works.[12] Chadwick, on
the other hand, harmonizes this dissonance by stating, "Justin is not afraid
of these analogies. He can even use them to argue that Christianity is so

---

as if from him by the sowing of seed and from those who were called his brothers and
their children as well. For they—that is, the poets and storytellers—called them by the
names which each of the angels gave to himself and to his children." This assessment is
also found in *Dialogue with Trypho* 69.1 where Justin responds to Trypho's objection
that certain Christian doctrines resemble pagan myth: "My knowledge of the Scriptures
and my faith in them have been well confirmed by the things which he who is called
the Devil counterfeited in the fictions circulated among the Greeks." In *1 Apology*, this
theme is repeated on six different occasions by Justin: 21.4, 23.3, 25.3, 54.1–10, 56.1,
and 64.1–10.

9. *1 Apology* 54.2

10. Chadwick, *Early Christian Thought*, 11.

11. Contreras, "Christian Views of Paganism," 978–79.

12. Examples of this critique of Justin's writing style can be detected in Quasten and
Barnard. For instance, Quasten states, "The style of [Justin's] works is far from pleasant.
Not accustomed to adhere to a well-defined plan, Justin follows the inspiration of the
moment" (*Patrology*, 197). Barnard laments, "Justin is a somewhat rambling writer and
does not systematize his material carefully" (*First and Second Apologies*, 133n166).

nearly indistinguishable from the myths of paganism that it is inexplicable that it should be singled out for persecution by the government."[13] In other words, Chadwick argues that Justin never had the illumination of Christian doctrine in mind when establishing these analogies; rather, these contrived parallels served as mere "*ad hominem* debating points" aimed at disarming a pagan audience accustomed to persecuting Christians on the charge that their religion was a mere novelty.[14]

Although Contreras and Chadwick provide straightforward explanations that make Justin's diverse handling of myth comprehensible to the modern reader, it is my contention that both these solutions are somewhat inadequate. With regards to Contreras' stance, what the modern eye may perceive as a disjointed approach towards myth—have been deemed as such by Justin's ancient readers? No, as Justin's varied approach to myth should not be understood as inconsistent as Contreras has proposed; rather, Justin was merely tapping into an established pagan hermeneutic of ancient poetry where simultaneous suspicion yet reverence of these primeval stories was already in vogue (this phenomenon will be dealt with at further length later in this chapter).

With regards to Chadwick's stance, did Justin actually view these discernible parallels between the "so-called" sons of Zeus and the Christian Son of God analogies of his own making as Chadwick seems to contend? Here, too, I argue in the negative for in revisiting *1 Apol.*54.2 Justin announced that these perceptible similarities were of diabolical origin, "For when [the demons] heard through the prophets that the future coming of Christ was proclaimed . . . they threw many so-called sons of Zeus into the discussion." So in the apologist's estimation, he was not responsible for thinking up these parallels between the sons of Zeus and the Christian Son of God but rather he was in the business of observing where and when they occurred.

But going back to the objection of Contreras, were there any conventions within the classical world that shared a comparable "simultaneous receptivity and hostility" or incorporation yet separation towards the work of the Poets?[15] I offer below a brief preview of three such cases that I will be

13. Chadwick, "Justin Martyr's Defence of Christianity," 284–85.

14 Martindale is also in agreement with Chadwick that Justin has only *ad hominem* in mind when making these analogies: "[Justin] argued purely *ad hominem*. He said: You ought not to accuse us of telling incredible stories about Christ, such as His Virgin Birth, because you tell quite as strange things about your own heroes and gods; moreover, said he, you place these miraculous episodes in atrocious settings, and, even in the actual episode, immortality of hideous and unnatural sorts is often in-woven" (*St. Justin the Martyr*, 125–26).

15. Norris, *God and World*, 43.

building upon throughout this work: (1) the ancient response to the inspiration of the Muses, (2) the typological tendencies within pagan literature, and (3) the ancient expectations placed on philosophers regarding the poets. It is my hope that by establishing these parallels, I can demonstrate that Justin's diverse approach to myth was not considered an unusual phenomenon to his ancient audience and thereby opening up a fresh reconsideration of what Justin was attempting to accomplish in his interactions with these ancient stories.

ANCIENT RESPONSE TO INSPIRATION OF THE MUSES

It was commonly held in the pagan world that the source of inspiration behind the work of the poets were the Muses, the nine daughters of Zeus and Mnemosyne (Memory) who were the patronesses of poetry and music.[16] While revered as the divine impetus behind the creative genius of the likes of Homer and Hesiod, it was also paradoxically understood that these goddesses often fed well-crafted mistruths to the poets. The classic proof-text demonstrating such a sentiment within the ancient world is found in Hesiod's proem of the *Theogony*.[17] In it, Hesiod recalled that upon their initiation of him into the role of poet on Mt. Helicon the Muses openly boasted about the whimsical nature by which they would transmit their revelations, "We know how to say many lies that are similar to the true things, and we know how to speak true things, when we wish."[18]

---

16. Macpherson, *Four Ages of Man*, 187. Macpherson points out that while the Greeks viewed that all nine muses collectively inspired the entirety of the arts without distinction, it was the Romans who would assign definitive artistic roles to each: Calliope (epic poetry), Clio (history), Euterpe (flute-music), Terpsichore (dance), Erato (lyric poetry), Melpomene (tragedy), Thalia (comedy), Polyhymnia (rhetoric), and Urania (astronomy).

17. Thalmann, *Conventions of Form and Thought in Early Greek Epic Poetry*, 149–52.

18. Hesiod, *Theogony, Works and Days, Testimonia*, 27–8. Lantana theorizes that Hesiod was referring to the works of Homer as containing "lies that are similar to the true things" while his own work upheld truth: "Si ammette in genere che l'espressione 'menzogne simili alla verità' vada riferita alla poesia omerica : di fronte allo splendido quadro omerico della vita della società cavalleresca nel medioevo ionico, che contrastava così duramente con l'esperienza quotidiana di una vita tanto più misera ed angusta, legata a valori profondamente diversi, Esiodo avrebbe sentito e condannato la poesia omerica come menzogna, investendo se stesso delle divina missione di annunciatore della 'verità,' e mostrendosi così come il prime sostenitore di una concezione 'didascalica' della poesia" (*Poetica Pre-Platonica*, 24). On the other hand, Pietro Pucci argues that Hesiod's firsthand knowledge of the Muses' operations did not preclude him from experiencing their notorious deception: "It is indeed a remarkable proof of his faith that, having exposed the doubleness of the Muses' *logos*, Hesiod feels neither

There was, thus, a wide spectrum of how the philosophers in the ancient world accounted for this acknowledged co-mixture of truth and falsehood within poetry[19] ranging from outright rejection (e.g., Xenocrates and Zoilus of Amphipolis) to toleration by viewing these false mythical elements within poetry as clever teaching devices that helped proliferate truthful ideas (e.g., Strabo and Aristotle).[20] Yet according to the classical scholar Pietro Pucci, the common person in the ancient world resigned themselves to embracing this "doubleness" within poetry as the inherent risk that came with receiving this gift from the gods, "The odd nature of the divine gift deserves our attention because it constitutes the 'mythical' foundation and explanation for the ambiguous quality of the Muses' *logos* . . . In contrast to human gifts—which are desirable, precious, and generally dispensable—the gift of the gods assumes a curiously paradoxical quality."[21] As it was understood that Zeus' gifts paradoxically brought forth benefit as well as harm to its recipients (e.g., the creation of Pandora), his daughters' gift of poetry were of similar "mixed value" combining both true and mythical accounts the difference of which humanity could not ironically discern without the aid of the Muses themselves.[22]

Building upon Pucci's divine gift theory, classical scholars William Thalmann and George Walsh provide two additional insights stemming from ancient poetry's accepted "doubleness" that can aid us in deciphering Justin's own murky approach to myth. Thalmann states that the false,

---

excessive alarm nor wariness. Only the Muses can know if their discourse is truth of a lie disguised as truth, but Hesiod does not seem apprehensive. Yet he should. For the reader perceives that the doubleness of the Muses' *logos* affects even the song of Hesiod" (*Hesiod and the Language of Poetry*, 1).

19. An excellent, succinct outline of ancient philosophers who argued for and against the mythic elements within poetry can be found in a chapter of Feeney's *Gods in Epic* called "The Critics: Beginnings, and a Synthesis" (q.v., Feeney, *The Gods in Epic*, 5–56).

20. Strabo the historian argued that because the *Odyssey* was ultimately a geographical lesson that, "Homer must be excused . . . if he mixed fantastic elements in his stories because they are meant to inform and instruct" (*Geography*, 1.73). While the Stoic philosophers argued that deep, spiritual truths could be mined from these spectacular accounts via the allegorical method, Aristotle in his *Poetics* felt that a criteria of truth and falsehood was altogether irrelevant when it came to these poems due to a télος or purpose stating that "it is all right if the poem thereby achieves what it aims at, that is, if in this way the surprise produced either by that particular passage or by another is striking. An example is the pursuit of Hector" (Feeney, *Gods in Epic*, 28–9).

21. Pucci, *Hesiod and the Language of Poetry*, 3.

22. Ibid., 8–13. Another classical scholar, Thalmann, also remarks, "Poetry is presented as a divine gift, with the mixed value typical of all such gifts. The Muses, as we have seen, are no different after all from other divinities; they deal out their favors arbitrarily" (*Conventions of Form and Thought in Early Greek Epic Poetry*, 149).

mythical elements the Muses infused within poetry were deemed acceptable within ancient Greco-Roman society because without this gift of "mixed value" it was conceded that humanity would be deprived of an, "act of mediation between man and god, by which man is granted knowledge that would normally be denied him."[23] In other words, the ancients believed receiving this form of divine revelation, notwithstanding its deceptive elements, was better than receiving nothing at all from the gods. Therefore, Justin's varied approach to myth should not be understood as inconsistent as Contreras has proposed; rather, Justin was merely tapping into an established pagan hermeneutic of ancient poetry where simultaneous reverence and suspicion of these primeval stories was in vogue.

But according to Walsh, even the false, mythical elements were never categorically discounted by the ancients, "If lies are like 'real things,' and if these things are the subject of the song, it seems possible that an audience can learn something from the Muses' lies since the likeness of lies and facts suggest that lies are only partly deceptive."[24] Such an example of this propensity can be seen in the unique approach specifically employed by the poet Stesichorus (640—555 BC) that may shed some light on what Justin was attempting to do in his own interaction with myth.[25] According to Plato's *Phaedrus* (243a), Stesichorus wrote a poem that followed the traditional Homeric narrative explaining Helen's presence in Troy the result of her misdeeds as an adulteress and husband-deserter. But shortly after penning this account, Stesichorus was struck with blindness of which he believed was Helen's punishment for his complicity in passing on the erroneous Homeric narrative regarding her life.

In a desire to recover his sight as well as set the record straight, Stesichorus composed a *palinode* or recantation that honored Helen by declaring she never went to Troy but rather an "image" (εἴδωλον) of her did so instead,

---

23. Ibid., 151.

24. Walsh, *The Varieties of Enchantment*, 26–27.

25. My primary argument here is not that Justin was directly influenced by Stesichorus but rather that there was a classical precedent that corroborates his movement of separation and incorporation of myth thereby giving weight to the notion that Justin's audience would have not found his approach a novelty. Still, there are several clues in Justin's works that betray that he probably was aware of this revisionist tactic of Stesichorus: (1) Justin brings up a woman named Helen that was considered the first thought that emanated from the Gnostic Simon (*1 Apol.* 26.3). Although Justin's allusion does not tell us much about this Helen, Irenaeus in *Against the Heretics* 1.23.2 elaborates in more detail regarding this same Helen stating that the Gnostics believed that she was a reincarnation of the same Helen who struck Stesichorus blind. (2) Justin demonstrates an extensive firsthand knowledge of Plato's *Phaedrus*, which is incidentally the source from which the legendary story of Stesichorus is originally recorded.

"That story is not true, you did not go in the well-decked ships, nor did you come to the citadel of Troy."[26] After the composition of the *palinode* to Helen, Stesichorus sight was miraculously restored, which was taken as a sign of Helen's vindication.

If one closely inspects Stesichorus' revisionism of the life of Helen, one can pick up a movement of separation from the ancient tradition resembling that of Justin Martyr's. Classical scholar Denis Feeney describes the explicit, as well as, implicit claims at work within this approach to Greco-Roman poetry:

> Stesichorus, then, surveys his (already multivocal) tradition, and not only disassociates himself from this tradition, but also from an early production of his own which the tradition had led him to compose. He explicitly denounces that 'version' or 'story' (logoς) as not 'true' (etumoς), thereby implicitly asserting that his new version *is* 'true.'[27]

As Stesichorus explicitly exposed what in his estimation were lies originally transmitted by the Muses to tarnish the reputation of the virtuous queen of Sparta, Justin in similar fashion declared that the stories of the Greek gods were deceptive imitations fabricated to dishonor the Logos. But the deconstruction of the traditional account is only one part of the equation for both Stesichorus and Justin. As Feeney so insightfully points out, Stesichorus' approach is also reconstructive in nature as he ended up implicitly affirming that his version of Helen's story (although at first glance a novelty) was actually the older and truer account that the Muses in their arbitrariness initially decided to withhold. According to Feeney, Stesichorus' prayer at the beginning of his *palinode* is most likely a beckoning to the Muses to divinely assist him in his revisionist project, "Hither, again, goddess, lover of song."[28] If this be the case as Feeney suggests, then "Stesichorus is indulging in a feat of tremendous panache, calling upon the Muse, the guarantor of poets' 'truth,' to collaborate with him in setting right the version which the two of them had earlier given the world."[29]

It helps our thesis to see how Justin shared a similar outlook to the pagan world regarding the inherent "doubleness" of truth and falsehood contained within the writing of the poets. But he would, of course, abandon the classical notion that the Muses were those responsible for this phenomenon (in fact, he never once mentioned the Muses in his writings) by recasting

26. Page, *Poetae melici Graeci*, 192.

27. Feeney, *Gods in Epic*, 15.

28. Page, *Poetae melici Graeci*, 193.

29. Feeney, *Gods in Epic*, 15–16.

whom he believed to be the two actual sources at work behind the poets: (1) the Logos and (2) the Demons. For Justin, all that was considered truthful within the poets was promulgated by the Logos (2 *Apol.* 13.2–3) while all the deceptive elements contained therein he attributed to the demons (*1 Apol.* 54.2). So unlike Stesichorus who believed that the Muses had to be persuaded to rectify false accounts they originally set into motion, Justin argued that the Logos was sent to remedy lies as well (i.e., the stories of mythical gods) the propagation of which it was not responsible for.

In another sense, though, even the myths fashioned by the demons could be understood as the property of the Logos, albeit stolen and then perversely re-shaped. I contend that while Stesichorus simply substituted the previous Homeric account of Helen's life with his own rendition, Justin's act of replacement was far more sophisticated. The Christian apologist actually sought to reverse myth's deceitful effects by exploiting the very parallels meant to hinder Christian belief: unveiling the truth regarding these demonic imitations and then, in turn, using this exposé as a form of corroborating evidence to argue that an ancient anticipation of the incarnation of the Logos indeed existed within pagan literature (albeit demonic). Jean Daniélou describes how Justin sought to reverse the effects of myth by transforming a stumbling block to faith into a stepping stone for it, "Mythology may be the work of demons, but the Fathers [Justin especially] still see it as the perversion of a primitive revelation, traces of which are preserved within it, in particular in the form of borrowings from the Bible, which represents the authentic version."[30]

TYPOLOGICAL TENDENCIES WITHIN PAGAN LITERATURE

It has been a common misconception that typology was a hermeneutical exercise developed exclusively within Christian circles as they attempted to establish continuity between the emerging New Testament as well as its predecessor, the Hebrew Scriptures. While it would be accurate to state that the Church's pursuit to connect these two sacred texts was a successful one, it would be inaccurate to say that the Christian tradition held a monopoly on this form of intertextual interpretation.[31]

---

30. Daniélou, *Gospel Message and Hellenistic Culture*, 75.

31. Frye, *The Great Code*, 80–90. Frye demonstrates the pervasiveness of the typological method arguing for its application even within non-Christian ideological histories such as Marxism and Judaism.

In fact, just a generation prior to the arrival of Christ (between 29 to 19 BC) Virgil penned the Roman epic poem, the *Aeneid*, which classical scholars have identified as possessing a remarkable typological correspondence with that of Homer's *Illiad* and *Odyssey*. John Taylor remarks, "Virgil is to Homer as the New Testament is to the Old. Authoritative texts from the past are reworked in a different language, and with a different message. These are our two supreme examples of intertextuality, the new texts empowered by the prolonged allusion to great predecessors."[32] In other words, as the New Testament writers sought to demonstrate the resemblance between their Lord with the venerable Old Testament figures such as Abraham, Moses, and David, Virgil did the same by comparing the great Trojan patron of the Julian household, Aeneas, to the Greek heroes such as Odysseus, Achilles, and Heracles.[33]

Virgil's *Aeneid* was a widespread text by the time Justin arrived on the scene, demonstrating to all Roman citizens how vanquished, "Greece . . . was for the Romans both a subservient colony and the ancient source of their own culture, with all the hierarchical implications of this dual identity."[34] As one can guess, the *Aeneid* accomplished what can be characterized as an incorporation and separation from Greek culture through the use of a typology possessing the twofold movement of (1) incorporation when Virgil linked characters or themes in his epic poem with that of Homer [*argumentum ad similia*] as well as a (2) separation when he then portrayed the character or theme in the *Aeneid* as surpassing its Greek predecessor [*argumentum a fortiori*] both in glory and honor.[35]

---

32. Taylor, *Classics and the Bible*, 85.

33. An exhaustive summary of the various typological connections between Homer's *Iliad* and *Odyssey* and Virgil's *Aeneid* can be found in a chapter of Leithart's *Heroes of the City of Man* called "*Patria* and *Pietas*: Virgil, *The Aeneid*" (q.v. *Heroes of the City of Man*, 213–272). A few of the more intriguing typological connections Leithart elaborates upon are: (1) the *Aeneid* is a retelling of the Homeric epics in reverse order with books 1–6 alluding to the *Odyssey* and books 7–12 alluding to the *Iliad*—a rhetorical move to signal similarity yet difference between these epics; (2) Aeneas' journey surpasses that of Odysseus in greatness because his is not a return, but a journey to an unknown place; (3) Virgil used the same Homeric description of Odysseus' Ithaca (*Odyssey* 13.109–117) to describe Dido's Carthage (*Aeneid* 1.217–233)—again, another rhetorical move by the poet to assert the greatness of Rome above both cities; (5) while Achilles and Odysseus motivations were solely for their personal glory and reputation, Aeneas emulates the noble attitude of the Trojan prince, Hector, being more concerned with protecting and preserving his community than with the attainment of personal glory.

34. Manguel, *Homer's the Illiad and the Odyssey*, 51–2.

35. Taylor, *Classics and the Bible*, 87–92.

The importance of the *Aeneid* is not so much that it prepared Justin's future audience to read texts typologically (the Jewish heritage had much to contribute here also)[36] but that Virgil's epic poem did so in relation *to myth*, thus forcing the reader to compare and contrast distinctive Roman stories of gods and heroes with that of their ancient Greek counterparts found in the *Iliad* and *Odyssey*. This is a crucial point because one of my fundamental arguments is that Justin employed typological exegesis to compare and contrast Greek myth with the narrative of the emerging New Testament (i.e., the Old Testament being read Christologically). Since Justin's learned Roman audience would have been familiar with Virgil's triumphalistic methodology towards Greek culture, I contend that they would have seen precisely how Justin, too, employed a typological framework akin to that of the great Latin poet.[37]

So while Christians and pagans concurrently exercised this form of intertexual exegesis with respect to their sacred writings (i.e., New Testament with Old Testament, Virgil with Homer), on what grounds can we posit that Justin crossed-over the religious divide by establishing typological correspondence between biblical teaching and pagan poetry? Is there any evidence from the 2nd century demonstrating that such a convention was at work within Justin's intellectual context? Such attestation does indeed exist in the form of Irenaeus' critique of the Gnostics whom this early church father accused of crafting *centos* or literary devices that weaved together disparate verses "plucked" (κέντρων) from Homer's poems to express a heretical Christian message.[38] Below is the cento that Irenaeus reproduced in *Against the Heretics* 1.9.4 (with Homeric references inserted)[39]:

36. Shotwell, *The Biblical Exegesis of Justin Martyr*, 12–20.

37. While I am arguing that Virgil's *Aeneid* played a pivotal role in preparing Justin's audience to typologically interact with Greek myth, it is interesting to note that there is not a single instance within Justin's writings where the apologist made a clear allusion to this renowned Roman poet. This is despite the fact that the *Aeneid* had been long translated into the Greek by Polybius, the freedman of Emperor Claudius according to Seneca (*To Polybius* 8.2; 10.2) and that many first- and second-century "Greek-speakers not only were familiar with Virgil, they held his works in high regard" (MacDonald, *Does the New Testament Imitate Homer?*, 9). Finally, the fact that Justin's headquarters was based in Rome in accordance to his testimony in the *Martyrdom of the Holy Martyrs* makes Justin's omission of Virgil's great epic to legitimate the Roman empire (a work he and his students in Rome would have been familiar) a glaring one. A hypothesis I would like to propose for this omission is that Justin deliberately ignored the great Roman epic as a discursive stratagem, forcing his reader to exchange this national antitype to Homer's writings that they had been raised upon (i.e., *Aeneid*) for an entirely new one (i.e., the Christian Scriptures).

38. Wilken, "The Homeric Cento in Irenaeus, 'Adversus Haereses' I, 9,4," 26.

39. It is important to note that the construction of centos did not originate from

Thus speaking, he sent forth from the house, deeply groaning
(*Odyssey* 10.76)
The man Hercules, conversant with mighty deeds (*Odyssey* 21.26)
Eurystheus, son of Sthenelos, of the seed of Perseus (*Iliad* 19.123)
To bring from Erebus the dog of hateful Pluto (*Iliad* 7.368)
And he came forth like a mountain lion, haughty in his strength (*Odyssey*
6.130)
Rapidly going through the city, while all his friends followed
(*Iliad* 24.327)
Both maidens and youth, and patient old men (*Odyssey* 11.38)
Lamenting him with pity as destined for death (*Iliad* 24.328)
But Mercury and gleaming-eyed Minerva escorted him
(*Iliad* 11.626)
For she knew well in her own mind the cares of her brother
(*Iliad* 2.409)[40]

Although Irenaeus never disclosed the cento's meaning, Daniélou theorizes that the poem was perhaps an attempt by the Gnostic Valentinus to illuminate the Christian teaching of the Father sending the Son to the depths of Hell in order to defeat death, an immense task that resembled the perilous missions of King Priam to the tent of Achilles and, even more similarly, Heracles and Odysseus' own expeditions into the realm of the dead.[41]

Intertexual cross-over, as demonstrated above, should therefore not come as a surprise given that an emerging Christian society in the second century, made up primarily of converts from paganism, would have been naturally inclined to perceive connections between the sacred texts on which they had been raised and the sacred texts they had just recently come to accept. So it is within the Gnostic centos such as the example furnished by Irenaeus that we get the first clear-cut expressions of Homeric poetry

Gnosticism, but were in existence early on within the classical tradition: "The preserved centos by Aristophanes and Petronius evidence that centos are likely appear in literature as soon as there exists a suitable prototext (indeed Homer may be regarded as the first ever prototext), and an educated reader (or even, as in the case of Aristophanes, listener-viewer)" (q.v. Stehlikova, "Centones Christiani as a Means of Reception.," 11).

40. Irenaeus, *Against the Heresies*, trans. Unger, 47–8.

41. Daniélou, *Gospel Message and Hellenistic Culture*, 85–6. There is differing opinions over the origin of this *cento* furnished by Irenaeus. Wilken argues that although it is certainly Gnostic in authorship that there is no way for us to know who exactly composed (q.v. "The Homeric Cento in Irenaeus," 29), while Heinrich Ziegler came to the conclusion that Irenaeus composed it by himself to provide an example of a Gnostic cento (q.v. *Irenaeus der Bischof von Lyon*, 17).

interacting typologically with Christian thought, though in an aberrant way according to the bishop of Lyon.

Although not explicitly labeling the cento as an exercise in typology, David Meconi provides an explanation of this literary device that supports the notion that it should be understood as such: "The cento is a curious construct of antiquity and contemporaneity: ancient in that it is formed wholly by canonical words of the revered past, contemporary because it meets its readers as an entirely new theme manipulated for current concerns and purposes never intended by the original author."[42] While it seems that the Gnostics were using these literary devices in full force by the second century, Meconi states that it took awhile for the first truly Christian *cento* to arrive upon the scene—not until the fourth century when a wealthy aristocratic woman, Faltonia Proba, (c. 320–370) composed one.[43]

This should immediately beg the question of why it took so long for the Christian community to incorporate the use of the *cento*. I contend that much of their reluctance probably stemmed from the early Gnostic use, or better yet abuse, of this literary device that perpetuated their notorious syncretistic tendencies towards paganism. Valentinus, for example, was known for calling Homer a Christian prophet—a proclamation that certainly drew the ire of ecclesiastical leaders of that time.[44] Therefore for a Christian to employ this form of poetry in the early centuries would have put them at risk of probably being considered a Gnostic. More germane to our discussion is to what degree did the prevalence of these Gnostic *centos* during Justin's time play a part in shaping his varied approach to myth? Although somewhat of a speculation, Justin's desire to combat the Gnostic tendency that fluidly merged pagan and Christian belief as demonstrated in their centos would be a plausible explanation behind why he so quickly followed up his incorporation of myth with a bold proclamation of his separation from it as well.

---

42 Meconi, "The Christian Cento and the Early Church's Appropriation of Prophet and Muse." Using the helpful categories previously established by Stehlikova (i.e., prototext, metatext), Meconi further asserts that centos were read on "two separate but ever-interpenetrating planes" (a trademark of typological exegesis), with the first plane, the *prototext*, the reader encountering Homeric phrases with which they would have been familiar followed by the second plane of the *metatext* that the reader's new literary tradition (i.e., Scripture) informed them how to newly understand these texts.

43. Meconi, "The Christian Cento and the Evangelization of Christian Culture," 109–32. Meconi asserts that the emergence of the centonic method within Christian circles was largely due to the rising Christian aristocracy's response to Emperor Julian's project to reinstitute paganism in the Roman Empire.

44. Daniélou, *Gospel Message and Hellenistic Culture*, 82.

ANCIENT EXPECTATIONS ON PHILOSOPHERS
REGARDING THE POETS

Perhaps a better sense of what Justin was doing with myth can also be ascertained if his diverse use of these ancient narratives was understood in the light of the ancient expectations placed upon his chosen vocation as philosopher. Justin's bearing of the *pallium* certainly set him apart from many of the other second-century Christian thinkers categorized as apologists for only a few among them were also considered professional philosophers by trade.[45] What is the significance of this distinction? Within the Greco-Roman world leading up to the time of Justin, a perception had emerged that an inextricable link existed between the ancient poets (e.g., Homer, Hesiod) and those who deemed themselves explicitly and solely as philosophers. While the work of the poets was seen as inspired by the gods, the philosophers were viewed as those who could cipher the myths for truth they did contain.[46]

By virtue of holding the occupations of both apologist and philosopher, Justin's diverse use of myth should therefore come to us as no surprise. As an apologist, he certainly sought to persuade his audience how Christian belief was superior to the Roman ancestral religion. Yet as a philosopher, Justin was expected to interact with the stories that served as the very fabric of the paganism he sought to eschew.[47] Myth was a form of religious dis-

45. Besides Justin, the only other two apologists who have been identified as being professional philosophers were Aristides (by Eusebius in *Eccles. Hist.* 4.3.2) and Athenagoras (as described in the title of his *Supplication for the Christians*). Although Tatian and Militiades do not qualify as professional philosophers, both were considered to be students of Justin's distinctive school of Christian philosophy (q.v. *Patrology*, 220–28).

46. Malherbe, "Athenagoras on the Pagan Poets and Philosophers," 216. This relationship between poet and philosopher described by Malherbe is corroborated by the testimony of the Stoic Philosopher, Cornutus, who argued a century prior to Justin that the earliest theology was transmitted by the poets via the use of myth: "One day you shall have a more perfect exegesis of the genealogy of Hesiod, who, in my view, took over some things from philosophers more ancient than himself, and added other things of his own in more mythical vein, whereby most of the ancient theology was destroyed" (Cornutus, *Theologiae Graecae compendium* 31.12, quoted in Woollcombe, "The Biblical Origins and Patristic Development of Typology," 52n2).

47. Wilken argues that Justin was successful in establishing Christianity as a competing philosophical school to the likes of Platonism and Stoicism. Wilken believes that the testimony of Galen, a pagan contemporary to Justin, as firm evidence of this: "[Galen] . . . is not much impressed by Christians he knew, but what he says about them is quite different from the earlier comments of Pliny, Tacitus, and Suetonius. Galen calls the Christians a philosophical school. He believes that as a school the Christians are quite inferior to other schools he had investigated, but that the important point is not whether Galen found Christian teaching superior but that he was willing to recognize

course by which his audience were raised upon from their youth in order to grasp concepts of the divine.[48] In other words, to ask a philosopher of Justin's time to expound about the divine without the use of this theological language (i.e., myth) would have been practically impossible and theoretically nonsensical.

There is no better example to demonstrate the pervasiveness of myth as the language of religious discourse than in the case of Plato where he explicitly banned the works of Homer from his ideal Republic. The great disciple of Socrates viewed poetry as the bane to any society because instead of encouraging men to experience the true and the good directly, relegated them to a mere vicarious experience of these qualities through the art of imitation. Despite this condemnation, even Plato as philosopher could not escape the discursive use of Homer of which Alberto Manguel aptly describes as the "unavoidable reference" in the ancient Greco-Roman world, "The paradox is apparent in Plato: for all of art's supposedly noxious influence, Homer retains pride of place in Plato's library, surfacing at every occasion to illuminate a passage or provide a poignant reference: there are 331 references to Homer and his works in Plato's *Dialogues*."[49]

I contend that Justin experienced a similar phenomenon as the philosopher whose teachings he deemed closest to that of Christianity (1 *Apol.* 59). While the apologist certainly took his stand to mark Christianity's separation from Greco-Roman myth, he, like Plato, could not avoid incorporating mythical references, the absence of which would have severely hampered his efforts to persuade minds saturated with these narratives.

DYNAMIC APPROACH TO MYTH

The explanations provided by Chadwick and Contreras therefore represent two poles of a long-standing debate in regards to whether Justin ultimately held a negative or positive attitude towards these pagan narratives.[50] It is my contention that this binary approach (i.e., negative versus positive) used by previous scholarship to help explain and clarify the confusion surrounding Justin's diverse use of myth has been a major source of the problem. By

the Christian movement as a school at all" ("Toward a Social Interpretation of Early Christian Apologetics," 447–48). By establishing Christianity as a legitimate philosophy and himself as the teacher of this school, Justin would have been under the general expectation to interact with myth.

48. Lamberton, *Homer the Theologian*, 189.

49. Manguel, *Homer's the Illiad and the Odyssey*, 35–41.

50. I provide a full discussion of this scholarship in the portion of my literature review on "Justin's Approach to Mythology."

trying to conform the entirety of Justin's mythical allusions into mutually exclusive categories pertaining to his overall attitude of them (i.e., negative or positive), the dynamism in his approach towards these pagan stories has gone relatively ignored.[51] It is my contention that the three cases I have explored above regarding the Muses, typology, and philosophers and poets in the ancient world give weight to a dynamic approach to myth in the thought of the apologist.

In order to hasten a departure from this way of understanding Justin's use of myth, it is important that the terminology needs to be modified. Instead of using the term "negative" to describe instances where Justin is critical of myth, this work will use the expression "Justin's separation from myth" in its place; in lieu of the word "positive" to characterize occasions where the apologist looks favorably upon myth, the phrase "Justin's incorporation of myth" will be used instead. This altered phraseology is important as it shifts the emphasis from determining *how* Justin viewed myth (i.e., negative or positive) to investigating *what* Justin sought to accomplish in making these allusions to myth: separate or incorporate. It is my contention that when seen from this dynamic movement of incorporation and separation, the continuum of mythical allusions in *1 Apology* renders an observable pattern of pedagogy.

LITERATURE REVIEW OF JUSTIN'S APPROACH TO MYTHOLOGY

In this survey of literature, there are three schools of thought I have identified upon which this project shall build upon: (1) Justin's complete denigration of myth [Carl Andresen], (2) Justin's partial denigration of myth [Günter Glockmann], and (3) Justin's dynamic incorporation and separation of myth [Jean Daniélou, Peter Widdicombe].

Justin's complete denigration of myth

In the problem statement, I argued that the binary approach (i.e., negative versus positive) that has been historically utilized by scholarship to determine Justin's overall attitude to myth has proved to be counterproductive. A key figure whose ideas have come to perpetuate this approach amongst

---

51. The only monograph to my knowledge to entertain a positive and negative tension in Justin's approach to myth is by Günter Glockmann (q.v. *Homer in der frühchristlichen Literatur bis Justinus*, 116–88).

recent scholarship is Carl Andresen.[52] Working off Elyseé Pélaguad's 19th century suggestion that Celsus in *The True Logos* (which has been reconstructed from Origen's *Against Celsus*) was directly responding to Justin's *Apologies*, Andresen gave this obscure theory prominence by championing it as a central theme in his groundbreaking work, *Logos und Nomos*.[53] Andresen even goes on to argue that if one fails to supply Justin's thought as a backdrop to that of Celsus' thought, the project of the infamous pagan critic of early Christianity cannot be properly understood.[54]

Therefore the misgivings that Celsus declared in a general sense against Christianity in *True Logos*, Andresen projects specifically onto Justin.[55] In particular, this includes Celsus' displeasure with a stream of Christian thought he had encountered, which, in his estimation, violently fragmented Greek culture by selectively accepting elements of its philosophy but then rejected the work of the poets altogether.[56] By identifying Justin as the source responsible for this unnatural bifurcation of the ancient tradition that Celsus portrayed in his diatribe, Andresen has developed a popular narrative that has informed not only Chadwick but a whole host of contemporary scholars who all argue that although Justin could be somewhat accepting of Greek philosophy, the same of which could not be said regarding his approach towards Greek mythology.[57]

---

52. The profound influence that Andresen has had upon Justin scholarship regarding the *Apologies* has been recently noted by Slusser, according to whom there are two streams of thought that have developed over the past fifty years in Justin scholarship: "the Justin of the Apologies" versus "the Justin of the Dialogue." The first stream was forged by Andresen in the 1950s whose studies focused upon Justin as a philosopher while the second was commenced by Skarsaune in the late 1980s who focused upon Justin as a biblical interpreter (q.v. "Justin Scholarship: Trends and Trajectories," 15–16).

53. Droge, *Homer or Moses?*, 76.

54. Andresen, *Logos und Nomos*, 350: "[D]aß einzelne Argumente der Polemik von Kelsos überhaupt nicht verständlich sind, wenn sie nicht als Antworten auf die Apologetik Justins verstanden werden, für die Klärung ihrer beiderseitigen Beziehung Bedeutung zubilligen müssen."

55. Ibid., 363.

56. Ibid., 371. Celsus viewed the work of the philosophers and poets as an indissoluble whole that could not be easily separated. Malherbe points out the symbiotic relationship the ancients understood between the philosophers and the poets as they were, "inextricably connected, for the poets were considered to be inspired, and it was deemed the duty of the philosopher to interpret the myths for the truth they did contain" ("Athenagoras on the Pagan Poets and Philosophers," 216).

57. Besides Chadwick, see Boys-Stones, *Post-Hellenistic Philosophy: A Study of its Development from the Stoics to Origen*, 178; Bray, "Explaining Christianity to Pagans: The Second-Century Apologists," 16; Droge, *Homer or Moses*, 72–81; Holte, "Logos Spermatikos: Christianity and Ancient Philosophy according to St. Justin's Apologies," 109–68; Saldanha, *Divine Pedagogy: A Patristic View of Non-Christian Religions*, 48–51;

Justin's partial denigration of myth

The polarized depiction of Justin's approach to Greek culture has been challenged by Günter Glockmann who argues that such a portrait does not account for 2 *Apology* 13.2–3 where Justin placed the poets (i.e., those responsible for transmitting myth) on equal standing with the philosophers. The apologist wrote:

> Praying and fighting with all my might to be found a Christian, I confess not that the teachings of Plato are alien to those of Christ, but that they are not in all ways the same as them, just as neither are those of the others, Stoics, poets, and prose-writers. For what each of them proclaimed was good, when he saw from a part of the divine spermatic logos what is connatural to it.[58]

In light of this passage, Glockmann offers a nuanced way of understanding how the apologist approached myth. He takes the three categories Ragner Holte had previously developed in order to delineate how Justin perceived the relationship between Christian truth and pagan philosophy, rendering them applicable to the works of the pagan poets as well: (1) logos-spermatikos, (2) loan theory, and (3) demon theory.[59] When Justin framed the work of the poets with the first two categories in mind, Glockmann argues that he was handling these narratives in a positive manner.[60] But when

and Wright, "Christian Faith in the Greek World: Justin Martyr's Testimony," 80.

58. Glockmann, *Homer in der frühchristlichen Literatur bis Justinus*, 157: "Gerade diese Schlußerklärung kann freilich auch zeigen, daß für Justinus die Frage nicht lautet 'Christian truth—truth in philosophy,' wie es nach Holtes Ausführungen scheinen könnte, sondern umfassender 'christliche Wahrheit—Wahrheit im Heidentum.' Der Apologet nennt nämlich App. 13, 2 nicht nur Philosophen, Plato und die Stoiker, sondern auch ποιηταί und συγγραφεῖς schlechthin, und App. 13, 5 spricht er wieder von συγγραφεῖς πάντες."

59. Holte, "Logos Spermatikos," 164. Following the cue of Holte, Glockmann argues for the direct action of the *logos spermatikos* upon the poets when they were able to deliberate on issues of what we would call "general revelation." To exemplify this, Glockmann uses Justin's quote of Menander (*1 Apol.* 20.5) where the poet ridicules the worshipping of idols (Glockmann, *Homer in der frühchristlichen Literatur*, 164). In regards to "loan theory," Glockmann uses the example of *1 Apol.* 18.5 where Justin alludes to "Homer's pit" as a pagan analogue to the Christian doctrine of hell borrowed from the teachings of Moses and the Prophets (ibid., 158–59). In contrast to *logos spermatikos*, loan theory deals with aspects of what we would call "special revelation." Finally, "demon theory" is a deviant form of loan theory where the demons mimic the special revelatory prophecies in Moses and the Prophets for the purpose of deception.

60. Ibid., 158: "Justinus mußte folglich entweder auf die Logos-Spermatikos-Theorie oder auf die Anleihen-Theorie zurückgreifen, wenn er bei heidnischen Dichtern, Philosophen oder anderen Autoren auf positiv zu wertende Parallelen zum christlichen Glauben stieß."

it came to the work of the poets that was within the realm of demon theory (primarily allusions to the gods), Glockmann posits that Justin viewed all such instances negatively.[61]

Although Glockmann should be lauded for providing a much needed corrective to ascertain better Justin's approach to myth, his assessment of the apologist's attitude in regards to the last category is not entirely accurate. As mentioned previously, the willingness of Justin to point out the resonant attributes shared between the so-called sons of Zeus and that of Christ in chapters 21 and 22 of *1 Apology* reveals a friendliness to these mythical characters that does not fit Glockmann's facile categorization.

Justin's dynamic incorporation and separation of myth

Jean Daniélou builds upon this dichotomy by arguing that Justin's negative and positive attitudes of myth should not be viewed as contradictory, but actually as complementary. For Daniélou, this nuanced understanding of the mythological phenomena in Justin's writings opens up a world where the apologist could have perceived refracted intimations of the coming of Christ within the ancient Greco-Roman narrative itself. Therefore, Justin recruited the myths in a similar vein to how he recruited Old Testament texts that foreshadowed, in his estimation, the Incarnation.

> Christianity, in its penetration of the Graeco-Roman world, expressed itself not only through the philosophical categories of that world, but also through its symbolism . . . just as the truths of Greek philosophy derived from that same Word who was to become incarnate in the Christ, so the symbols of Greek religion too were "hierophanies" which constituted distant prefiguring of the mysteries of Christ.[62]

To describe these mythical pre-figurations as "hierophanies," Daniélou draws from the historian of religions, Mircea Eliade, to argue mythical events and figures are vague appearances of the sacred throughout history (as opposed to the much clearer foreshadowings known as "theophanies").

---

61. Ibid.: "Derartige heidnische Parallelen zu christlichen Aussagen gelten dem Apologeten also als dämonische Kontraoffenbarungen. Die Dämonen—Theorie scheidet aus diesem Grunde als Erklärung für die von Justinus positiv gewerteten heidnisch-christlichen Analogien aus, zu denen die oben besprochenen homerischen ja an erster Stelle zu rechnen sind. Man wird dieser Theorie in Verbindung mit denjenigen Justinstellen wieder begegnen, an welchen der Apologet in negative Sinne auf das homerische Epos anspielt."

62. Daniélou, *Gospel Message and Hellenistic Culture*, 82.

Daniélou thus implies that although Justin perceived them as useful that he also understood them to be of inferior quality to the Christological prophecies directly revealed through Moses and the Prophets.[63] This insight offered by Daniélou dovetails quite nicely with Justin's movements of incorporation and separation with myth I am arguing for here. If anything, I will take the dynamism in Justin's approach to these demonically inspired stories of which Daniélou merely suggests and will advance it by framing these allusions within the context of Christian pedagogy.

A recent work that argues for a more dynamic understanding of how Justin approached myth is by Peter Widdicombe. Widdicombe confirms two instances in which Justin actually allegorized myth: (1) in the case of Hermes as an interpretative λόγος of all [1 Apology 21.2] and (2) in the case of non-sexual conception of Athena from the mind of Zeus [1 Apology 64.5].[64] The fact Justin was even willing to allegorize myth, a method widely known to be employed by pagan thinkers to preserve the honor of the ancient poets from both Christian and non-Christian scrutiny,[65] hints at something more than a negative valuation of myth was occurring in the thought of Justin.

By demonstrating Justin's positive use of myth in his employing the allegorical method in these two particular instances, Widdicombe argues that Justin should be understood as ultimately having, "an ambivalent attitude to the myths" and that he used "the phenomenon of the myths both

63. Justin seemed to show this attitude towards pagan philosophy as well, even wearing the philosopher's outward dress (i.e., the pallium) in order to gain an audience (*Dial.* 1.1–2). But once he made his connection as a philosopher, he jettisoned the very thing that gained him the initial interest of his audience. When Trypho the Jew asked Justin to talk philosophy with him, Justin responded by asking Trypho to abandon the pursuit of philosophy (which was filled with inconsistencies and contradictions) in favor of the truth present in his own sacred text: "'How,' I asked, 'can you gain as much from philosophy as from your own lawgiver and prophets?'" (*Dial.* 1.3).

64. Widdicombe, "Justin Martyr, Allegorical Interpretation, and the Greek Myths," 234–39. Widdicombe actually misses a third instance where Justin allegorized myth: the aforementioned story of Heracles at the Crossroads between Virtue and Vice in 2 *Apol.* 11 (Carena, "La critica della mitologia pagana negli Apologeti greci dei II secolo," 34: "Così il mito di Eracle al bivio era diventato anche per i cristiani pura allegoria dell'animo umano in presenza della vita").

65. Rivière, *Saint Justin et les apologistes du second siècle*, 50–51: "La mythologie païenne—ou plutôt les mythologies disparates et touffues que le paganisme officiel connaît dans son sein—renfermait, outre le vice radical de son principe polythéiste, une multitude de details visiblement absurdes ou immoraux. Sans doute quelques esprits plus élevés s'efforçaient de les atténuer en subtils symboles; mais prises au sens littéral—et c'est bien ainsi qu'elles avaient cours dans la masse—ces histoires de dieux et de déesses offraient à la verve satirique des Apologistes une abondante et facile matière. Ils ne se privèrent pas de l'exploiter."

negatively and positively to bolster his argument for the uniqueness and the superiority of the Christian faith."[66]

While Widdicombe's discovery of these allegories provides an excellent point of departure from previous overarching assessments of Justin's attitude to myth, his conclusion that Justin was "ambivalent" towards them is far too simplistic. Such an appraisal by Widdicombe seems to suggest that the apologist's interest in dealing with these ancient stories was solely for rhetorics. Although argumentation and persuasion certainly play a large role in Justin's pedagogy of myth, Widdicombe overemphasizes this aspect to the point of grossly ignoring the six different occasions in *1 Apology* alone where Justin declares the diabolical origin and purpose behind the myths. Such repeated insistence by the apologist certainly betrays an attitude towards myth that is anything but indifferent. While the schema of incorporation and separation I am proposing in this paper explores the rhetorical aspects of Justin's mythical allusions, it also takes into consideration the apologist's strong convictions about the demonic inspiration of these pagan narratives.

The main shortcoming in both Daniélou and Widdicombe is that they argue for a dynamic movement within Justin's use of myth but attempt to do so within the same binary framework of positive and negative, which has been shown to be problematic. This project will depart from this faulty paradigm altogether by not emphasizing "how" Justin viewed myth (i.e., positive and negative) but by focusing on "what" Justin sought do with myth (i.e., incorporation and separation).

CONCLUSION

Besides arguing that Justin's audience would have not found his varied approach to myth unusual, what ultimately cinches this is assuming the newer perspective that Justin composed *1 Apology* with an internal audience in mind. A proponent of this view, Wayne Kannaday, spells out how this paradigm shift beckons us to question our traditional assumptions of what the text was designed to accomplish, "Readers of apologetic literature, therefore, must beware of confusing the designated addressee of the apology with the genuine intended audience . . . Justin and his successors were, most of all, strengthening the belief of believers, not convincing the antagonistic. They

---

66. Widdicombe, "Justin Martyr, Allegorical Interpretation, and the Greek Myths," 234.

were offering those of like mind but fragile faith some matrix of rationality on which to pin their piety."[67]

If Justin were writing *1 Apology* with the intent of strengthening the "belief of believers" as Kannaday suggests, why would the apologist constantly allude to the symbols of an ancient religion his audience was tempted to revert back to? While Justin's ultimate goal was that his readers decisively abandon their ancestral religion, he also perceived a resource of images from this same tradition that could be utilized to reinforce belief in the Christian faith. It is my contention that these two very different approaches of pagan narratives within the thought of Justin can be best harmonized when understood within the framework of a simultaneous incorporation of myth (guided mostly by typology) and a separation of myth.

67. Kannaday, *Apologetic Discourse and the Scribal Tradition*, 40. Kannaday applies this new paradigm to reevaluate how scholars should think about the scribal tradition within the early church.

2

Shifting the Paradigm

FROM EXTERNAL TO INTERNAL AUDIENCE[1]

IN THE INTRODUCTION, I demonstrated how three perspectives offered by classical scholarship (i.e., the "doubleness" of the Muses, the prevalence of pagan typology, and the perceived dependence of philosopher upon poet) support a fresh reconsideration of what Justin was seeking to accomplish in his diverse use of these pagan narratives. While these insights will play no small part in driving my thesis, another important scholarly contribution responsible for giving my overall argument its shape would have to be the debates regarding who was the intended audience for Justin's *1 Apology*.

The conventional understanding, of course, has been that Justin wrote this work for an external audience targeted either for an educated pagan readership with the emperor Antoninus Pius and his son, Marcus Aurelius, particularly in mind. This traditional approach to *1 Apology* has been very influential within scholarship.[2] For example, the previously mentioned

1. I credit the master's thesis of Haddad for orienting me to the recent scholarly conversation surrounding the destination of *1 Apology*. Although his discussion was very helpful, my conclusion regarding primary audience differs vastly from his (q.v., "The Appropriateness of the Apologetical Arguments of Justin Martyr," 48–62).

2. This is affirmed by the prevailing historical metanarrative that assumes that the work of the Apologists served as an important watershed or "hinge" in Christian discourse, representing the transition from texts written solely for an internal audience (i.e., Apostolic Fathers) to texts targeted towards an external one. An excellent representative of this historiography is found in Karen Bullock who distinguishes the Apostolic Fathers from the Apologists by stating that the likes of Clement of Rome and

theory of Chadwick that Justin's allusion to myth was nothing more than a form of *captatio benevolentiae* is built upon the premise that the apologist was writing to an outside audience unsympathetic to the Christian cause. In addition, this historical backdrop for *1 Apology* has experienced wide acceptance within traditional scholarship given the fact that the text begins with a direct address to the Roman emperor and his sons (*1 Apol.* 1.1).

Yet, this contextual assumption regarding the audience of *1 Apology* has come under recent scrutiny by Harry Gamble (1995) and Lorraine Buck (1996). While Gamble disputes the existence of an external audience based upon established circulation patterns of second-century texts, Buck discounts the idea of an outside readership for *1 Apology* by theorizing that this writing should be understood as a literary fiction that served the intellectual needs of Justin's early Christian community. While there is a line of scholarship going as far back to 1930 who entertained the possibility that Justin actually composed *1 Apology* with an internal audience in mind (e.g., A.D. Nock, Kurt Aland, Robin Lane Fox, and Ramsey MacMullen), according to Buck "none of these scholars . . . argued this position at any length."[3] I will provide a fuller treatment later in this chapter of both Gamble and Buck's respective arguments for *1 Apology*'s internal audience and its impact upon our understanding of how Justin interacted with myth.[4]

This change of thought regarding the audience of *1 Apology* has far-reaching implications. André Wartelle, who seems to argue for both an external and internal audiences for *1 Apology*, anticipates how entertaining an internal audience for the text expands the possibilities behind Justin's recruitment of these mythical analogies. Not only does he perceive in Justin's analogies an attempt to secure the goodwill of those who persecute

---

Ignatius of Antioch wrote, "simple, practical, discipleship materials used by the church for training and encouragement in the Christian way," while the Apologists in distinct contrast "used philosophical categories to explain the Christian faith to a pagan world. They were often addressed to the state authorities, defending Christians against false charges" (*The Writings of Justin Martyr*, 2–3).

3 Buck, *Second Century Greek Christian Apologies*, 262–63. The texts of Nock, Aland, Fox, and MacMullen that Buck refers to as arguing for an internal audience for *1 Apology* but not doing so at any length are as follows: Nock, *Conversion: The Old and the New in Religion*, 192; Aland, *Über den Glaubenswechsel*, 32; Fox, *Pagans and Christians*, 515; MacMullen, *Christianizing the Roman Empire*, 21.

4. It is interesting to note that Minns and Parvis sidestep the issue of internal audience versus an external one altogether in the introduction of their critical edition. Their main debate is whether *1 Apology* was intended just for the imperial family or whether the Senate and People were included as well; they make the judgment that it was only intended for the imperial family. Once this is established, the majority of the section consists of biographical backgrounds of Antoninus Pius, Verissimus, and Lucius, the formal addressees of *1 Apology* (q.v. *Justin, Philosopher and Martyr: Apologies*, 34–41.

Christians (i.e., external audience) but also a demonstration for his an internal audience of how these ancient stories served a preparatory role for the eventual incarnation of the Logos.[5]

Although Wartelle's argument for multiple audiences in *1 Apology* provides an excellent framework to clarify what Justin's interactions with myth would have meant to a Christian and non-Christian respectively, his theory of multiple audiences is too vague as it lacks an adequate explanation regarding how copies of *1 Apology* went about being transmitted to each respective group. Based upon the insights provided by Gamble and Buck, I will argue that an external, pagan audience only came in contact with Justin's arguments through the mediation of Christians who in their conversations with their pagan counterparts shared what they themselves had read from *1 Apology*.

So in order to further highlight the importance of approaching *1 Apology* as a text meant for internal consumption, I have provided a concise survey below of the three schools of thought regarding the immediate audience for Justin's *1 Apology*: (1) the Roman emperor and his sons, (2) the educated pagan masses, (3) and Christians. In so doing, I will argue how the emergence of this third school of thought (i.e., internal, Christian audience) forces us to reevaluate Justin's interaction with myth.

1st school: Roman emperor and his sons

Given the opening inscription of *1 Apology* (1.1), which addresses emperor Antoninus Pius and his sons Verissimus and Lucius, the traditional understanding of the immediate recipients of *1 Apology* has simply been that the letter was directed to the Roman emperor and his sons.[6] A representative of this school of thought is Wolfram Kinsig who describes how the emperor's reception of Justin's *1 Apology* subsequently led to its proliferation to the pagan masses. Given his command of the ancient conventions surrounding how *libelli* or petitions were handled within the Roman empire, Kinsig

---

5 Wartelle, *Apologies*, 257: "L'argumentation de Justin dans ce chapitre ressemble fort à une *captatio benevolentiae*, et l'on peut sa montrer plus exigeant que lui sur le bien-fondé de certains rapprochements. Il n'en reste pas moins que son étonnants bienveillance s'exprime par sa doctrine du λόγος σπερματικός, du Verbe répandu, ensemencé partout dans le monde comme une préparation au Christ dans le monde païen, Plutôt que par un plat souci de concordisme."

6. Erhardt, "Justin Martyr's Two Apologies," 5; Grant, "Forms and Occasions of the Greek Apologists," 216; Guerra, "The Conversion of Marcus Aurelius and Justin Martyr," 171–87; Jaeger, *Early Christianity and Greek Paideia*, 26–28; Keresztes, "The Literary Genre of Justin's First Apology," 99–110.

explains how Justin could submit *1 Apology* directly to the emperor and yet could have written it with the general public also in mind. According to Kinsig, once the emperor finished reading a petition he would have his officials post it for a month at the "Porticus of the Trajan Springs" with his reply attached for all to read.[7] Therefore, Justin was able to gain a broad readership of *1 Apology* by manipulating the petition process; he wrote a general apology for the Christian faith dressed up in the language of petition.[8]

This explanation has recently come under criticism most notably by Lorraine Buck. Although Buck provides a myriad of reasons to discount the traditional understanding of *1 Apology*'s destination, two particular concerns tend to dominate her argument: (1) the unusual length of *1 Apology* as a legal petition and (2) the illicit status of Christianity at the time of the text's composition.[9] Buck points out that given the heavy time constraints placed upon a Roman emperor, petitions were to be, "between 150 and 200 hexameter lines in length, that is, short and precise" in order for them to be accepted.[10] Being sixty-eight chapters in length, the *1 Apology* far surpasses these required parameters and according to Buck would have been quickly excluded from the petition process. Compounded by the fact that Christians during Justin's milieu did not have legal recourse to submit a petition to the emperor in the first place given their illegal standing in the empire, Buck ultimately concludes that *1 Apology* should be regarded as a "literary fiction."[11] The earliest evidence of an emperor, in fact, replying to members of the early church is not until the third century where according to Eusebius (*Ecclesiastical History* 7.13) the Egyptian bishops were able appeal to Gallienus because the emperor had bestowed legal standing to Christians during his reign.[12]

As a defender of the traditional understanding of *1 Apology*'s destination, William Schoedel addresses the objection regarding its undue length by suggesting that Justin was responsible for introducing a new form of literature, what he calls an "apologetically grounded petition . . . It is a mixed form that as such appears to have no real precedent in the Greco-Roman literary tradition."[13] Schoedel goes on to argue that the length of *1 Apology*

---

7. Kinsig, "Der Sitz im Leben der Apologie," 303.

8. Ibid., 310.

9. Buck, "Athenagoras's Embassy: A Literary Fiction," 211–13.

10. Ibid., 210. These parameters are based from the limits prescribed by Menander's famous *Handbook on Rhetoric*.

11. Buck, "Justin Martyr's *Apologies*," 54–55.

12. Millar, *The Emperor in the Roman World*, 240n1.

13. Schoedel, "Apologetic Literature and Ambassadorial Activities," 78.

also becomes a non-factor if Justin made his defense in person with the document functioning as a mere reference work he would hand to the emperor who scanned through it at his discretion; indeed, such precedence can be found in first-century Judaism where Philo and Josephus utilized this very approach.[14]

Although this theory by Schoedel may meet the concerns regarding the length of *1 Apology*, it does not take into account that the Jewish apologists he mentioned were functioning under the status of *religio licitas* while Justin was not. Given the proscriptions on Christianity spelled out by Hadrian's Rescript, an oral defense of Christianity by Justin before the emperor would have been considered nothing less than suicide.

2nd school: Educated pagan masses

This school of thought reverses the order of how *1 Apology* was transmitted; that is, Justin's immediate audience was the educated pagan masses whom he hoped would eventually bring it to the attention of the emperor.[15] A worthy representative of this position is W. H. C. Frend who argues for a more "ground roots" approach where copies of the text were distributed to the general public as open letters to the imperial government. According to Frend, it was Justin's hope that such a format would gain a sympathetic reading thereby providing a surge in public interest that would eventually propel the text into the hands of the emperor.[16]

Although Frend's theory seems more plausible than the one stated by Schoedel, it still suffers from the same deficiency: How could Justin have averted his execution for so long after openly identifying himself as a Christian in a treatise distributed to the general public (*1 Apol.* 1.1), "I, Justin, son of Priscus and grandson of Bacchios who both come from Flavia Neapolis in Syria Palaestina"? Buck makes the excellent point that Christians were constantly exposed to the threat of *delation* or being turned over to the authorities, "by their pagan neighbours and relatives and would thus have been loath to distribute Christian literature to those who could easily denounce them to the authorities as Christians."[17]

---

14. Ibid., "Apologetic Literature and Ambassadorial Activities," 59–69.

15. Barnard, *The First and Second Apologies*, 6; Chadwick, "Justin Martyr's Defence of Christianity," 275; Daniélou, *Gospel Message and Hellenistic Culture*, 9; and Haddad, *The Appropriateness of the Apologetical Arguments of Justin Martyr*, 54.

16. Frend, *The Rise of Christianity*, 234.

17. Buck, *Second Century Greek Christian Apologies Addressed to Emperors*, 263.

It is important to note that while Justin alongside several of his companions eventually suffered martyrdom in AD 165 when they were identified as Christians by the Roman authorities, the beginning of *The Martyrdom of the Holy Martyrs* states that their incarceration was not due to the censorship of their teacher's works. Rather, the basis for why they were brought before the prefect, Rusticus, was that he and his companions had been found wanting in their participation of the state mandated worship of the gods.[18]

3rd school: To Christians

As mentioned previously, notable scholars since the 1930s have suggested that *1 Apology* should be understood as a text that was posed primarily towards an internal audience. Scholars such as Ramsey MacMullen based their position solely on the fleeting comment of Tertullian in *The Soul's Testimony* §1 where he said, "no one turns to our literature who is not already Christian."[19] But it was not until the mid-90s that this position was treated in depth by Harry Gamble and Lorraine Buck respectively.

Gamble in *Books and Readers in the Early Church* (1995) substantiates the theory that *1 Apology* was written towards an internal audience based upon how 2nd century authors in the Roman empire, both pagan and Christian, traditionally relied on an internal network of social relations to disseminate their texts. Following this model, Justin would have initially distributed copies of *1 Apology* to his close friends sympathetic to his ideas. By virtue of being inspired by his message, his friends would in turn have the text transcribed at their own expense circulating the copies, "along paths of

18. *Martyrdom of the Holy Martyrs* §1, "In the time of the lawless partisans of idolatry, wicked decrees were passed against the godly Christians in town and country, to force them to offer libations to vain idols; and accordingly the holy men, having been apprehended, were brought before the prefect of Rome, Rusticus by name" (*ANF*, 1:305). According to Eusebius (*Ecclesiastical History* 4.16.1), he states that the mastermind that tipped off to the authorities that Justin and his companions were Christians was the Cynic philosopher Crescens who did so out of retribution for constantly being routed by the apologist in public debates. Osborn questions the ancient church historian's testimony stating, "Eusebius has grasped the motive for [why Crescens would want to take] Justin's life but he has exceeded the evidence for the cause of his death." While we have evidence of Justin suspecting that Crescens was plotting against him (*2 Apol.* 3.1) and even a claim from Tatian that Crescens had turned in both he and his teacher to the authorities, "endeavouring to inflict on Justin, and indeed on me, the punishment of death" (*Exhort. to the Greeks* §19), there is no indication from the *Martyrdom of the Holy Martyrs* itself that Justin and his companions were before the prefect, Rusticus, on account of Crescens' machinations (q.v., Osborn, *Justin Martyr*, 9). Also see Bisbee, "The Acts of Justin Martyr: A Form-Critical Study," 136.

19. MacMullen, "Two Types of Conversion to Early Christianity," 177.

friendship or personal acquaintance."[20] In Gamble's estimation, this would have been a limited social circle made up exclusively of fellow Christians.

Although Gamble does not entirely preclude the possibility that Justin could have also produced copies of *1 Apology* for pagan readership, he casts serious doubts upon this likelihood. He states, "That the apologies were written not merely for Christian but for also pagan consumption has consequences for my conception of their publication and circulation . . . Propaganda, more than other types of literature, requires a greater effort of distribution. We can only guess how widely Christian apologies circulated among pagans, but we know that they were rapidly disseminated in Christian circles."[21]

While Gamble supports the view of an internal audience based upon publication and circulation patterns of the ancient world, Buck further buttresses this position by arguing why Justin's *1 Apology* should be understood as a "literary fiction" and not an actual address to the imperial court. She bases this upon the opening address to the emperor and his sons in *1 Apol.* 1.1, "To the emperor Titus Aelius Hadrian Antoninus Pius Augustus Caesar, and to Verissimus his son, philosopher, and to Lucius, the son of Caesar by nature and by Pius by adoption." Despite having the appearances of formality, Buck points out "three inexcusable errors" Justin committed in the opening address that betray *1 Apology* as a letter never intended to reach the emperor: (1) "Caesar" would have never been placed after "Augustus" but rather "emperor," (2) the names of the sons of an emperor were to never appear in official address, and (3) Justin fails to ascribe the title "Caesar" to Marcus Aurelius [i.e., Verissimus] who had gained that designation ten years prior to the composition of *1 Apology*.[22] Buck goes on to argue that Justin's *1 Apology* as a whole does not possess the necessary tone of "obsequiousness" characteristic of an authentic imperial *libellus*.[23]

If Justin were writing to a Christian audience, what benefit did they receive from reading this fictional appeal to the emperor and his sons? It provided a model for how his students could argue the case for Christianity over and against paganism—even towards those at the highest levels of society. It also helped solidify those wavering in their newfound Christian faith. Regarding the former, Walter Wagner contends that this format served as an, "in-school model prepared by the master teacher for use by his students.

---

20. Gamble, *Books and Readers in the Early Church*, 85.

21. Ibid., *Books and Readers in the Early Church*, 111–12.

22. Buck, "Justin Martyr's Apologies," 51.

23. Ibid., 53. For a short rebuttal of Buck's position, see Moll, "Justin and the Pontic Wolf," 146–47.

By working with the document—both in form and content—students learned not only the techniques of rhetoric and philosophy but also their master's theology."[24] Regarding the latter, Buck argues:

> The *Apologies*, moreover, were no doubt an important means of confirming Christian truths. Given that second-century Christians lived in fear of incrimination, incarceration, and execution and were thus tempted, on a daily basis, to revert to their ancestral—and much safer—religion, the *Apologies* would have provided that much needed reassurance that the Gospel for which they might forfeit their lives was true.[25]

Recent monographs have been published with this emerging presupposition in mind, exploring how elements of early Christianity like heresy (Karen King) and the scribal tradition (Wayne Kannady) should be reconsidered.[26] Yet there has not been a work to date that has applied this premise to Justin's approach to myth exploring why the apologist would constantly allude to these pagan narratives when writing to a Christian audience. This work will seek to fill this void.

CONSTRUCTING A JUSTINIAN PEDAGOGY OF MYTH

I contend, therefore, that the primary key to unlocking Justin's diverse use of myth is to read *1 Apology* from the perspective of early Christian converts pondering a return back to their ancestral religion. While one means of staving off such a relapse was to attack paganism head-on by exposing the absurdities found within its foundational myths, Justin was also aware that these same stories were still held in high esteem amongst his readership (hence their temptation to revert back) due to the integral role they had served in both shaping as well as ordering ancient society.[27] For this reason, Justin could not steer his wavering audience back into the fold by merely demolishing these revered narratives "for the sake of demolishing" as was the

---

24. Wagner, *Christianity in the Second Century*, 159.

25. Buck, *Second Century Greek Christian Apologies Addressed to Emperors*, 273.

26. King, *What is Gnosticism?*; Wayne Kannaday, *Apologetic Discourse and the Scribal Tradition.*

27. Wilken describes the importance of the stories of the ancestral gods within ancient Greco-Roman society, "In what did true piety consist? Excessive religious zeal was not pious. Not plowing for religious reasons was impious. People who spent whole days in prayer and sacrifice were not pious. The truly pious life was one devoted to the gods in accord with the noble ideals which had been transmitted for centuries" (q.v. "Toward a Social Interpretation of Early Christian Apologetics," 440).

custom of his young contemporary and satirist, Lucian of Samosata (c. AD 125–180).[28] Rather, Justin was compelled to interact with myth in a manner that would ultimately engender confidence within his audience towards the Christian faith they had recently come to profess.[29] He would accomplish this, ironically, through the very stories he sought to deconstruct by identifying select elements from them that could lend support to radical notions of Christian belief such as Jesus Christ being both divine and human. Justin, in fact, would be the only second century apologist to appeal to the ancient concept of demigods (i.e. their divine-human makeup) as a sort of pagan precedent that foreshadowed the doctrine of the Incarnation.[30]

---

28. Carena, "La critica della mitologia pagana," 26–27: "Luciano demolisce per demolire: le colpe e le debolezze degli dèi li abbassano al grado umano, li screditano nella stima degli uomini. Il mondo olimpico cade, ma questa rovina non è oggetto che di ironia: Luciano vuole svelare compiutamente l'intima assurdità e risibilità di questo mondo crollante, ma di rado, o mai se il *De sacrificiis* non è suo, giunge allo sdegno. Negli apologeti invece, anche in quelli che ricorrono a frizzi ed ironie, prorompe aperta la condanna, quella condanna che cade sui presunti dèi impotenti, ridicoli, malvagi da parte del Dio unico, santo e onnipotente: essi demoliscono per far posto alla nuova fede . . . se Luciano resta un letterato, un retore, sia pure di ingegno e di gusto tale da non confondersi con i contemporanei, gli apologeti sono anche apostoli, nei quali l'ardore della causa che vogliono sostenere prevale sullo spirito di critica." This tendency we see in Justin to not demolish myth "for the sake of demolishing" was a task taken on by poets and philosophers long before the apologist arrived upon the scene. In the previous chapter, an example from the poets (i.e., Stesichorus) and the philosophers (i.e., Plato) were provided with the former appealing to the Muses in order to right the story regarding Helen (ibid., 9–12) while for as much as the latter openly impugned the works of Homer found the poet to be "the unavoidable reference" alluded to him 331 times (ibid., 17–19). Brisson insightfully points out that Plato was not contradicting himself: "When Plato uses *muthos* in a nonmetaphorical way, he does two things: he describes and he criticizes. With the help of this term, he describes a certain type of discursive practice while expressing his judgment on its status in relation to that of another discursive practice he considers superior" (*How Philosophers Saved Myths*, 15).

29. Although Norris works off the old paradigm that Justin wrote towards an external audience, he perceives that Justin's approach to myth could not be solely be deconstructive in nature: "In this connection the Apologists found themselves with two jobs on their hands. They were obliged to expound certain distinctive points of Christian teaching in a way that would make their meaning clear to people who habit of thought raised a barrier to understanding. But at the same time as they attempted this, they were bound to indicate both how Christian teaching differed from other points of view, current or traditional, and how it was superior to them" (*God and World in Early Christian Theology*, 43).

30. Andresen, *Logos und Nomos*, 364: "Ganz davon abgesehen, daß die Parallele jüngeren Datums ist, befriedigt sie vor allem nicht in dem Punkte, daß die für Kelsos charakteristische Reihe: die Dioskuren, Herakles und Dionysos bei Tertullian nicht erscheint. Der einzige Apologet, der nicht nur die gleichen Halbgötter, sondern vor allem auch die gleiche Thematik des christlichen Inkarnationsproblemes mit ihnen zusammenbringt, ist Justin."

Yet for Justin, establishing this resonance between paganism and Christianity was an incomplete project in itself—the pagan foreshadowing now had to be deemed obsolete because the original it copied and mimicked from (i.e., Moses and the Prophets) was now in the possession of his audience.[31] To hasten this abandonment, Justin not only had to demonstrate how their newfound faith was distantly echoed in the narratives of their ancestral religion but he also had to show how this Christian belief they now staked their lives upon was the complete fulfillment and manifestation of the truth only vaguely hinted at within these pagan stories.

Resonance and myth

This is where the previously mentioned insights in classical scholarship regarding ancient poetry's accepted "doubleness" and the pagan typology of myth can be of great assistance: the former affirms resonance at work while the latter, fulfillment.[32] In fact, it is the notion of poetry's accepted "doubleness" that allows us to discount the prior claim of Carlos Contreras that Justin was being "flagrantly inconsistent" in his use of myth. Rather, we can now understand the apologist's diverse usage of these narratives as compatible with how pagans for centuries had accustomed themselves to receive these "lies that are similar to truth things" (as Hesiod came to describe myth): on the one hand, openly acknowledging that these fabulous tales were distortions of the truth but on the other hand, still showing appreciation for this ambiguous gift bestowed upon them by the gods by attempting to extract from them some remnant of truth buried under all the layers of deception.[33] Justin's audience, mainly composed of pagan con-

---

31. Here is where one can see Platonic Idealism in Justin's thought as he beckons his audience to abandon corrupted forms in favor of the pure idea on which those forms are based. For Justin, both pagan philosophy and mythology contained corrupted forms of the pure idea of the Incarnation contained in Moses and the Prophets with philosophy being less corrupt than that of mythology. One can pick up this impulse in Justin's understanding of philosophy when Trypho the Jew asked Justin to talk philosophy with him. Justin responded by asking Trypho to abandon the pursuit of philosophy (which was filled with inconsistencies and contradictions) in favor of the truth present in his own sacred Jewish text: "'How,' I asked, 'can you gain as much from philosophy as from your own lawgiver and prophets?'" (*Dial.* 1.3)

32. Brown marvels at the fact that very little work has been done to study the revelatory insights the classical past had upon Christian doctrine. In an ecumenical age where studies in comparative religion flourish, the most obvious comparison is often neglected (q.v. *Tradition and Imagination*, 169–172).

33. Veyne captures how our modern binary notions of truth and error are often incompatible with the dynamism exhibited in ancient Greco-Roman society toward

verts to Christianity, would have been trained from childhood to apprehend myth in this dualistic fashion (i.e., simultaneous suspicion and reverence) and subsequently would have not found it confusing or contradictory when encountering texts written in this vein.[34]

One of the clearest examples of where Justin exploited his reader's dichotomous hermeneutic of myth is in his interaction with the Greco-Roman mythological concept of the "divine man" (θεῖος ἀνήρ).[35] According to Charles Talbert, there were two classifications of divinity within Greco-Roman mythology in the Mediterranean world during Justin's time: (1) the eternals and (2) the immortals. While the gods of the Pantheon fell within the category of the eternals (e.g., Zeus, Poseidon, and Hades) coming from entirely divine pedigree (i.e., both father and mother were gods), heroes like Heracles and Asclepius were understood to be immortals in which one of their parents was divine (usually the father) while the other was human (usually the mother) making their semi-divine offspring susceptible to death.[36] It is this latter category of the immortals for which the θεῖος ἀνήρ of Greco-Roman mythology belonged.

myth: "Myth was a subject of serious reflection, and the Greeks still had not tired of it six hundred years after the movement of the Sophists . . . Far from being a triumph of reason, the purification of myth by *logos* is an ancient program whose absurdity surprises us today. Why the Greeks go to the trouble of wishing to separate the wheat from the chaff in myth when they could easily have rejected both Theseus and the Minotaur, as well as the very existence of a certain Minos and the improbable stories tradition gave him? We see the extent of the problem when we realize that this attitude toward myth lasted for over two millennia" (*Did the Greeks believe in their Myths?*, 1).

34. Purves makes the excellent point that in criticizing myth, Justin relied upon a long established tradition where pagan thinkers before him paved the way by making the deconstruction of these fabulous stories an acceptable practice in the eyes of the ancient reader: "Justin declares it to have been the work of demons; he scorns and ridicules its idolatry; he points out its contradictions, and denounces its impure stories and shameless rites. He could safely do so, for pagan writers themselves had already done the same" (*The Testimony of Justin Martyr to Early Christianity*, 81). Justin himself marvels in *1 Apol.* 4.9 how many pagan thinkers are lauded for their critique of myth: "Some of them in their teaching denied the gods and those of them who were poets proclaimed the promiscuity of Zeus as well as of his sons, and you do not bar performers who take up their teaching. Rather, you give prizes and rewards for those who are in good voice when they offer insult to them."

35. It is important to note that I am narrowing the concept of θεῖος ἀνήρ as it relates to the gods of Greco-Roman mythology and not to wonder-workers, magicians, charismatic sages, and wizards from the first and second century (e.g., Apollonius of Tyana). By doing so, I am able to sidestep the controversy of the θεῖος ἀνήρ as it relates to this subgroup whose agreed upon characteristics are often "flexible and subject to change" (Flinterman, "The Ubiquitous 'Divine Man,'" 83).

36. Talbert, "The Concept of Immortals in Mediterranean Antiquity," 420: "The concept of immortals must be understood within the context of a distinction between

There are four trademark characteristics that made up a θεῖος ἀνήρ: (1) they possessed an extraordinary birth involving a divine parent,[37] (2) they earned a state of immortality on the basis of their virtuous "services rendered to humankind,"[38] and (3) were ultimately honored by the gods through some form of ascent into heaven either living alongside the eternals or being installed as a constellation in the sky.[39] This concept of heavenly ascent usually necessitated a final characteristic upon the θεῖος ἀνήρ that they (4) experience some form of death followed by the disappearance of their bodies. This vanishing was taken as a sign by the ancients as confirmation of the θεῖος ἀνήρ having experienced a heavenly ascent, "witnessed to by such circumstances as there being no remains of his body to be found."[40]

The key passage signaling Justin's exploitation of the concept of θεῖος ἀνήρ for Christian purposes is 1 Apol. 22.1, "The Son of God who is called Jesus, even if he were only an ordinary human being, would be worthy to be called a son of God because of wisdom." According to Talbert, Justin can be seen in this assertion manipulating the second characteristic of the θεῖος

two types of divine beings, the eternals and the immortals. This typology is mentioned at least as early as Herodotus (Hist., 2.43, 145–46) who says that Heracles and Dionysos were gods that had a beginning to their existence and had not existed eternally. Herodotus' distinction between those deities that are eternal and those that are immortal but have had a beginning was recognized and commented on by Plutarch near the end of the first or the beginning of the second century C.E."

37. Rose, "Herakles and the Gospels," 128: "The first characteristic of the θεῖος ἀνήρ, then, is that his begetting and birth should be out of the common."

38. Knox, "The 'Divine Hero' Christology in the New Testament," 231–232: "But they had lived on earth and earned their immortality by the services they had rendered to mankind. The most prominent figures in this class were Heracles, Asclepius (who was, however, normally confined pretty strictly to his purely medical duties) and Dionysus: and of these Heracles was the most prominent in the tradition of popular philosophy."

39. Talbert, "The Concept of Immortals in Mediterranean Antiquity," 422: "When one spoke of an immortal in the Greco-Roman world, therefore, he meant a mortal who had become a god, and this was usually expressed in terms of an extraordinary birth (one of his parents was a deity) and an ascension into heaven (witnessed to by such circumstances as there being no remains of his body to be found)."

40. Talbert also states that in some cases, ascent was confirmed by eyewitness reports of the immortalized ascending into the heavens ("The Concept of Immortals in Mediterranean Antiquity," 421: "Since the second characteristic is crucial, whenever Mediterranean peoples spoke about the immortals, constant in their description was the explicit or implicit idea that 'he was taken up into heaven.' Some evidence of this ascent is usually given. Either his ascent to heaven was witnessed or there was no trace of his physical remains"). Justin seems to be alluding to such a sentiment in his reader when in 1 Apol. 21.3 he states, "If you deem them worthy to be made into gods you also bring forward someone who swears that he has seen the cremated Caesar going up to heaven from the pyre."

ἀνήρ by distancing the virtuous life of Jesus with those of the sons of Zeus. In the prior passage, he had just critiqued the υἱοὶ τοῦ Διὸς in *1 Apol.* 21.4 for their notoriety in not only living immoral lives but through their poor example, "persuading to corruption those who are being educated. For all think that it is good to imitate the gods." For Justin, the sons of Zeus had disqualified themselves as legitimate candidates for attaining immortality because they were such poor exemplars for humanity.[41]

Yet Frances Young argues that Justin's audience prior to even encountering the apologist's critique of the lifestyles of the υἱοὶ τοῦ Διὸς would have already been steeped in doubt regarding their viability as legitimate θεῖος ἀνήρ, "no one knows quite how seriously to take many of these professions of belief and worship: the ruler-cult seems to have become a half-mocked convention performed solely for political reasons and probably not affecting the bulk of the populace, and the traditional mythology could certainly be treated with skepticism at least by the educated."[42] So why would Justin argue for something that his audience would have already affirmed? It is my contention that such a move by Justin was his way of tapping into the suspicion his audience already held towards the sons of Zeus as true "divine men."

But as stated previously in the chapter, Justin did not deconstruct myth "for the sake of demolishing" it and his interaction with the category of θεῖος ἀνήρ as it pertained to the sons of Zeus was no exception. While Justin capitalized on the suspicion his audience held regarding the sons of Zeus as "divine men," he would simultaneously engage his reader's reverence for the mythical notion of apotheosis by applying the blueprint for a θεῖος ἀνήρ upon the life of Jesus, "It is only a short distance from this conviction that Jesus is the true reality of which the immortals are only demonic imitations to an explicit employment of the pattern as a conceptual tool in Christology."[43] This will be quite apparent when we discuss the thematic progression of Justin's Pseudo-Creed Sequence (*1 Apol.* 21.1f) later in this chapter as it will exhibit a demonstrable correspondence with the four characteristics of the θεῖος ἀνήρ thusly outlined.

One can also detect the apologist's manipulation of this simultaneous suspicion and reverence towards myth in the pattern of how Justin incorporates myth and separates from myth. For instance in *1 Apol.* 21, Justin begins the chapter with the proposition that distinctive features of the life

41. Ibid., 420n7: "Justin seems to be aware of and involved in the debates over what constitutes the true *theios aner* in *1 Apol.* 22.1"

42. Young, "Two Roots of a Tangled Mass?," 102.

43. Talbert, "The Concept of Immortals in Mediterranean Antiquity," 433.

of Christ possessed a similar ring to those of the so-called sons (λεγομένους υἱούς) of Zeus that had been relayed within ancient myth: "And when we say that the Logos, which is the first offspring of God, was born without sexual intercourse as Jesus Christ our teacher, and that after his crucifixion, death, and resurrection he went up to heaven, we introduce nothing stranger than those you call the sons of Zeus." After this claim of similitude, Justin paraded a select list of mythical allusions regarding features of the sons of Zeus he felt resonated with that of the life of Christ (1 Apol. 21.2–3), "Justin finds analogues to Christian beliefs in Greek mythology in order to make Christian teaching understandable to pagan readers."[44]

But immediately after this roll call of the gods, we see an abrupt shift in Justin's stance as he goes to great lengths to attach disclaimers to the very analogies he just identified warning about the irrationality, as well as, the immorality these myths perpetuated within those who imbibed of them (1 Apol. 21.4–6). So in the first half of chapter 21 we can see incorporation of myth at work as Justin tapped into the innate reverence his audience had for these stories, but in the second half we witness the occurrence of partial separation from myth as he continued to build upon the suspicion his audience already possessed regarding these narratives.

While there will be a full treatment of incorporation of myth and separation from myth towards the end of this chapter, it is important at this juncture to distinguish between *partial* separation from myth and *full* separation from myth. Instances of *partial* separation of myth are often in close proximity with instances of incorporation of myth (Table 1.1). The reason behind this phenomenon is that the *partial* separation from myth allowed Justin to employ an *argumentum a fortiori* for the incorporation of myth he was employing. On the other hand, instances of *full* separation from myth were to convince his audience that they needed to abandon the pagan religious text in favor of the Christian one.

This dual action of incorporation of myth followed by the separation thereof is not just limited to chapter 21, either. Rather, one can observe in Table 1.1 this oscillating pattern occurring throughout the whole of 1 Apology: sections consisting of incorporation of and partial separation from myth (§ 21- 22, § 30- 53) dynamically interweaved with sections entirely dedicated to full separation from myth (§ 23- 29, § 54- 66). Out of the 47 total instances where Justin alluded to Greek myth, there is only a slight

---

44. Ferguson, *Church History*, 74. The gods and heroes that Justin alludes to are in this order: Hermes, Asclepius, Dionysius, Heracles, Castor and Pollux, Perseus, Bellerophon and Pegasus, Ariadne, and the Cult of the Emperor. In chapter 3, I will expand and theorize how underlying elements of each allusion provided weight to different aspects of the Incarnation of the Logos.

difference in frequency between incorporation of myth and full separation from myth: 18 of the instances are of the variety where Justin leveraged his audience's inherent reverence for myth to illuminate Christian doctrine (i.e., incorporation of myth) while 20 can be characterized as a complete opposing movement (i.e., full separation from myth). The remaining 9 are partial separation from myth, which we discussed earlier as being closely tethered to instances of incorporation of myth (Table 2.1).

Table 2.1
Justin's allusions to Greek myths in 1 Apology and their movements[A]

Greek god or hero	chapters
Achilles, Thetis, Briseis, and Briareus	§25.2 (FS)
Adonis	§25.1 (FS)
Antiope	§25.2 (FS)
Aphrodite	§25.1 (FS)
Apollo son of Leto	§25.1 (FS)
Ariadne	§21.3 (I)
Asclepius	§21.2 (I); §22.3 (I), 4 (PS), 6 (I); and §54.10 (FS)
Athena	§64.5 (FS)
Bellerophon/Pegasus	§21.2 (I) and §54.7 (FS)
Cronos and Zeus	§21.5 (PS)
Cybele (Magna Mater) and Attis	§27.4 (FS)
Dionysus son of Persephone and Semele	§21.2 (I); §22.3 (I), 4 (PS); §25.1 (FS); and §54.6 (FS)
The Dioscuri (Sons of Leda)	§21.2 (I)
Elysian Fields	§20.4 (I)
Ganymede	§21.5 (PS) and §25.2 (FS)
Heracles	§21.2 (I); §22.3 (I); §22.4 (PS); and §54.9 (FS)
Hermes	§21.2 (I) and §22.2 (I)
Minos and Rhadamanthus	§8.4 (I/PS)
Odysseus	§18.5 (I) and §18.6(PS)
Persephone (Core)	§25.1 (FS) and §64.4 (FS)
Perseus/Danaë	§21.2 (I); §22.5 (I/PS); and §54.8 (FS)

Zeus and his sons	§4.9 (FS); §21.1ff (I); §22.1 (I); §33.3 (PS); §54.2, 6 (FS); §55.1 (FS); and §56.1 (FS)
I = Incorporation, PS= Partial Separation, FS = Full Separation	
A. This table has been adapted from the index constructed by Peter Lampe to track all mythical allusions throughout the entirety of Justin's extant works (q.v. *From Paul to Valentinus*, 265–66).	

It is important to note that despite this very close correspondence between the movements of incorporation and full separation, Justin's overall application of this dichotomous hermeneutic should still be understood as being asymmetrical. Although the quantity of occurrences may be similar, the intensities by which Justin employed each respective movement are vastly different.[45] In other words, while one can describe his project to establish resonance between Christian doctrine and Greek myth as somewhat guarded, the same cannot be said of his critique of myth, which could properly be characterized as "vehement."[46] Justin's desire to emphasize the weaknesses in myth over and against the possible redeeming qualities they could provide his readers reveals an impulse within the apologist to have his audience place less and less faith in these refracted pre-figurations of the Logos.

So while Justin worked with his audience inherent simultaneous suspicion and reverence to myth early on in *1 Apology*, by the time one gets towards the end of the work the apologist has shattered this tension altogether placing his full energies in further bolstering his reader's suspicion towards these pagan religious narratives. Pierre Prigent has pointed out that in chapters 54 to 66 Justin virtually repeats the montage of mythical analogies to the life of Christ he established in chapters 21 and 22 but this time goes to great lengths to expose the diabolical origin behind these Greco-Roman

---

45. Glockmann, *Homer in der frühchristlichen Literatur bis Justinus*, 194: "[I]st, so zeigt sich unter Berücksichtigung aller einschlägigen Stellen, daß Justins Verhältnis zu Homer ganz deutlich sowohl von positiven als auch von negativen Momenten bestimmt wird, daß aber die negativen weitaus dominieren."

46. Chadwick aptly captures the high degree by which Justin accentuated his movements of separation from myth: "Towards pagan cult and myth he is vehemently negative: They are crude, superstitious, and immoral both in content and in practical influence" ("The Gospel a Republication of Natural Religion in Justin Martyr," 238). This is where Chadwick's assessment is of great aid to us as there is no way that Justin could have desired that his wavering audience continue to perpetuate their reverence for these myths after the lengths in which he goes to deconstruct them.

religious narratives.[47] Therefore, Justin viewed these illuminating connections that could be made between pagan myth and Christian doctrine as only provisional in nature and by the time his reader had finished *1 Apology* needed to be persuaded that they make the transition to a tradition that was more safe and secure, "Effectively Justin has adopted a positive attitude to pagan glimmerings of the truth, not so much to praise aspects of Hellenistic culture as to boost the status of Christian revelation. He wanted to encourage those who already highly prized the pearl of Greek culture to discover a pearl of considerably greater worth elsewhere."[48]

A "guarded" typology of myth

In order to hasten the departure of his audience's confidence in these pagan narratives, Justin would begin arranging them within a typological framework with the mythical allusion serving as the type (§21–22) and the Christological fulfillment as prophesied by Moses and the Prophets assuming the role of the antitype (§30–53).[49] In *1 Apol.* 23.1, Justin pronounced the Christological foreshadowings that were faintly detectable in myth of inferior quality to those fully evident within Moses and the Prophets, "And in order that this too might now become plain to you, only the things which we say and which we learnt from Christ and the prophets who came before him are true, and they are older than all those who were writers." While one of the motives behind such a claim was to establish an *argumentum ad an-*

---

47. Prigent, *Justin et l'Ancien Testamente*, 160.

48. Keith, "Justin Martyr and Religious Exclusivism," 68.

49. The description of §21–22 as type material and §30–53 as antitype material is my categorization of what Justin is doing with myth and the emerging New Testament narrative and not explicitly described as so by the apologist. According to Goodspeed, Justin did use the term τύπος five different times as it relates to a type-antitype framework but only in relation to the Old Testament and the emerging New Testament narrative. Also, these instances occur within *Dialogue with Trypho* alone: §40.1 (Passover Lamb/Christ); §41.1 (Offering of Flour/Eucharist); §41.4 (Circumcision/Resurrection); §114.1 (the holy Spirit's action in creating type-antitype correspondences); and §140.1 (Jacob/Christ) (*Index apologeticus*, 275). But Justin does utilize the term σύμβολος in *1 Apol.* 55.1–2 (Goodspeed, *Index apologeticus*, 259), which is closely linked to the concept of τύπος and was discussed by the apologist in the context of mythmaking: "But nowhere and about none of the so-called sons of Zeus did they imitate crucifixion. For it was not understood by them, as the things said concerning it were said symbolically (σύμβολικῶς), as was made clear earlier. This, as the prophet said beforehand, is the great symbol (σύμβολον) of his strength and rule." So the type-antitype relation fits here as Justin argued that demons tried to detect the christological σύμβολος or "type" in Moses and the Prophets and end up developing false antitypes (i.e., sons of Zeus) that competed with the one, true antitype.

tiquitatem to allay concerns his readers may have had regarding the antiquity (or the lack thereof) of their newfound faith,[50] Justin more importantly set up the stage for a chronological argument where the similarities between the Christological prophecies in Hebrew Scriptures and the myths of Greek Poetry stemmed from the latter being a demonic knockoff of the former.[51]

Gerald McDermott constructs the historical schema Justin would have understood how this process came about. McDermott uses the apologist's interaction with the myth of Dionysus as his example: (1) a fallen angel or an offspring of one [i.e., a demon] took on the name Dionysus [*2 Apol.* 5.6], (2) the demonic forces eventually stumbled upon the prophecy in Gen. 49:11 about the prince of Judah who, "washes . . . his robe in the blood of grapes" [*1 Apol.* 54.5], (3) since they already had given the name Dionysus or "god of wine" to one of their own, used this Christological foreshadowing to flesh out the character of the new deity [i.e., Dionysus], (4) with the final result of the original prophecy being passed onto the poets in the marred form of "Dionysus is the son of Zeus . . . the discoverer of the vine . . . [with] wine among his mysteries . . . and they taught that he was torn in pieces and that he has gone up to heaven" [*1 Apol.* 54.6].[52]

Yet, Justin recognized that an either outright ignoring or rejecting these ancient narratives (as Chadwick has suggested) would have been counterproductive to his cause. That is, since these stories were deeply etched within the memory of his readers, a historical reckoning of them needed to be provided in relation to the advent of Christianity. While an aspect of Justin's project was thus to expose myth as a diabolical product meant to inhibit Christian belief, as an apologist he also recognized within these same myths refracted truths that could be utilized as evidence that a pagan, pre-Christian anticipation of the Logos in ancient history did indeed exist (albeit demonic). Typology thus allowed him to balance the tension between these two diverse interests by allowing Justin to incorporate aspects of these stories to bolster Christian belief and yet at the same time uphold Christianity's supremacy over that tradition.

In his definition of typology, the renowned archetypal critic Northrop Frye provides a concise explanation of how the correspondence of type and

---

50. Frend, "Old Testament in the Age of the Greek Apologists," 140.

51. Zeegers-vander Vorst, *Les citations des poètes grecs chez les apologistes chrétiens*, 319: "Rappelons-nous par exemple le cas d'Homère tel qu'il est compris dans le cadre de la théorie des emprunts. Aux yeux des apologistes, Homère a énoncé certaines vérités bien proches du christianisme. Mais si le Poète a pu de la sorte préparer l'annonce de la Bonne Nouvelle, c'est dans la mesure où il fut le disciple des prophètes juifs, dont les chrétiens sont les authentiques héritiers."

52. McDermott, *God's Rivals*, 91–92.

antitype allows the writer to both draw upon and yet be lord over the revered past held by his audience:

> Typology is a figure of speech that moves in time: the type exists in the past and the antitype in the present . . . What typology really is as a mode of thought, what it both assumes and leads to, is a theory of history, or more accurately of historical process: an assumption that there is some meaning and point to history, and that sooner or later some event or events will occur which will indicate what that meaning or point is, and so become an antitype of what has happened previously.[53]

As many Christian writers prior to Justin (as well as the apologist himself) imbued new meaning and significance to the stories of Israel's history by viewing them in light of the recent Christ event, Justin would go the additional step of providing his readers what would be the first sustained treatment of how the venerated myths of his audience's past needed to be understood within this new economy.[54]

Now this begs the question of whether Frye's definition of typology can technically be applied to Justin's approach to myth. Frye's definition assumes that a "type" is a *historical* event in the past that foreshadows another *historical* event in the present and/or future (i.e., antitype). There are several occasions in *1 Apology* where Justin insisted on the non-historicity of the myths, "But what was foretold by these the evil demons, myth-making through the poets, spoke as having happened" (*1 Apol.* 23.3) and "those who hand down the myths invented by the poets supply no demonstration to have been said by the working of the evil demons for the deception and misdirection of the human race" (*1 Apol.* 54.1).

But the fact that Justin goes to great lengths to attack the historicity of these myths suggests that Justin's audience was still operating under the premise that these pagan narratives were indeed factual.[55] As established

---

53 Frye, *The Great Code*, 80.

54. Although *Acts of the Apostles* contains glimmers of the supercession of Christianity over paganism in the accounts of Paul and Barnabas in Lystra (Acts 14) and the Aeropagus sermon (Acts 17), the author of Luke/Acts treatment could hardly be described as lengthy and sustained.

55. Glockmann, *Homer in der frühchristlichen Literatur bis Justinus*, 180: "Vermittels der Dichter setzten sie Mythen (sc. über andere Göttersöhne) in die Welt und sorgten sodann dafür, daß diese Mythen allgemeine Verbreitung fanden und als Tatsachen anerkannt wurden (sc. mit der Absicht, daß die Heiden den von den Christen verkündigten Gottessohn mit den von den Dichtern in so unwürdiger Weise geschilderten vermeintlichen Göttersöhnen auf ein und dieselbe Stufe stellen und sich so das Verständnis der christlichen Botschaft verbauen möchten)."

earlier in this chapter, Justin's handling of myth had less to do with his own attitude towards these pagan narratives and more to do with how best to leverage the current paradigm his audience held with regards to them (e.g., simultaneous suspicion and reverence) in order that he might advance the Christian message. Therefore, Justin initially employed a typological framework between myth and the emerging New Testament narrative, not because he believed in the historicity of the myths but rather because his audience did.

I argue the primary type-antitype movement within *1 Apology* exists in the relationship of sections §21–22 to §30–53 where the former is replete with mythical allusions serving as type and the latter contains an exposition of Christological fulfillment acting as the antitype. The main obstacle that has probably prevented this identification within previous scholarship is that the apologist nearly ceased from referring to myth altogether in the antitype section giving way to Moses and the Prophets as the essential proof texts.[56] In my estimation, the dearth of mythical allusions in the latter section of *1 Apology* can be understood as a rhetorical move Justin affirming that typological correspondence was very much at work. As stated previously, Justin knew many of those within his internal audience felt the temptation to revert back to the ancient religion. This abrupt change of religious narratives (i.e., Moses and the Prophets in the place of the myth of the Poets) on the part of Justin was his way of modeling the switching out of sacred texts that needed to occur amongst his readers.

The key text that inextricably links §21–22 and §30–53 in a typological framework is *1 Apol.* 31.7 described by Oskar Skarsaune as the "Creed Sequence." Meanwhile, Skarsaune interestingly labels §21–22 (the material I have identified as *type* material) the "pseudo-Creed Sequence" because the resonant themes Justin established between the sons of Zeus and the Incarnate Logos in this section make-up part of the "Creed Sequence" found in *1 Apol.* 31.7.[57] The "Creed Sequence," in turn, works as a typological pivot that serves as an outline for §30–53 or what I have deemed as the *antitype* material. In the new critical edition of *1 Apology* edited by Paul Parvis and Denis Minns, they, in fact, provide the chapter numbers in §30–53 that correspond to each element outlined in the *1 Apol.* 31.7 otherwise known as the "Creed Sequence," "Well then, in the rolls of the prophets we found out

---

56. There are only a total of five instances of mythical allusion in this section: *1 Apol.* 33.3, 36.2, 44.7–10, 44.12, and 53.1.

57. Skarsaune, *The Proof from Prophecy*, 139–50. Although Skarsaune identifies this fascinating relationship between the two sections, Skarsaune does not explore any further whether the elements found within the "pseudo-Creed sequence" (1 Apol. 21–22) could have been used by Justin as illuminative material for 1 Apol. 30–53.

Lord Jesus Christ, proclaimed ahead of time as drawing near, being born of a virgin [§ 33.1–34.2], and growing to manhood [§ 35.1], and healing every disease and illness, and raising the dead [§ 48.1–2], and being resented and not acknowledged [§ 49.1–7] and being crucified, and dying [§ 35.2–10, 38.1–7, 50.1–11], and rising again [§ 38.5], and going to the heavens [§ 53:4–11], and being called, the Son of God, and we found certain people sent by him to every race of people to proclaim these things [§ 39.1–3; 40.1–4; 45.5], and that it was people from the gentiles rather who believed in him [§ 53.4–11]."[58]

Out of the total of nine elements outlined in the Creed Sequence, five of them are included in the Pseudo-Creed Sequence in *1 Apol.* 21–22 . . . (1) being born of a virgin, (2) healing every disease and illness, and raising the dead, (3) being crucified, and dying, (4) rising, and (5) going into the heavens. The inclusion of these particular themes for the Pseudo-Creed Sequence is hardly incidental when one takes into consideration our previous discussion of Justin's extensive interaction with the mythological concept of θεῖος ἀνήρ here in this section. The blueprint of a true "divine man" as understood by Justin's audience virtually overlaps with each theme contained in the Pseudo-Creed Sequence: (1) being born of a virgin conforms with the category of extraordinary birth, (2) healing every disease and illness, and raising the dead fits nicely with the criteria of virtuous services rendered to humankind earning immortality, (3) dying, and (4) rising again, and going to the heavens corresponds to the pagan understanding of heavenly ascent.

Although technically "rising again" and "going into the heavens" were understood by Justin as two distinct themes, especially when handled in the context of working off the full-fledged Creed Sequence, he conflated these two concepts when working within the realm of Pseudo-Creed Sequence. I posit that this was due in large part to the lack of any instances of immortals dying and then returning back to their human condition in Greco-Roman myth—rather from their death they would go on to deification.[59] Hence, I will mirror Justin's propensity to conflate these two themes when dealing with them in the context of Pseudo-Creed Sequence by handling them as one broader theme as well.

---

58. Minns and Parvis, *Justin, Philosopher and Martyr,* 167nn5–13

59. Rose admits that trying to find a parallel of resurrection in the pagan world especially when it came to dealing with a θεῖος ἀνήρ was impossible to find: "The story of the Resurrection is, of all the incidents in the traditional life of Jesus, the hardest to parallel, a fact that much inclines me to believe that his disciples really had some very vivid subjective experience of a nature to convince them that he was still alive and powerful." (q.v. Rose, "Herakles and the Gospels," 140).

By virtue of their minds being saturated with these pagan narratives, Justin's immediate audience would have made the connection between sections §21–22 and §31–53, "Today we read these texts with a cultural competence radically different than from those for whom they were written; ancient readers could detect allusions invisible to all but the best-trained classicists."[60] To help alleviate the historical distance of the modern reader, it is important to become re-oriented with the mythical stories that Justin merely alluded to as a type. Although this seems at first glance an insurmountable task, there is a niche of controllable literature that explores these stories as they relate specifically to Justin.[61] These resources will be helpful in bringing to light key elements within these pagan stories that would have resonated as a type within the minds of Justin's audience.

At the same time, the typological method utilized in this project will advance the scholarship of these works by providing a guiding principle to the myriad of parallels merely offered by these authors. Frye laments how such an interpretive method by itself ultimately leaves the reader in want, "The only trouble with this is that while parallels are suggestive and even tantalizing, and endless diffusion of analogies does not seem to be getting anywhere, much less nearer an understanding of universal symbolism. To adapt a phrase of Wallace Stevens, there is a continuous dazzle that never yields to clarity."[62] By serving as a corresponding antitype, the Christological fulfillment material in §30–53 provides the criteria by which to validate or invalidate a suggested parallel or analogy.

In a way, Justin's typological method was not all too different from that of great Roman poet, Virgil. Although readers of the *Aeneid* would have perceived that the Roman poet was making clear typological connections with Homeric gods and heroes throughout his epic, it was quite clear from the title of his work the identity of the central *type* to whom the Homeric types paled in comparison: Aeneas the ancient Trojan prince and proto-Roman.[63] In the same manner, Justin typologically connected Homeric gods

60. MacDonald, *Does the New Testament Imitate Homer?* 2.

61. Aune, "Heracles and Christ," 3–19; Ciholas, *The Omphalos and the Cross*; Dölger, "Christus und 'der Heiler' Asklepios bei Justinus"; Fédou, "La vision de la croix dans l'oeuvre de saint Justin"; Hamman, "Dialogue entre le christianisme et la culture grecque," 41–50; Joly, "Parallèles païens pour Justin, Apol. I, 19," 473–81; Rahner, *Greek Myths and Christian Mystery*; Story, "The Cross as Ultimate in the Writings of Justin Martyr," 18–34. Trakatellis, *The Pre-Existence of Christ in Justin Martyr*; Zeegers-vander Vorst, *Les citations des poètes grecs chez les apologistes chrétiens*.

62. Frye, *The Great Code*, 92.

63 Markos, *From Achilles to Christ*, 209: "Aeneas is presented again and again as a type or prefiguring of Augustus: a literary device that allows Virgil either to praise or criticize his emperor by praising or criticizing the actions and choices of his hero."

and heroes with the Incarnated Logos in *1 Apology*, but made it clear that his central type was that which foreshadowed the arrival of the Logos was Moses and the Prophets (*1 Apol.* 30–53). As Virgil's type, Aeneas served as the superior contemporary to the Homeric heroes of Achilles and Odysseus due to his unrivaled *pietas* towards gods, family, and community. As Justin's archetype, Moses and the Prophets act as the superior predecessor to Greek myth because Moses and the Prophets are faithful messengers of the foreshadowings of the Logos—unlike myth that not only stole from Moses and the Prophets but caricatured their message in such a way as to defame the Logos and to ultimately bring undue spiritual harm upon the reader. In so doing, Justin begged of his audience to hasten their abandonment of the stolen and corrupted pre-figurations of the Logos found in myth in favor of the pure, unadulterated, and trustworthy ones easily discernable within Moses and the Prophets.

It is important to point out that there is not one instance in Justin's *1 Apology* (or any of his works for that matter) where he ever alluded to the *Aeneid* directly.[64] Given this silence, how can a relationship between Virgil's typology as seen in his epic poem and Justin's *1 Apology* even be established? The solution, I believe, lies in the fact that Justin's *1 Apology* was not alone in its quiet subversion of the reigning typological framework of that day, Virgil's *Aeneid*. Marianne Palmer Bonz in her book *The Past as Legacy* outlines a whole corpus of rival typologies, pagan and Christian, which emerged upon the scene in the first century to address the Roman public's rising discontent with Nero—the last emperor of the Julio-Claudian dynasty (the dynasty, of course, officially endorsed by the *Aeneid*). Amongst the pagans, the first was Lucan's *Bellum Civile* (AD 61), which was penned during Nero's rule and typologically linked the decadent emperor not to the magnanimous Aeneas but rather the destructive uncle of Augustus and destroyer of the Roman Republic, Julius Caesar. This rendition formed according to Bonz, "a kind of

---

64. Lampe suggests that because Justin supposedly "blundered" in *1 Apol.* 31.2 making Ptolemy Philadelphos (d. 247 BC) a contemporary of Herod the Great (d. 4 BC), this misstep betrayed his unfamiliarity with many Latin works, including Virgil's *Aeneid*. His rationale is that Justin, "could have read [in the *Aeneid*] that in the first century B.C. a charming woman named Cleopatra sat as the last descendent upon the Ptolemaic throne" (Lampe, *From Paul to Valentinus*, 269). But in defense of what appears to be a gross anachronism on Justin's part, Minns and Parvis argue that Justin was not referring to Herod the Great but the Jewish ruler over Israel during the reign of Ptolemy: "[T]he meaning here would not be 'Herod, who was then ruling the Jews,' but 'the Herod who was then ruling the Jews,' as though 'Herod' were a title of principality similar to 'Caesar' or 'Augustus'" (*Justin, Philosopher and Martyr*, 165n4). While an explanation such as this does not help prove that Justin ever read the *Aeneid*, it does sidestep Lampe's claim that Justin never did.

negative salvation history in which the Roman people move ever closer to disintegration and ruin under the rule of the Julio-Claudian family."[65]

Once the Flavian dynasty came into power after the demise of Nero and the year of the three emperors in 69, other competing typological frameworks to the *Aeneid* popped up such as the *Argonautica* of Valerius Flaccus (AD 70–79) and the *Thebaid* of Statius (80–92).[66] In essence, each poem sought to solidify the notion that the Flavian emperors were the true fulfillers of the Roman destiny—not the Julio-Claudian family that had been endorsed by Virgil's *Aeneid*. Bonz goes on to argue that even Justin's Christian predecessor, the author of *Luke-Acts*, got into the typological fray by providing a uniquely Christian response to the well-renowned Virgilian framework by, "recasting his community's sacred traditions in a style and manner that would make the Christian claim a powerful and appealing rival to the ubiquitous and potentially seductive salvation claims of imperial Rome [whether found in the *Aeneid* or its pagan counterparts]."[67] As argued by Bonz, predecessors to Justin both pagan and Christian had set up the typological battleground or stage where the apologist could then provide his own rendition of how the venerated myths of his readers measured against the emerging Christian narrative.

From Traditional Binary Approach to Dynamic Approach

The application of the classical insights of the "doubleness" of poetry and pagan typology towards Justin's interaction with myth allows us to depart from traditional binary paradigms within scholarship that have sought to conform Justin's overall approach to myth as either being positive (viz., Carlos Contreras) or negative (viz., Henry Chadwick). By understanding that Justin framed his diverse approach to myth based upon his audience's simultaneous reverence and suspicious of these stories, the categories of positive and negative are no longer useful.

Instead of stalling at the question of *how* Justin viewed myth (i.e., negatively or positively), now we can focus our energies upon *what* Justin was actually doing with it. This assertion was first brought up by Peter Widdicombe in his 1997 article, "Justin Martyr, Allegorical Interpretation, and

---

65. Bonz, *The Past as Legacy*, 68.

66. Ibid., 61–86. According to Bonz, Valerius Flaccus's *Argonautica* typologically links Vespasian to the legendary Jason while Statius' *Thebaid* typologically links the Julio-Claudian family to the house of Oedipus (who brings disorder to Thebes/Rome) while at the same time linking Domitian to Theseus (the restorer of Thebes/Rome).

67. Ibid., 86.

the Greek Myths" where he suspected that these binary categories of under-standing Justin's approach to myth have all but become obsolete.[68] Wid-dicombe argues that the few instances in which Justin actually allegorized myth (a method that pagans employed to protect these stories from disre-pute) should be a clear signal to us that any attempt to determine Justin's overall attitude to myth is an unfruitful endeavor.

Although I disagree with Widdicombe's conclusion that Justin's harsh critique of myth can simply be ignored, I agree that much can be gained if one has the freedom to explore what the apologist was seeking to con-vey in his mythical allusions without being hampered by the limitations of a predetermined category (i.e., positive versus negative) looming in the background. I contend that in order for this change in paradigm to occur, though, the language used to describe Justin's interaction with myth needs to be revamped entirely. Instead of labeling Justin's approach to myth as being positive or negative, I will replace the former label of "positive" to the phrase *incorporation of myth* and the label of "negative" to *separation from myth*. This change in nomenclature helps us look past Justin's attitude to myth (positive versus negative) to what Justin was attempting to argue through his interactions with these pagan narratives.

At this juncture, some insights from modern scholarship that helped me to formulate these two categories are worth mentioning. An excellent description of what I envision *incorporation of myth* encompassing is found in thought of Louis Markos who asserts that pagan narratives can be used to bolster the pre-eminence of Christian doctrine by acting as "glimpses, road signs, pointers to a greater truth that was someday to be revealed liter-ally and historically in a specific time and place."[69] As a C. S. Lewis scholar, Markos implements Lewis's approach to account for how the story of Christ could sound strikingly similar to pagan myths of dying and rising gods: Jesus was the myth made fact.[70]

An example of this can be seen in the parallels that resonate between Dionysus (as depicted in Euripides's *Bacchae*) and Jesus Christ. John Taylor describes in detail the various connections the Greco-Roman mind would have immediately perceived when confronted by the stories of both figures:

> Dionysus comes as a god in human form (and not just a fleeting appearance as the Olympians in Homer typically do). He comes in disguise to his own domain. Unrecognized, he is rejected

68. Widdicombe, "Justin Martyr, Allegorical Interpretation, and the Greek Myths," 234–35.

69. Markos, *From Achilles to Christ*, 248.

70. Lewis, "Myth Became Fact," 66–67.

specifically by members of his own family ('his own received him not'). He faces hostility and unbelief from the ruling powers of the city, but is welcomed by the meek and lowly. He works miracles. Dionysus as a prisoner answers the questions of Pentheus in a studiedly enigmatic way, so that we sense it is the interrogator who is really on trial.[71]

The modern reader is, therefore, at a distinct disadvantage not having the full, vivid story in their memory to which Justin only briefly alluded. Such a deficiency prevents one from perceiving implied connections Justin may have anticipated that his original audience would have made given their complete familiarity with the pagan narratives.[72] This project will seek to bridge that gap by reengaging the mythical stories that Justin merely alluded to as a type.

In regards to *separation from myth*, Peter Leithart contends that pagan narratives antithetically positioned in relation to Christianity can still serve to illuminate Christian belief. This is accomplished when the characteristics of the two are purposefully held in stark contrast to one another, "None of these poems or plays teach the wisdom of Christ in a direct way. Rather, by wrestling to evaluate these books biblically, we are led to discover biblical truth that we might otherwise have overlooked. Pagan literature can, rightly used, give us an important entry into the mind and culture of fallen humanity, and even sharpen our understanding of the Christian worldview."[73] In essence, these mythical narratives according to Leithart can serve as a literary foil accenting Christian doctrine in the mind of the reader.

In her analysis of how to consider separatist discourse amongst early church thinkers, Karen King offers a fresh way to think about separation from myth besides understanding it as merely a sort of disclaimer for the apologist's incorporative use of these pagan narratives. King argues that the attempt of Irenaeus, for instance, to downplay the so-called Gnostics in *Against Heresies* was less about defining Gnosticism and more about establishing an internal self-definition of Christianity. In other words, by discounting Gnostic conceptions of God, Irenaeus conversely eliminated

---

71 Taylor, *Classics and the Bible*, 62.

72. Hatch remarks about the pervasiveness of these narratives within the collective memory of those in the ancient world, "The main subject-matter of . . . literary education was the poets . . . They were read as we read the Bible. They were committed to memory. The minds of men were saturated with them. A quotation from Homer or from a tragic poet was apposite on all occasions and in every kind of society" (*The Influence of Greek Ideas on Christianity*, 30).

73. Leithart, *Heroes of the City of Man*, 21–22.

attributes of how the Christian God was to be understood thereby cobbling out a distinctive social identity for proto-orthodox Christians.[74]

In the same manner, I contend that when Justin exercised *separation from myth* by describing the pagan gods as deceptive, unbecoming of divinity, and disorderly that he was not only conversely framing how the Christian God was to be understood (i.e., true, pure, and perfect) but Justin was mapping out a distinctive Christian social identity as well. Therefore, I will adopt King's method of the socially interpreting separatist discourse amongst early church thinkers to analyze the instances where Justin exercised *separation from myth* in *1 Apology* especially in §23–30 and §54–66.[75]

King's method to interpret separatist discourse is based on the premise that the audience had a familiarity with the heretical system being used as a foil to Christianity. But given the esoteric nature of Gnosticism, it is questionable whether the majority of Irenaeus' audience would have been versed with the contours of this secretive religious system. On the other hand, King's method to interpret separatist discourse dovetails nicely with Justin's situation where his internal audience would have been completely familiar with all the various classical myths to which the apologist alluded.

---

74. Gruen also challenges how we should think about separatist discourse in ancient Mediterranean societies: "While ancient societies certainly acknowledged differences among peoples (indeed occasionally emphasizing them) could also visualize themselves as part of a broader cultural heritage, could discover or invent links with other societies, and could couch their own historical memories in terms of a borrowed or appropriated past. When ancients reconstructed their roots or fashioned their history, they often did so by associating themselves with the legends and traditions of others. That practice affords a perhaps surprising but certainly revealing insight into the mentalities of Mediterranean folk in antiquity. It discloses not how they *distinguished* themselves from others but how they transformed or reimagined them for their own purposes. The "Other" takes on a different shape. This is not rejection, denigration, or distancing—but rather appropriation. It represents a more circuitous and more creative mode of fashioning a collective self-consciousness" (*Rethinking the Other in Antiquity*, 3–4).

75. King, *What is Gnosticism?*, 20–52, 239–47.

3

Incorporation of Myth

ESTABLISHING TYPOLOGICAL CORRESPONDENCE
BETWEEN §21–22 AND §30–53

IN THIS CHAPTER, I shall demonstrate my typological theory of myth as it pertains to *1 Apology* by identifying interchanges occurring between the type material in §21–22 with that of the antitype material in §30–53. While such an endeavor requires some theological imagination, the typological relationship between these two respective sections should naturally curb what Northrop Frye describes as the temptation to create "diffusive analogies that do not seem to get anywhere."[1] Therefore, the resonances teased out from Justin's mythical allusions serving as type must be substantiated from the scriptural content present in the corresponding antitype material.

The antitype material, understood by Justin as the clearest portrayal of the history of Christ derived from his extensive citations of Old Testament prophetic passages deemed most tried and true[2], imposes a sort of typological trajectory upon the mythical allusions mentioned by Justin in the type material. The awareness of this trajectory is crucial because Justin's reference to events concerning the gods (e.g., Dionysus being torn to pieces) are characteristically brief and without much elaboration. Yet, I posit that each allusion to myth would have brought the entire story for which it belonged

1. Frye, *The Great Code*, 92.

2. *Dialogue with Trypho* 1.3: "'How,' I asked [Trypho], 'can you gain as much from philosophy as from your own lawgiver and prophets?'"

to the forefront of his reader's consciousness. Although this opens up fascinating possibilities for mining Christological resonances amongst the related yet unmentioned narratival aspects surrounding Justin's mythical allusions, this could also potentially create the problem of parallelomania highly warned about by Frye.[3]

This is where being mindful of the typological trajectory, set into motion by the antitype material, provides invaluable direction as well as limits on the sort of Christological resonances that can be legitimately teased out from these stories. In order to ensure such a methodology is actively at work, I shall treat the two respective sections in reverse fashion dealing with the antitype material before the type material. So as I go about in this chapter treating the four Christological themes contained in the Pseudo-Creed Sequence (virgin birth, healing ministry, passion, and resurrection/ascension), I will begin the treatment of each theme mapping out that particular theme's typological trajectory based upon the antitype material and in so doing develop parameters that make the selection process for silent elements of narration surrounding Justin's mythical allusions one that is purposeful and with direction.

While Justin obviously prioritized the value of the Old Testament fulfillment passages over that of his allusions to myth, this should not diminish how important his inclusion of the latter was to his overall argument of *1 Apology* especially when one takes into consideration the pagan background of his audience. Oskar Skarsaune has identified Justin's argument in the antitype material as being thoroughly Jewish in nature pointing out the distinctive Messianic Christology that drives Justin's scriptural exegesis in §30–53. Skarsaune marvels at how this approach employed by Justin all but defies modern historiographies that tend to portray a situation in the early church where an exclusively Jewish argument such as this one would have been incommensurable to a second century Gentile reader.

> It would have been futile, Pinchas Lapide maintains, if [Justin] in Rome had proclaimed the Son of David to be the anointed *Jewish Messiah.* 'They would not know what he was talking about.' Perhaps, but that was exactly what Justin did, prompted by (one could answer) his faith in the Old Testament as holy Scripture.[4]

3. Samdel, "Parallelomania," 1: "We might for our purpose define parallelomania as that extravagance among scholars which first overdoes the supposed similarity in passages and then proceeds to describe source and derivation as if implying literary connection flowing in an inevitable or predetermined direction."

4. Skarsaune, *Incarnation: Myth or Fact?*, 62. Lapide quotes from his book *Jøder og kristne: Bidrag til en dialog*, 94.

In highlighting what appears to be a mismatch of message to audience, Skarsaune entertains a possible scenario where the apologist was forced to defend how Christ was the fulfillment of Old Testament Messianic promises in order to retain Christianity's Jewish roots. This was due to the emerging threat of Gnosticism and Marcionism, which either possessed an indifferent attitude towards the Old Testament (i.e., Gnosticism) or tried to sever ties from the Jewish Scriptures altogether (i.e., Marcionism).[5] Although this is an interesting theory by Skarsaune, I contend that there is a better way to understand how Justin went about mediating a thoroughly Jewish argument to a Gentile audience. By first convincing his reader that hints of this Messianic Christology was detectable in the narratives of their ancestral religion (§21–22), such as Jesus being of divine birth, dying, and rising into the heavens, Justin was able to prepare his reader's theological palate for the eventual full digesting of his robust Messianic argument in §30–53 that Jesus was the Anointed One whom the Hebrew Scriptures had long anticipated. In this case, Justin's allusions to myth in §21–22 played no ancillary role in Justin's *1 Apology* as the Christological resonances that Justin detects therein serve as a theological translator or even "adapter" that makes what would have initially been foreign to a Gentile mind on its own terms, now meaningful.[6] The fact that in §21–22 he introduced a Pseudo-Creed Sequence that is a partial version of the full Creed Sequence brought up later in *1 Apology* betrays a movement where Justin was slowly acclimating his Gentile audience to the full-blown Jewish Messianic argument he would introduce them to in §30–53.

An important issue that needs to be brought up at this juncture is the unsystematic manner by which Justin elaborated upon the themes of the Pseudo-Creed sequence throughout §21–22 and what provision I have put into place to offset this issue. Instead of following the natural progression of the Pseudo-Creed sequence (virgin birth, healing ministry, passion, and resurrection/ascension), Justin arranged his mythical allusions in this section in a serpentine and staccato fashion making it difficult to provide a sustained analysis of the corresponding themes that lie beneath his exposition. So instead of treating Justin's allusions to the gods on the basis of their chronological ordering within the type material, I will follow the thematic progression of the Pseudo-Creed sequence lifting out each mythical allusion and placing them into the respective theme to which they belong (*1*

5. Ibid., *Incarnation: Myth or Fact?*, 62–64.

6. Knox, "The 'Divine Hero' Christology in the New Testament," 242: "All that we have is the use of a common stock of ideas, ultimately religious, but adopted by rhetoric and popular philosophy, and carried over into the liturgical and homiletic language of the Hellenistic world, including that of the Church."

Apol. 21.1f): (1) extraordinary birth, (2) Christ's healing ministry, (3) his suffering and death, and (4) his resurrection and ascension into Heaven. In so doing, below is an arrangement of Justin's mythical allusions throughout the type material (§21–22) ordered on the basis of the Christological theme to which they belong within the Pseudo-Creed sequence:

Justin's allusions to Perseus begotten of Danaë (§21.2, §22.5), Ganymede (§21.5), and Hermes (§21.2, §22.2) fall within the category of elements dealing with extraordinary birth.

- Justin's allusion to Asclepius in §22.6 belongs to the theme of Christ's healing ministry.

- Justin's allusions to Asclepius (§21.2), Dionysus (§21.2), and Heracles (§21.2) fit in the theme of Christ's suffering and death.

- Finally, Justin's mentioning of the Diocuri (§21.2), Bellerophon (§21.2), Ariadne (§21.3), and Caesar (§21.3) are allusions relating to the theme of resurrection and ascension.

Since the majority, if not all, of these mythical allusions deal with the concept of the sons of Zeus and his relations in either begetting or impacting the lives of these particular θεῖος ἀνήρ in some form or fashion, allusions to the lightning god will be ever present amongst all of the themes. It is important to note that the focus of this chapter will be on Christological resonance and resemblance in Justin's allusions to myth, while the next chapter (Ch. 4) will be dealing with the same loci of themes but with Justin's separation from myth in mind as he sought to hasten his audience's departure from these once venerated religious narratives.

"Being Born of a Virgin"

The biblical passages for the antitype material regarding this Christological theme are found in *1 Apology* 33.1–34.2.[7] The Old Testament fulfillment passages cited therein by Justin are Isaiah 7:14 and Micah 5:1–2 while he recruited texts from the Gospel writers Luke (1:31–32) and Matthew (1:20–21, 2:6) to corroborate that the Hebrew Scriptures he had cited were indeed fulfilled in the arrival of Jesus.[8]

---

7. Minns and Parvis, *Justin, Philosopher and Martyr*, 167n5.

8. Ibid., 173nn5 and 7, 175nn4 and 6. Skarsaune, "Justin and His Bible," 76: "In Justin there is not yet a canonical text of the New Testament books, not even the Gospels. And there is not yet any clear delimitation of exactly which documents should be considered authoritative above others, once we are outside the category of *Memoirs* or Gospels."

In constructing a typological trajectory from the Scripture passages in the antitype material, the basic contours would look like this: (1) Christ was prophesied in Isa 7:14 that he would be born of a virgin (παρθένος) signifying he was of supernatural parentage—a characteristic that received further affirmation by Justin when he translated the name "God with us" (§33.1) directly into the Greek (Μεθ᾽ ἡμῶν ὁ θεός) instead of adapting the transliterated version of the name from the LXX (Ἐμμανουήλ)[9], (2) the prophecy of the Virgin Birth in Isa 7:14 is then confirmed by the account of Mary and Joseph in Luke 1:31–32 and Matt 1:20–21 who are both approached and comforted by an angel regarding the miraculous birth that she is about to participate, (3) followed by the significance of the child that will be born (i.e., "he will save his people from their sins"), and finally ending with (4) the proclamation that the very place of his birth (i.e., Bethlehem) having been predicted long before by the Old Testament prophet, Micah (5.1–2), and then verified by the Gospel writer, Matthew (2.6).

Perseus, begotten of Danaë (21.2; 22.5)

In the type material, Perseus is brought up regarding his supernatural birth: "And if we allege birth through a virgin, consider this the same as in the case of Perseus" (§22.5). As Justin argued that Christ's birth was of supernatural origin, he explicitly took advantage of the case of Perseus whose father was reputed to be the Greek god, Zeus.[10] Furthermore, as Christ's mother was a virgin at the time of her impregnation—so, too, was the mother of Perseus, Danaë.[11] Also as the power of God "overshadowed" (ἐπεσκίασεν) Mary so that she would conceive (§33.4), the approach of the thunder god disguising

---

9. In *Dialogue with Trypho* 67, Trypho argued with Justin on how the LXX has the wrong Greek word (παρθένος) to represent "young woman" in the Hebrew text (𝔐almah). Trypho asserts that the Greek word that better approximates "young woman" should be the word νεᾶνις. Trypho goes on to say that child spoken of in Isaiah 7:14 is actually Hezekiah, who was yet to be born but Justin responds to Trypho by charging him for "putting faith in his teachers who had tampered with the text of the Septuagint in order to make the text of Isaiah apply to Hezekiah." This semantic tug-of-war reveals how much Justin is unwilling to capitulate on the divine parentage of Jesus (q.v. Sweeney, "Modern and Ancient Controversies over the Virgin Birth of Jesus," 154).

10. Diodorus Siculus, *Library of History* 4.9.1; Herodotus, *Histories* 7.61; Hesiod, *Shield of Heracles*. 229; Homer, *Illiad* 14.310; Pseudo-Hyginus, *Fabulae* 155.

11. Rose, "Herakles and the Gospels," 116: "According to Plutarch [Numa 4, cf. quaest. conuiu. 718 b.], the Egyptians were of opinion that although no mortal man could be the lover of a goddess, it was possible for a god's πνεῦμα to 'draw near to a mortal woman and implant in her certain beginnings of birth.'"

himself as a golden shower to impregnate the imprisoned Danaë would have rang familiar in the minds of Justin's readers.[12]

But another similarity not mentioned by Justin that would have reso-nated with his readers was that as the prophets Isaiah and Micah predicted the birth of Jesus, so too did the oracle of Apollo prophecy about the child who was to be born from the daughter of King Acrisius. Even specific details regarding the significance of their lives were foretold: Jesus was to be born in Bethlehem (Mic. 5:1–2) and the one who "will save his people from their sins" (Matt 1:20–21) while the son of Danaë was predicted to be the killer of his grandfather, which was fulfilled later in Perseus' life when he accidently struck King Acrisius with a discus.[13]

Given the nature of typology, there is a movement to establish similar-ity (*ad similia*) followed by a movement where the antitype figure surpasses its counterpart in greatness (*a fortiori*) also known as a partial separation from myth. With the figures of Perseus and Danaë, such a dynamic can be demonstrated. While the name of Mary's child was pronounced prior to his birth in several instances both in Isa 7:14 ("God with us") as well as by the angel Gabriel (Jesus), Danaë's child did not receive such acclaim other than that he would be the one who would kill his grandfather.[14] Also the respective circumstances surrounding Mary and Danaë's virginity are vastly different. While Mary was a virgin on the basis of her virtuousness and choice, Danaë was a virgin due to her father locking her up in a bronze tower so that no man would be able to impregnate her.[15]

---

12. Labriolle, *La Réaction Païenne*, 118–19: "Des vestiges de legendes paiennes restent discernables au fond de plusiers de leurs croyances: l'affirmation que le Christ serait ne d'une vierge visitiée par l'espirit saint rappelle les fables de danae, de mela-nippe, d'Augé et d'antiope"; Ovid, *Metamorphoses* 4.604: "Acrisius, the son of Abas, sprung from the same stock, who forbade the entrance of Bacchus within the walls of his city, Argos, who violently opposed the god, and did not admit that he was a son of Jove. Nor did he admit that Perseus was son of Jove [Zeus], whom Danaë had conceived of a golden shower"; Lycophron, *Alexandra* 838.

13. Pseudo-Hyginus, *Fabulae* 63: "When Acrisius was detained there by a storm, Polydectes died, and at his funeral games the wind blew a discus from Perseus' hand at Acrisius' head which killed him. Thus what he did not do of his own will was ac-complished by the gods."

14. It is interesting to note that the name *Perseus,* which Danaë gives to her child at his birth, means "avenger" in the Greek to accentuate that he would live to avenge her father who had unjustly locked her up in the tower (q.v. Evslin, *Heroes, Gods, and Monsters of the Greek Myths*, 112).

15. Horace, *Carmen Saeculare* 3.16; Pausanias, *Description of Greece* 2.23.7; Sophocles, *Antigone* 947.

Another stark contrast that Justin's readers could have noticed is that Zeus seduced Danaë.[16] No such manipulation or coercion would occur in the Gospel accounts as the angel Gabriel came to announce God's favor on Mary encouraging both her and Joseph to be willing participants in this miraculous occurrence they would soon experience. In relation to this, Justin was also critical of Zeus sexually gratifying himself with the virgin Danaë (1 Apol. 33.3) while the Christian God preserved both His honor and that of Mary by causing, "her to be pregnant not through intercourse but through power" (1 Apol. 33.6) It is important to note that while Zeus in the guise of a golden shower actually made contact with Danaë (pouring himself into her lap), no such indiscretion is reported of the Christian God in His overshadowing movement (1 Apol. 33.4). So while Danaë no longer was a virgin after her encounter with Zeus, Mary's chastity was in contrast completely preserved.

To further highlight the profligate nature of Zeus, Justin reminds his reader not only of the whole myriad of other maidens to have been sexually taken advantage of by the god of lightning but also of the rape performed by Zeus upon even a man, "enslaved by love to evil and shameful pleasures, had sex with Ganymede and with the many women he debauched, and this his own children did similar things" (1 Apol. 21.5). According to the poetic tradition, Zeus abducted this Trojan prince and sexually violated him making Ganymede his eventual winebearer.[17] Plato even accused the Cretans of fabricating this story in order that their decadent lifestyles might have divine license, "And we all accuse the Cretans of concocting the story about Ganymede. Because it was the belief that they derived their laws from Zeus, they added on this story about Zeus in order that they might be following his example in enjoying this pleasure as well" (Laws 636c).[18] Justin, of course,

---

16. Pseudo-Apollodorus, The Library 2.4.1: "When Akrisios later learned that she had given birth to Perseus, not believing that Zeus seduced her, he cast his daughter out to sea with her son on an ark. The ark drifted ashore at Seriphos, where Diktys recovered the child and brought him up"; Homer, Iliad 14.319.

17. Homeric Hymn 5 to Aphrodite 204: "Verily wise Zeus carried off golden-haired Ganymedes because of his beauty, to be amongst the Deathless Ones and pour drink for the gods in the house of Zeus, a wonder to see, honored by all the immortals as he draws the red nectar from the golden bowl . . . deathless and un-aging, even as the gods"; Statius, Silvae 3. 4.13: "Pine-clad Ida . . . pride herself on the cloud of a holy rape [of Ganymede]—for surely she gave the High Ones him at whom Juno [Hera] ever looks askance, recoiling from his hand and refusing the nectar"; Euripides, Iphigenia at Aulis 1051; Homer, Iliad 20.232; Ovid, Metamorphoses 10. 152; Pindar, Olympian Ode 1.40; Pseudo-Apollodorus, The Library 3.141; Pseudo-Hyginus, Astronomica 2.16, 29; Theognis, Fragment 1.1345.

18. Plato, Laws, trans. Bury, 41.

would share the same sentiment regarding how myths like this encouraged corrupt behavior in its readers (*1 Apol.* 21.4).

Hermes (21.2, 22.2)

In the type material, Hermes is alluded to on two instances to expand upon a different dimension surrounding his supernatural birth: (1) "Hermes the explanatory word [λόγον] and teacher of all"[19] [§21.2] and (2) "But if in fact we say that, in a special manner and not ordinary birth, he was born from God, as we said before, as Logos [λόγον] of God, consider this the same as your calling Hermes the logos who announces things that come from god." [§22.2]. While Justin's allusions to Perseus and Danaë focused on the miraculous qualities surrounding the birth itself, these references to Hermes were an attempt by the apologist to highlight another extraordinary aspect behind the birth of Jesus: his preexistent qualities.[20] He would do this, of course, by arguing he was the eternal Logos of God, which in Justin's Middle Platonic categories was the very instrument by which the divine revealed itself to the world.[21]

In both instances, Justin is leveraging an emerging pagan understanding of Hermes as λόγος to illuminate how Jesus is to be understood as λόγος within Christian belief. Given the prevalent Stoic conception of λόγος as not being a person but rather a rational principle imparted to man, coupling

19. Minns and Parvis omit this allusion from their critical edition suggesting that it was an addition "supplied by a redactor who has supposed that when Hermes is mentioned in *1 Apol.* 22.2 the back-reference there 'as we said before' means that there must be an earlier reference to Hermes, when it need be no more than a reference to the origin of Jesus a Son of God" (q.v. *Justin, Philosopher and Martyr*, 133n1). But Widdicombe has pointed out that it was a common practice within the classical tradition to utilize ἑρμηνεύω (*1 Apol.* 21.2) and ἄγγελος (*1 Apol.* 22.2) in tandem when describing Hermes as λόγος: "Plato in the *Cratylos* 407e had suggested the derivation and had linked ἑρμηνεύς with ἄγγελος, describing Hermes as interpreter and messenger. Heraclitus . . . alludes to *Cratylos* 407e, styling Hermes as τὸν ἑρμηνεύοντα and as ἄγγελος. Philo too was familiar with the allegory. While he never identifies Hermes with the Logos, in *Legatio ad Gaium* 99 he describes Hermes as 'the interpreter (τὸν ἑρμηνέα) and the prophet of God' and refers to him as διάγγελος" (q.v. "Justin Martyr, Allegorical Interpretation, and the Greek Myths," 237). For Minns and Parvis to omit the Hermes allusion in *1 Apol.* 21.2 would be to break up this terminological coupling (ἑρμηνεύω . . . ἄγγελος) that seemed to be a convention within the philosophical tradition for how Hermes as λόγος was described.

20. Machen, *The Virgin Birth of Christ*, 318. According to Machen, there is for Justin "the close connection between the doctrine of the virgin birth and the doctrine of the preexistence of Christ. That connection unquestionably exists."

21. Edwards, "On the Platonic schooling of Justin Martyr," 23.

Jesus with Hermes would allow Justin to establish the personhood of the λόγος through a mythical allusion his audience would be quite familiar. In his first reference to Hermes in *1 Apol.* 21.2, Justin employs a subtle, yet clever etymological argument to explain further the role of the messenger god with the full intent of transposing that notion onto Christ: Ἑρμῆν μέν, λόγον τὸν ἑρμηνευτικὸν.[22] This wordplay using the adjectival participle ἑρμηνευτικὸν would have been a catchy way of illuminating the role of Jesus as λόγος. So while the deity Hermes had been given the primary task of "explaining" the express will of the gods (not his own)[23] to the world, in a similar fashion Jesus was responsible for solely conveying the will of the one who sent him.

In *1 Apol.* 22.2, Justin highlighted the fact that Hermes was assigned the role of the messenger god "who announces" (ἀγγελτικὸν) divine things to humankind below on behalf of the other eleven gods of Mount Olympus (yet being one of the gods of Mount Olympus himself)[24] made his figure an attractive candidate to parallel with that of Jesus: as Hermes interacted with humanity yet upheld his high standing as one of the twelve gods of the Pantheon, so too, did the Son of God come down and mingle with humanity still upholding his divine status as well.[25]

As stated previously from the antitype material, Justin went at great lengths to emphasize the deity and perhaps preexistence of the Messiah prophesied about in Isa 7:14 by ensuring that the significance of his name did not go unnoticed by his Gentile reader. Instead of settling for Ἐμμανουήλ, which was a bald transliteration of the Hebrew word for "God with us" (עִמָּנוּאֵל) in the LXX, Justin took the initiative to offer the translation in its place (i.e., Μεθ' ἡμῶν ὁ θεός) ensuring that his non-Jewish audience

---

22. Widdicombe, "Justin Martyr, Allegorical Interpretation, and the Greek Myths," 237. Widdicombe argues that this etymological argument to establish Hermes role was something that he did not invent but rather borrowed from the philosophical tradition: "The allegorical interpretation of Hermes' name and role was a common-place in the allegorical tradition and presumably Justin could have taken it from a number of sources."

23. Ovid, *Metamorphoses* 2.743: "I [Hermes] am he who carry my father's messages through the air. My father is Jove [Zeus] himself"; Pseudo-Apollodorus, *The Library* 3.115: "And Zeus made Hermes his personal herald and messenger of the gods beneath the earth"; Hesiod, *Theogony* 938; Homer, *Odyssey* 5.4; *Orphic Hymn 28 to Hermes*; Pausanias, *Description of Greece* 8.32.4.

24. Philostratus the Elder, *Imagines* 1.26: "Birth of Hermes . . . He is born on the crest of Olympus, at the very top, the abode of the gods . . . The mountain rejoices in him for its smile is like that of a man and you are to assume that Olympus rejoices because Hermes was born there."

25. Homer, *Odyssey* 19.135, and *Iliad* 24.333; *Homeric Hymn 18 to Hermes*; *Homeric Hymn 29 to Hestia*; *Orphic Hymn 28 to Hermes*.

fully apprehended its meaning. It is interesting to note that while both Perseus and Hermes were technically considered sons of Zeus due to having the same father, they were qualitatively different types of deities as Perseus was understood to be an "immortal" while Hermes an "eternal."[26] As discussed in the previous chapter, this designation of Perseus as an immortal while that of Hermes as an eternal had much to do with the status of each of their mothers: while the former had a human mother (i.e., Danaë), the latter had a divine one (i.e., the Titaness, Maia).[27] Therefore, the status of Hermes as an "eternal" would assist Justin in communicating how the Son of God both preexisted and yet walked amongst humanity.

Yet the one quality that is not explicitly mentioned by Justin but shared by both Hermes and Jesus is that despite their presence here in the world below, their divine statuses are both upheld mainly because of their remarkable faithfulness as messengers for the one who sent them. For instance in *Odyssey* 5.97, the nymph Calypso with sumptuous feast prepared so as to distract the messenger god asked why he so often visited her. He would reply, "You, a goddess, have questioned me, a god, upon my coming, and I will speak my word truly, since you ask me to. It was Zeus who bade me come here against my will. Who of his own will would speed over so great space of salt seawater, great past telling? Nor is there at hand any city of mortals who offer to the gods sacrifice and choice hetacombs. But it is in no way possible for any other god to evade or make void the will of Zeus, who bears the aegis." In the same manner, Jesus in the antitype material is understood as one who will be faithful to perform the mission of the one

---

26. This begs the question if Justin contradicted himself when identifying Perseus as a son of Zeus (i.e., an immortal) and Hermes as a son of Zeus (i.e., eternal) as demonic imitations of Christ as the Son of God with the former having a human mother while the latter a divine one. But if we take into account that Justin held that the demons took guesses trying to determine the makeup of the Son of God who was to come (i.e., Human? Divine? Semi-divine?), then to the apologist these varying constitutions of the sons of Zeus depicted in myth was a demonic guesswork at play. In fact, the notion that a wholly divine being (i.e., an eternal) could walk amongst humanity was according to Frances Young the first heresy in the early church: "Pagan mythology could envisage a docetic incarnation, Jewish legend could envisage the coming of an angel in disguise. The association of historical or contemporary personages with the appearance of the gods was occasionally made, but hardly seems to have been taken seriously. Is it any wonder that the first Christian heresy was docetism?" ("Two Roots of a Tangled Mass?" 119).

27. Talbert, "The Concept of Immortals in Mediterranean Antiquity," 420. Aeschylus, *Libation Bearers* 683; *Alcaeus Frag* 308; Apollodorus 3.112; Hesiod, *Theogony* 938 & *Astronomy Frag* 1; *Homeric Hymn 4 to Hermes, Homeric Hymn* 17, *Simonides Frag* 555; Ovid, *Fasti* 5.79

who sent him, "for from you will come forth a leader who will shepherd my people." (Mic. 5:1–2)

"Healing every disease and illness, and raising the dead"

The biblical passages for the antitype material regarding this Christological theme are found in 1 *Apology* 48.1–2, "And also that it was foretold that our Christ was going to cure all illnesses and raised the dead, listen to the things that are said. They are these 'At his coming the lame shall leap like the deer, and the speech of the stutters shall be clear, the blind shall see again, and lepers shall be made clean, and the dead shall be raised, and they shall walk about.'"[28] The Old Testament fulfillment passages cited by Justin in text above are from Isa 35:5–6 and 26:19 respectively.[29]

In constructing a typological trajectory from the Scripture passages in the antitype material, the basic contours would look like this: there is an elevation in benefit to humanity as the antitype material here transitions from Isaiah 35:5–6 to 26:19. While the first two passages employ the literary device of *merism* to describe the comprehensiveness of Christ's healing powers by listing four contrasting types of physical miracles (i.e., restoring sight, opening deaf ears, making the lame walk, and the mute speak) he was able to perform, the last instance (Isaiah 26:19) would serve for Justin the crescendo of the extent of the coming Messiah's ability to heal: that he was capable of even raising the dead. According to the prophetic passages, his healing ministry was being awaited upon with great expectation by all.

Asclepius (21.2; 22.3–4; 22.6)

In the type material, Asclepius is alluded to on two instances regarding his ability to heal and raise people from the dead: (1) "Asclepius, who was also a healer, after being struck by lightning" [§21.2] and (2) "But when we say he made well the lame and paralytics and those blind and that raised the dead, our saying these things will seem to be like the things said to have been done by Asclepius" [§22.6]. Minns and Parvis argue that Justin was so impressed with the resemblance of Asclepius' purported ability to heal and to raise the dead with that of Jesus that he incorrectly included the healing god amongst the sons of Zeus.[30] Although they are technically correct that Asclepius was

---

28. Minns and Parvis, *Justin, Philosopher and Martyr*, 167n7.

29. Ibid., 203n10.

30. Ibid., 133n1: "Asclepius is at best only a grandson of Zeus (on his father's

actually the son of Apollo, Justin seemed to be following a poetic tradition that tended to bundle Heracles, Dionysus, and Asclepius together as the ideal figures making up the θεῖος ἀνήρ, "The most prominent figures in this class were Heracles, Asclepius (who was, however, normally confined pretty strictly to his purely medical duties) and Dionysus: and of these Heracles was the most prominent in the tradition of popular philosophy."[31]

While on the surface they appear to imitate each other in powers, the Gentile mind would have been attuned to the stark qualitative differences that lay behind their ability to heal and raise the dead. Just as in the case of Perseus and Danaë, Justin probably anticipated that his audience could intuit a typological movement of *ad similia* to *a fortiori* (i.e., partial separation from myth) between Asclepius and Jesus by merely placing them side by side, "Justin established an analogy between the works of Asclepius and those of Christ, with the intent, of course, of proving Christ superior to Asclepius."[32]

One of the differences that would have immediately stood out in this coupling was that the divinity of the medicine god was often questioned because he supposedly learned his healing art from a mere mortal, the Centaur Chiron.[33] In contrast, the antitype material gives no such indication that Jesus obtained his healing powers from another but that those abilities were intrinsically and innately his.

Another aspect that would stand out in the mind of the reader is how vastly different their healing ministries were received. While Jesus acts of healing are reported to be thoroughly commended throughout the antitype material, the same cannot be said of Asclepius. While Justin mentioned that Asclepius was "struck by lightning" (§21.2), he never explicitly brought up the reason why Zeus struck him dead—that is, on account of bringing back

---

side—and great-great grandson on his mother's side)." Minns and Parvis incorrectly argue, though, that "an 'ascent to heaven' does not form part of his [Asclepius] mythology," as the mythological tradition does contain an account where Asclepius eventually ascends to heaven: "[Constellation Opiuchus:] The Serpent-Holder. Many astronomers have imagined that he is Aesculapius, whom Jupiter [Zeus], for the sake of Apollo, put among the stars" (Pseudo-Hyginus, *Astronomica* 2.14).

31. Knox, "The 'Divine Hero,'" 231–32. Maria Carena, "La critica della mitologia pagana negli Apologeti greci dei II secolo," 13: "Si concentrano gli attacchi di tutti gli apologeti contro Eracle ed Asclepio (che generalmente sono appaiati), a cagione della grande notorietà dei loro miti e della diffusione del loro culto."

32. Ciholas, *The Omphalos and the Cross*, 202.

33. Ibid., 61. Pindar, *Nemean Ode* 3.51: "Deeply wise Chiron brought Jason inside his stone dwelling, and next after him Asclepius, whom he taught the gentle-handed dispensation of medical remedies"; Apollodorus 3.10.3; Pindar, *Pythian Ode* 3.5; Pseudo-Apollodorus, *The Library* 3.118–122.

to life a man named Hippolytus for monetary gain.[34] F.J. Dölger insightfully points out what apologists like Justin were attempting to do when they brought up the greed that led to the sudden downfall of Asclepius: the death by lightning proved his mortality while his greed disproved his divinity.[35]

"Being Crucified and Dying"

The biblical passages for the antitype material regarding Christ's crucifixion and death are found in *1 Apology* 35.2–10, 38.1–7, and 50.1–11 respectively.[36] This theme contains by far the most copious amounts of The Old Testament fulfillment passages in contrast to the other themes:

- Justin cites seven (7) passages in *1 Apol.* 35.2–10 [Isa 9:6, 65:2, and 58:2; Ps 21(22):17–19; Zeph 3:14–15; and Zech 9:9 while he uses texts from the apocryphal Gospel of Peter (3.7) to corroborate that the Hebrew Scriptures cited in this section were indeed fulfilled].[37]

- He cites six (6) passages in *1 Apol.* 38.1–7 [Isa 65:2; 50:6–8; Ps 22:18; 22:16; 3:5; and 22:8].[38]

- Finally for *1 Apol.* 50:1–11, Justin quotes only two (2) passages but the latter one is of extraordinarily length [Isa 53:12 and 52:13—53:8].[39]

All told, there are fifteen (15) passages here divided over three separate discourses. Despite using different sets of passages for each discourse, the three

---

34. Carena, "La critica della mitologia pagana," 13: "Asclepio trovò la morte in conseguenza della sua cupidigia per la quale aveva accettato di risuscitare un morto contro le leggi di natura"; Pindar, *Pythian Odes* 3.54: "Gold appearing in his hands with its lordly wage prompted even him to bring back from death a man already carried off. But then, with a cast from his hands, Kronos' son [Zeus] took the breath from both men's breasts in an instant; the flash of lightning hurled down doom"; Hesiod, *Catalogues of Women Fragment* 90; Ovid, *Fasti* 6.735; Pseudo-Hyginus, *Astronomica* 2.14, and *Fabulae* 49.

35. Dölger, "Christus und 'der Heiler' Asklepios bei Justinus," 243–244: "Die Betonung der Gewinnsucht des Asklepios diente also ursprünglich bei den christlichen Apologeten ganz im Sinne von Pluto dem Nachweis, daß Asklepios eben nur ein Mensch gewesen sein könne. Sollte der Blitztod die Sterblichkeit des Asklepios beweisen, so die Gewinnsucht die Nichtgöttlichkeit. So wird es auch verständlich, daß in späteren Texten die Gewinnsucht mehr gefühlsmäßig gegen die Göttlichkeit des Asklepios herageholt wurde, um das Ungeziemende und Unwürdige für einen Gott zu kennzeichnen."

36. Minns and Parvis, *Justin, Philosopher and Martyr*, 167n9.

37. Ibid., 177nn2, 4–7 and 179n2.

38. Ibid.,181nn5–8, 10.

39. Ibid., 207n2.

discourses read on similar lines regarding their description of Christ's passion. One immediate question that should come to mind is why did Justin invest so much antitype material for this one particular theme? A follow-up question is why did Justin erect three distinct discourses that basically recycled the same Passion story using different passages?

I assert that Justin's massive compilation of proof texts here is directly related to his argument in the type material (*1 Apol.* 22.3–4) that the Son of God's death by crucifixion is superior to the variegated deaths told regarding the sons of Zeus or θεῖος ἀνήρ (i.e., Asclepius, Dionysus, and Heracles) on the basis that, "the sufferings in which they died were not all of a kind" (§22.4). In other words, the diverse nature of their respective deaths betray the work of demons who in their desire to ape the actual death of the Son of God prophesied in Moses and the Prophets end up leaving multiple, inaccurate versions in their wake.[40]

So the massive compilation of Old Testament proof texts in the antitype material are meant by Justin to demonstrate their unanimity (in contrast to the poetic depictions of the sons of Zeus) in foretelling the consistent manner in which the Son of God would suffer and die. But why does Justin belabor the point—cycling through three separate discourses to say the same thing over and over again? Is this just another case of Justin's rambling prose or is there a purpose behind this repetition? I contend that the latter may very well be the case as it seems too coincidental that as he focused on three specific sons of Zeus and their varying deaths in the type material that he then went on to construct three distinct discourses in the antitype section, each essentially composed of different passages but rendering the same unanimous theme to the point of redundancy. Hence, this possible numerical correspondence between the sons of Zeus and the discourses mentioned above provides more weight to my thesis that a typology of myth, albeit a guarded one, was truly at work in *1 Apology*.

In constructing a typological trajectory from the Scripture passages in the antitype material, the basic contours would look like this: (1) the Messiah riding in to Jerusalem on a donkey [Zeph 9:9], (2) being crucified [Isa 9:6, 65:2, 53:4, 53:7–8 and Ps 22:16], (3) being mocked by the crowd present [Isa 58:2, 50:6–8, 52:14, 53:3, Ps 22:17–19, Gospel of Peter 3:7], (4) saving his people through his death [Zeph 3:14–15, Isa 53:12, 52:15, 53:5–6], and (5) eventually rising from the dead [Ps 3:5, Isa 52:13]. Also, despite the humiliation and suffering the Messiah would experience during his passion, the antitype material highlights that the one who sent him would not leave him but grant him strength during his time of anguish [Isa 50:6–8]. In

---

40. Van Winden, *An Early Christian Philosopher*, 43.

treating the sons of Zeus below, I will omit Asclepius from our discussion as the nature surrounding his death by the lightning bolt of Zeus has already been brought up in the previous theme.

Dionysus (21.2)

In the type material, Dionysus is discussed in one instance regarding his death: "Dionysus after being torn apart" (§21.2). While there were multiple traditions regarding the career of Dionysus, the one Justin was alluding to here regarding the god being "torn apart" (διασπαραχθέντα) was from the Cretan myth of Dionysius Zagreus (the first Dionysus). While the classical account of Dionysus stated that he was the product of Zeus and the mortal, Semele, this version from the Orphic Mysteries identifies his actual mother as Persephone, queen of the Underworld.[41]

While Justin is silent regarding the circumstances surrounding the cruel death of Zagreus, his audience would have been quite familiar with the story. Through an act of brazenness on the part of Zeus, his bastard child Zagreus is installed upon the throne of heaven and armed with his father's lightning bolts.[42] This incited the jealousy of his wife Hera who then plotted Zagreus' demise by inspiring the Titans to catch the infant god off guard by luring him away with toys and then seizing upon him to dismember him.[43] In addition, once the Titans had overtaken Zagreus it is said that

41. Barnard, *The First and Second Apologies*, 128n151. Diodorus Siculus, *The Library of History* 4.4.1: "Some writers of myth, however, relate that there was a second Dionysus [Zagreus] who was much earlier in time than the one we have just mentioned. For according to them there was born of Zeus and Persephone a Dionysos who is called by some Sabazius and whose birth and sacrifices and honours are celebrated at night and in secret" (Diodorus Siculus, *Library of History*, trans. Oldfather, 349–351); Hyginus, *Fabulae* 155; Nonnus, *Dionysiaca* 6.155; *Orphic Hymn 29 to Persephone*; *Orphic Hymn 30 to Dionysos*; *Orphic Hymn 46 to Licnitus*.

42. Nonnus, *Dionysiaca* 6.155: "By this marriage with the heavenly dragon, the womb of Persephone swelled with living fruit, and she bore Zagreus the horned baby, who by himself climbed upon the heavenly throne of Zeus and brandished lightning in his little hand, and newly born, lifted and carried thunderbolts in his tender fingers . . . But he did not hold the throne of Zeus for long."

43. Pseudo-Hyginus, *Fabulae* 150: "After Juno [Hera] saw that Epaphus [or Zagreus, both were identified with the Egyptian Osiris], born of a concubine, ruled such a great kingdom, she saw to it that he should be killed while hunting, and encouraged the Titanes to drive Jove [Zeus] from the kingdom and restore it to Saturn [Kronos]"; Diodorus Siculus, *Library of History* 5.75.4; Pausanias, *Description of Greece* 7.19.4, and 8.37.1.

they mocked the infant god before he died by giving him a *thyrsus* (a fennel stalk) in place of his rightful scepter.[44]

The elements of this story obviously resonate with many of those within the antitype material: (1) as an infant would rule over Olympus, so too a child from Israel mentioned in *1 Apol.* 35.2 was destined to rule over his people, "A child was born for us, and a young man was given for us, whose rule is on the shoulders" [Isa 58:2], (2) as this son of Zeus was coronated, so too did the Son of God experience a similar procession in *1 Apol.* 35.10, "Behold your king comes to you gentle, mounted on the colt of an ass" [Zeph 9:9], (3) as the infant god was surrounded by the Titans, so too was the Son of God in *1 Apol.* 38.2 surrounded by those who sought to harm him, "I placed my back for scourging and my checks for cudgeling" [Isa 50:6–8], (4) just as the infant god's authority was mocked so also in *1 Apol.* 35.6 was the Son of God's authority mocked, "They seated him on the judgment seat in ridicule and said 'give judgment for us.'" [Gospel of Peter 3:7], and as excruciating was the death of the infant god, so too in *1 Apol.* 50.8 would be the nature of the Son of God's own death, "This one bears ours sins and suffers for us, and we reckoned him to be in suffering and in calamity and in distress" [Isa 53.4].

The resonance between this story of Zagreus and the description of Christ's Passion in the antitype material cannot be denied. According to Michel Fédou, Justin was even mindful to use the same exact terminology that followers of the Orphic Dionysus-Zagreus tradition embraced (i.e., διασπαραχθέντα) to properly capture the import of Zagreus' death: a passion endured by their god.[45] Despite his horrible and excruciating death, Zagreus is brought back to life in a reincarnated form. Zeus was able to recover the infant's heart and transform it into a potion that he gave to Semele who ended up conceiving the younger Dionysus.[46] Again, this element in the story would have reverberated with Justin's testimony in the antitype material where the Messiah anticipated his own return from death in *1 Apol.* 38.5, "But I slept and slumbered, and I arose, because the Lord helped me"

44. Damascius, *Commentary on the Phaedo*, 1.170.

45. Fédou, "La vision de la croix dans l'oeuvre de saint Justin 'philosophe et martyr,'" 66: "Le participe 'diasparachtheis,' que Justin emploie à trois reprises, rappelle directement une idée très chère à la théologie orphique de Dionysos-Zagreus : celle d'une passion endurée par le dieu. Écho d'ube vieille légende suivant laquelle le jeune Dionysos, victime de ses frère les Titans, aurait été mis à mort et sauvagement 'dépecé.'" The three instances of Justin using this participle of "tearing apart" are found in *1 Apol.* 21.2, 54.6, and *Dial. Trypho* 69.2 (q.v. Goodspeed, *Index apologeticus*, 72).

46. Pseudo-Hyginus, *Fabulae* 167: "Liber [Zagreus], son of Jove [Zeus] and Proserpina [Persephone], was dismembered by the Titans, and Jove gave his heart, torn to bits, to Semele in a drink . . . she was made pregnant by this."

(Ps 3:5) and in *1 Apol.* 50.3, "For behold my servant shall understand, and he shall be lifted up and glorified exceedingly" (Ps 52:13).

Notwithstanding the fascinating confluence between Dionysus and Jesus in regards to their suffering, death, and return to life, again there is a typological movement that Justin's reader could have discerned just like in the previous cases I have proposed regarding Perseus, Danaë, and Asclepius (i.e., partial separation from myth). Unlike the infant Zagreus who was caught unaware by the Titans,[47] we get the sense in Justin's antitype material that the Son of God willingly offered himself up to those who sought to destroy him. Justin used the fulfillment passage of Isa 65:2 to demonstrate this of which is repeated twice, first in *1 Apol.* 35.3 and again in *1 Apol.* 38.1, "I stretched out my hands to a disobedient and gainsaying people, to those walking in such a way that is not good."

Heracles (21.2; 22.3–4)

In the type material, Heracles is brought up in one instance regarding his death: "Heracles after giving himself to the fire to escape from pain" (§21.2). This allusion from Justin is from the story of Heracles where he throws himself upon the burning pyre after his wife Deianira inadvertently gives him a robe tainted with the poisonous blood of the centaur, Nessus.[48] By his own volition and willpower, he lays down upon the fiery altar so that his mortality may be burned away so that his immortal part could be released to Mt. Olympus.[49]

Justin's selection of Heracles' death as an analogue to that of Christ's actually makes up for the aforementioned deficiency plaguing the mythical allusion to Dionysus (i.e, the infant god being killed against his will). In

47. Clement of Alexandria, *Exhortation to the Greeks* 2.15: "He was yet a child, and the Curetes were dancing around him with warlike movement, when the Titans stealthily drew near. First they beguiled him with childish toys, and then, these very Titans tore him to pieces, though he was but an infant."

48. Barnard, *The First and Second Apologies*, 129n152. Pseudo-Apollodorus, *The Library* 2.157: "In fear lest Herakles desire Iole more than herself [Deianeira], and in her belief that the blood of Nessos was truly a love-potion, she doused the robe with it. Herakles put it on and started the sacrifice, but soon the robe grew warm as the Hydra's venom began to cook his flesh"; Cicero, *De Natura Deorum* 3.28; Diodorus Siculus, *Library of History* 4.36.3 and 4.38.1; Philostratus the Younger, *Imagines* 16; Sophocles, *Trachiniae*, 558.

49. Macpherson, *Four Ages of Man*, 66. Ovid, *Metamorphoses* 9.262: "Now, while the Gods conversed, the mortal part of Hercules was burnt by Mulciber; but yet an outline of a spirit-form remained. Unlike the well-known mortal shape derived by nature of his mother, he kept traces only of his father, Jove."

regards to Heracles, his fortitude in the face of death closely resembles that of Jesus. But Roman Garrison points out that Justin's coupling of the death of Heracles with that of Jesus, of course, was not incidental but that the apologist was ultimately leveraging the comparison to argue for the superiority of the latter.[50]

Despite the steadfastness that Heracles exhibits in his death, the Gentile reader would have detected a qualitative difference between the two figures in regards to the motives behind their resolve: Heracles died for a selfish reason while Christ died for a selfless one. Heracles motive behind his death was to escape the great pain that was inflicted upon him when his wife Deianira inadvertently poisoned him with noxious blood of the centaur Nessus.[51] On the other hand, the antitype material is quite clear that the motive that drove Christ to endure his suffering was the hope that his death would serve as an atonement to save his people from their sins (*1 Apol.* 50.2, 50.9–10).

Another point of divergence between the Heracles suffering and that of Christ is that in the account of the *Trachiniae* where it appears that Zeus completely deserted his son, Heracles. Garrison remarks about the accusatory comments that Heracles son, Hyllus, directs towards Zeus at the end of the play:

> The words of Hyllus at the conclusion of *Trachiniae* are a virtual indictment of Zeus' responsibility: "You've seen dreadful dying and agony today and hideous suffering and nothing is here, nothing, none of all of it, that is not Zeus." The piety of Heracles means nothing. Despite his offering sacrifice at the altar of Zeus, and his seemingly scrupulous religiosity, Heracles is forsaken by Zeus. He who is considered to be the son of the god cries out "You, Zeus, reward my worship with disaster."[52]

Although there is certainly a scriptural tradition in regards to Jesus lamenting upon the Cross as having also been forsaken (Ps 22:1; Matt 27:46; and Mark 15:34), Justin is completely silent about it throughout all of *1 Apology.*[53]

50. Garrison, *Why are You Silent, Lord?*, 37–38.

51. Carena, "La critica della mitologia pagana," 13: "Gli apologeti mettono in luce non solo il supplizio di Eracle, ma ancora le cause di esso: Eracle si accese il rogo per il suo furore." If burning on the pyre was Heracles's relief from the pain caused by the poisonous blood of Nessus, then in some sense his death was not as noble because he went from a state of great pain (i.e., poisonous blood) to one of lesser pain (i.e., being burned by fire).

52. Garrison, *Why are You Silent, Lord?*, 44; Sophocles, *Trachinae*, 993–95.

53. Justin was certainly aware of the tradition of Jesus' crying out of Ps 22:1 on the Cross, "My God, my God, why have you forsaken me?" (Matt 27:46; Mark 15.34) as

Rather, the passages that Justin supplied in the antitype material testify of Christ being divinely upheld and supported during his time of suffering, "And the Lord became my help. Therefore I was not put to shame, but I set my face like solid rock and I knew that I will not be shamed. For the one who has vindicated me draws near." (*1 Apol.* 38.3)

"And Rising Again . . . and Going to the Heavens"

The biblical passages for the antitype material regarding this Christological theme of Christ rising again and going into the heavens are found in *1 Apology* 38.5, 45.1–5, and 51.6–7.[54] The Old Testament fulfillment passages cited by Justin are Psalms 3:5–6; 109(110):1–3; and 24:7–8.[55] As stated in the previous chapter, although "rising again" and "going into the heavens" are technically two distinct Christological themes for Justin especially when handled in the context of working off the full-fledged Creed Sequence, he had the tendency to conflate the two concepts when working within the realm of Pseudo-Creed sequence. Hence, I am mirroring Justin's propensity to conflate these two themes when dealing with them in the context of Pseudo-Creed Sequence by merging them in like fashion as well.

In constructing a typological trajectory from the Scripture passages in the antitype material, the basic contours would look like this: (1) Resurrection [Ps 3:5–6] followed by (2) Ascension into Heaven with power and dominion awarded to the risen Son of God [Ps 109 (110): 1–3] and a (3) Coronation of the ascended Son of God as he entered into Heaven [Ps 24:7–8].

The Dioscuri (21.2)

In the type material, the Dioscuri (also known as Castor and Polydeuces) are alluded to in one instance regarding their ascension to the heavens: "Dioscuri, begotten of Leda" [§21.2]. Leda, who was wife to king Tyndareus of Sparta, was impregnated by Zeus with the result of the birth of twins named Castor and Polydeuces.[56] They were called the Dioscuri, which liter-

---

he provides an extensive commentary on the phenomenon in *Dialogue with Trypho* 98–99.

54. Minns and Parvis, *Justin, Philosopher and Martyr*, 167nn10–11.

55. Ibid., 181n5, 199n2, and 209n3.

56. Pseudo-Hyginus, *Fabulae* 77: "Jupiter [Zeus], changed into a swan, had intercourse with Leda near the river Eurotas, and from that embrace she bore Pollux [Polydeukes] and Helen; to Tyndareus she bore Castor and Clytemnestra."

ally meant "sons of Zeus."[57] Although they were twins, Castor was mortal while Polydeuces was immortal.[58] So when Castor died, Polydeuces became so overwhelmed with grief over the loss of his brother that he was willing to give up his immortality in order that he might see Castor once again.[59] Zeus took pity on them both and agreed that Castor should spend alternately one day in the Underworld and one day in Olympus with the gods.[60]

Rendel Harris points out that in the Greek world this act of devotion by Polydeuces was considered the shining example of the, "higher form of love in sacrifice . . . divided immortality and shared mortality."[61] For their love for one another, they were purported to have been changed into the constellation Gemini, the Heavenly Twins.[62] With their ascension into the heavens, they were given rulership over all transactions down in the world below—thereby becoming "the guardians of public truth."[63]

In alluding to these beloved twins in Greek myth, Justin was setting the foundation for the antitype material where the self-sacrifice of Polydeuces and the reward of immortality that both he and his brother receive

---

57. Harris, *The Cult of the Heavenly Twins*, 4: "Hesiod in giving their descent makes them [Kastor and Polydeukes] both sons of Zeus"; Hesiod, *Catalogues of Women Fragment* 66.

58 Stasinus of Cyprus, *Cypria Fragment* 7: "Castor was mortal, and the fate of death was destined for him; but Polydeuces, scion of Ares was immortal."

59. Pindar, *Nemean Ode* 10 ep3—ep5: "Then with hot tears streaming and bitter groans, he cried aloud: 'O Father, [Zeus] son of Kronos, what release shall there be from sorrows? Grant that I too with my brother may die, great king, I beg thee. For glory is departed from a man robbed of his friends, and under stress of toils few mortals will abide faithful companions to share in the labor'"; Pseudo-Apollodorus, *The Library* 3.136–137.

60. Lycophron, *Alexandra* 564: "An the one pair [the Dioskouroi, Dioscuri] Hades shall receive: the others the meadows of Olympus shall welcome as guests on every alternate day, brothers of mutual love, undying and dead"; Ovid, *Fasti* 5.697; Pindar, *Pythian Ode* 11 ep4.

61. Harris, *The Cult of the Heavenly Twins*, 4.

62. Macpherson, *Four Ages of Man*, 179. Pseudo-Hyginus, *Astronomica* 2.22: "The Twins these stars many astronomers have called Castor and Pollux [Polydeukes]. They say that of all brothers they were the most affectionate, not striving in rivalry for the leadership, nor acting without previous consultation. As a reward for their services of friendship, Jupiter [Zeus] is thought to have put them in the sky as well-known stars . . . Homer states that Pollux granted to his brother one half of his life, so that they shine on alternate days"; Diodorus Siculus, *Library of History* Book 6, Fragment 6; Ovid, *Metamorphoses* 8.370; Pausanias, *Description of Greece* 8.2.4; Pseudo-Hyginus, *Fabulae* 80; Seneca, *Hercules Furens* 4.

63. Harris, *The Cult of the Heavenly Twins*, 56. Aelian, *Historical Miscellany* 1.30: "So as to be like Dioscuri to the poor wretches, 'saviours and benevolent guardians,' as those gods are commonly described."

(i.e., being transformed into a constellation), dovetails nicely with the self-sacrifice of Christ and the reward he received for his greater act of love (willing to die for the world, not just one person) by ascending into the heavens in glory. In similar fashion, as Castor and Polydeuces in their transformed state rule the world below, so too, does Christ rule the world below as stated in the antitype passage Psalm 109 (110):1–3, "The Lord said to my Lord: 'Sit on my right, until I make your enemies a footstool for your feet. The Lord will send forth from Jerusalem a scepter of power for you; and rule in the midst of your enemies. With you is dominion in the day of your power in the splendours of your saints'" (*1 Apol.* 45.2–4).

Bellerophon (21.2)

In the type material, Bellerphon is alluded to in one instance regarding his ascension into the heavens: "Bellerophon, from human beings, rose to heaven on the horse Pegasus" [§21.2]. Minns and Parvis are quick to point out that, "Bellerophon cannot be considered a son of Zeus equivalently to Asclepius, Dionysus, and Heracles."[64] Leslie Barnard also critiques this allusion by Justin stating, "Bellerophon's ride on Pegasus failed and he did not reach heaven. Justin's memory would appear to be at fault here or else he knew another myth."[65] Though Minns, Parvis, and Barnard make valid points regarding how Bellerophon does not belong to the same genus of heroes contained in this section whether by nature (Minns and Parvis) or by deeds (Barnard), it is important to note that Justin himself admits upfront in his allusion to Bellerophon that he was "from human beings" (καὶ τὸν ἐξ ἀνθρώπων) and thereby by Justin's own standards outside the purview

---

64. Minns and Parvis, in fact, have omitted this allusion altogether from their critical edition on this basis. They conjecture that the allusion here was added by a later editor who seeing the later allusion to Bellerophon and his horse Pegasus recorded in *1 Apol.* 54.7 coupled with the phrase "as we said before" looked for this previous allusion in his particular copy of *1 Apology* with no avail—it had been lost somehow in the transmission process. Therefore, Minns and Parvis theorize that he made the editorial decision to re-insert the allusion back into *1 Apol.* 21 (*Justin, Philosopher and Martyr*, 133n2). This is a somewhat problematic theory, as Prigent has observed that chapters 54 to 66 repeat the montage of mythical analogies to the life of Christ established in chapters 21 and 22 but this time goes to great lengths to expose the diabolical origin behind these Greco-Roman religious narratives (*Justin et l'Ancien Testament*, 160). If there is pattern of corresponding mythical allusions between these two respective sections as Prigent contends, a reasonable explanation for why Justin mentions Bellerophon in the last section but not in the first is in order.

65. Barnard, *The First and Second Apologies*, 129n155.

of a θεῖος ἀνήρ.[66] Although Bellerophon did not fit the profile of the semi-divines he mentioned previously within the type material, it appears that Justin found the notorious failed attempt of Bellerophon to ascend into the heavens an attractive analogue that could be leveraged to ultimately affirm the belief of Christ's ascension into Heaven.

Although he was a mere mortal born of a human father, Glaucus, and human mother, Eurymedes,[67] he accomplished so many heroic deeds in his career (including the famous slaying of the Chimera) and did so in such a virtuous manner that he would have gained immortality by the standards set out for a θεῖος ἀνήρ.[68] He even became the owner of the winged horse, Pegasus, who previously belonged to the son of Zeus, Perseus, demonstrating the heights of his stature as a human being.[69] But despite all this success, he was still not satisfied and sought to ascend to Mount Olympus on the back of Pegasus. Zeus was angered by his presumption and sent a gadfly to sting the horse, causing it to throw him off thus flinging the hero back to earth. Afterwards he wandered the world alone despised by gods and men.[70]

A notable element surrounding the ascent of Bellerophon into the heavens that can be easily overlooked is that he did so using his winged-horse, Pegasus. It appears that in alluding to Bellerophon, Justin is not only attempting to establish resonance with the Christological theme of heavenly ascension but perhaps also Christ's physical ascension into Jerusalem on "an ass's colt" (πῶλος) in a very similar fashion as that of his pagan counterpart

66. There is an entire tradition that viewed Bellerophon's father as the god of the sea, Poseidon (Hesiod, *Catalogues* Fragment 7; Pseudo-Hyginus, *Fabulae* 157). But with Justin asserting the "mortal origin" (καὶ τὸν ἐξ ἀνθρώπων) of Bellerophon, he is referring to the other tradition that viewed him as the product of entirely human pedigree.

67. Pseudo-Apollodorus, *The Library* 1.85.

68. Pseudo-Hyginus, *Fabulae* 57: "After reading the letter, Iobates was reluctant to kill such a hero, but sent him to kill the Chimaera, a three-formed creature said to breathe forth fire. This he slew, riding on Pegasus, and he is said to have fallen in the Aleian plains and have dislocated his hip. But the king, praising his valor, gave him his other daughter in marriage, and Stheneboea, hearing of it, killed herself"; Diodorus Siculus, *Library of History* 6, Fragment 9; Hesiod, *Theogony* 325; Oppian, *Cynegetica* 1.225; Pseudo-Apollodorus, *The Library* 2. 30–33; Pseudo-Hyginus, *Astronomica* 2.18.

69. Strabo, *Geography* 8. 6. 21: "Peirenê [a spring of the city of Corinth] was wont to rise over the surface and flow down the sides of the mountain. And here, they say, Pegasus, a winged horse which sprang from the neck of the Gorgon Medusa when her head was cut off, was caught while drinking by Bellerophon."

70. Pindar, *Isthmian Ode* 7.44: "Pegasus winged high threw down to earth his lord Bellerophontes, who thought to reach the abodes of heaven, and share the company of Zeus. Sweets gained unrightly await an end most bitter"; Horace, *Carmen Saeculare* 4.11.26; Nonnus, *Dionysiaca* 11.142 and 28.167.

(1 *Apol.* 32.6).[71] It is in this latter form of ascending where the plight of Bellerophon and that of the pre-resurrected Christ seem to derive similitude as there certainly was a sense of failure experienced by Christ's disciples when their teacher appeared to fall short of living up to the political expectations that they had of him. This is perhaps why Justin goes to great lengths in the antitype material to discuss not only the coronation that Christ experienced in his heavenly ascent (1 *Apol.* 51.6–7) validating the one he experienced during Passion Week, but also affirming that the risen Son of God was indeed awarded power and dominion (1 *Apol.* 45.1–5).

Ariadne (21.3)

In the type material, Ariadne is alluded to in one instance regarding her ascension into the heavens: "What do we say about Ariadne and those said, like her, to have been set among the stars?" [§21.3] Ariadne was renowned within the Greco-Roman poets for her willingness to betray her own half-brother, the Minotaur, and estrange herself from her royal family (her father being King Minos of Crete and her mother, the immortal Queen Pasiphae)[72] on account of falling in love with the Greek hero, Theseus. After the Athenian prince was able to slay the Minotaur through Ariadne's assistance, he took the Cretan princess with him on his voyage back to Athens with the intent of marrying her.[73] Unfortunately for Ariadne, Theseus had a change of heart while at sea and deserted her on the island of Naxos.[74] The mythological tradition surrounding Ariadne's emotional state after Theseus'

---

71. Bourgeois, *La sagesse des anciens dans le mystère du verbe*, 161: "Tandis que Béllérophon qui monte aux cieux sur Pégase combine deux événements: d'une part, l'Ascension, d'autre part les Rameaux quand le Christ monta sur un ânon (πῶλος)."

72. Apollonius Rhodius, *Argonautica* 3.997; Hyginus, *Fabulae* 224; Ovid, *Heroides* 4.59.

73. Pseudo-Hyginus, *Fabulae* 40–43: "After he [Minos] conquered the Athenians their revenues became his; he decreed, moreover that each year they should send seven of their children as food for the Minotaur. After Theseus had come from Troezene, and had learned what a calamity afflicted the state, of his own accord he promised to go against the Minotaur . . . when Theseus came to Crete, Ariadne, Minos' daughter, loved him so much that she betrayed her brother and saved the stranger, or she showed Theseus the way out of the Labyrinth. When Theseus had entered and killed the Minotaur, by Ariadne's advise he got out by unwinding the thread. Ariadne, because she had been loyal to him, he took away, intending to marry her."

74. Apollonius Rhodius, *Argonautica* 4.425; Ovid, *Heroides* 4.57; Ovid, *Metamorphoses* 8.173; Pausanias, *Description of Greece* 1.20.3; Philostratus the Elder, *Imagines* 1.5

abandonment was that of inconsolable grief resulting in the desire to end her own life.[75]

Instead, Dionysus saw the weeping princess and fell in love with her. In so doing, he married Ariadne and ended up siring four children with her.[76] Because of his great affection for Ariadne, she was immortalized at her death signified by the translation of her crown into a constellation of stars in the sky known as the Corona.[77] Malcolm Day makes an insightful comment regarding this movement in Ariadne's life from utter devastation to a state of deification, "Ariadne's betrayal by Theseus was a common theme among later poets and artists, especially the idea that life could be found through death as a result of divine intervention."[78]

Justin's Gentile reader was certainly aware of the sudden reversal of fortune that served as the colorful backdrop to her apotheosis of which the apologist briefly alluded. It is this drama in the account of Ariadne that

---

75. Ovid, *Metamorphoses* 8.175: "She [Ariadne], abandoned [by Theseus], in her grief and anger found comfort in Bacchus' [Dionysus'] arms. He took her crown and set it in the heavens to win her there a star's eternal glory [as the constellation Corona]; and the crown flew through the soft light air and, as it flew, its gems were turned to gleaming fires, and still shaped as a crown their place in heaven they take between the Kneeler [the constellation Hercules] and him who grasps the Snake"; Nonnus, *Dionysiaca* 47.265.

76. Pseudo-Apollodorus, *The Library* E1. 9: "Dionysos fell in love with Ariadne, and kidnapped her [from Naxos], taking her off to Lemnos where he had sex with her, and begat Thoas, Staphylos, Oinopion, and Peparethos."

77. Diodorus Siculus, *Library of History* 4.61.5: "He [Theseus] carried off Ariadne [from Krete] and sailed out unobserved during the night, after which he put in at the island which at that time was called Dia, but is now called Naxos. At this same time, the myths relate, Dionysos showed himself on the island, and because of the beauty of Ariadne he took the maiden away from Theseus and kept her as his lawful wife, loving her exceedingly. Indeed, after her death he considered her worthy of immortal honours because of the affection he had for her, and placed among the stars of heaven the Crown of Ariadne [the constellation Corona]"; Apollonius Rhodius, *Argonautica* 3.997; Aratus, *Phaenomena* 72; Hesiod, *Theogony* 947; Ovid, *Heroides* 6. 114; Pseudo-Hyginus, *Astronomica* 2.5; Ptolemy Hephaestion, *New History Book* 5.

78. Day, *100 Characters from Classical Mythology*, 103. Ovid, *Fasti* 3.459: "Straightway at the fall of night shalt thou see the Cnossian Crown [Ariadne]. It was through the fault of Theseus that Ariadne was made a goddess. Already had she happily exchanged a perjured spouse for Bacchus [Dionysos] . . . He [Dionysos-Liber] puts his arms around her [Ariadne], with kisses dried her tears, and 'Let us fare together,' quoth he, 'to heaven's height. As thou hast shared my bed, so shalt thou share my name, for in thy changed state thy name shall be Libera; and I will see to it that with thee there shall be a memorial of thy crown, that crown which Vulcan [Hephaestus] gave to Venus [Aphrodite], and she to thee.' He did as he had said and changed the nine jewels of her crown into fires. Now the golden crown doth sparkle with nine stars [the constellation Corona]"; Pseudo-Hyginus, *Fabulae* 224: "Mortals who were made immortal . . . Ariadne, whom Father Liber [Dionysos] called Libera, daughter of Minos and Pasiphae."

would come to resemble the same suddenness in change of situation experienced by Christ in his own resurrection: going from a state of utter humiliation embodied in his crucifixion and death to a state of complete exaltation where he is according to Justin's antitype material is officially coronated in heaven (*1 Apol.* 51.6–7) and given dominion over the cosmos (*1 Apol.* 45.1–5).

Caesar (21.3)

In the type material, the Caesars are alluded to in one instance regarding their ascension into the heavens: "And what do we say about your deceased emperors? If you deem them worthy to be made into gods you also bring forward someone who swears that he has seen the cremated Caesar going up to the heaven from the pyre" [§21.3]. The account Justin most likely was referring to was the famous testimony of the former government official in AD 14 present at the funeral of Augustus Caesar who claimed to see the form of the deceased emperor rise to the heavens while his body was burning on the funeral pyre.[79] In mentioning this allusion, Justin is addressing one of the criteria brought up in the previous chapter regarding what the ancients accepted as evidence that an ascent into heaven or apothesis had occurred for a θεῖος ἀνήρ (i.e., the testimony of eye-witnesses).[80]

This allusion would have reverberated with Justin's audience, especially when Justin use of Ps 24:7–8 as a declaration of Christ's triumphant reception upon ascending to the heavens (*1 Apol.* 51.6–7) was predicated by the eyewitness accounts of the disciples from books of Acts (1:9–11) who physically saw Christ rise into the heavens. What would make the eyewitness testimony regarding Jesus greater than that of Caesar Augustus is that Christ would have been understood as ascending bodily into the heavens while Caesar's remains stayed.

---

79. Barnard, *The First and Second Apologies,* 129–30n157. Suetonius, *The Life of Augustus* 100.3–4: "[H]e was carried on the shoulders of senators to the Campus Martius and there cremated. There was even an ex-praetor who took oath that he had seen the form of the Emperor, after he had been reduced to ashes, on its way to heaven. His remains were gathered up by the leading men of the equestrian order, bare-footed and in ungirt tunics, and placed in the Mausoleum."

80. Talbert, "The Concept of Immortals in Mediterranean Antiquity," 421.

CONCLUSION

In his article "Religions of the Gentiles as viewed by Fathers of the Church," Paul Hacker describes the paradoxical nature in which Justin implores his audience to eschew the myths of their ancestral religion—all the while exploiting these same ancient narratives to prove to his readers that these myths betray the anticipation (albeit demonic) of the Son of God's arrival.

> Justin's explanation of such resemblances is that the demons, who had heard that the Prophets foretold Christ's incarnation, inspired poets to invent myths depicting events of Christ's history in a distorted form. The similarity of some features of the myths with the gospel was intended to induce men, when they came to know about Christ, to attach no greater importance to him than to figures of fiction or marvelous stories. In this way the demons sought to delude men. By this drastic theologoumenon St. Justin elucidated two facts. First, the final event in God's economy is foreshadowed even in the religions of the Nations. Secondly, the truth contained in these religions is hidden and disfigured by demonic contexts.[81]

The first point Hacker establishes in regards to "the final event in God's economy is foreshadowed even in the religions of the Nations" is especially important here as it represents the central argument behind this particular chapter. That is, Justin was not of the belief that he was simply establishing random analogies between Christological themes and aspects of the so-called sons of Zeus. Rather, Justin argues in such a way that these similarities were not of his own design but rather that of demons who long ago caricatured the Christological prophecies of the Old Testament.

With this being said, it can be then stated that the typological movement for Justin is not really between the emerging New Testament narrative and that of Greek myth at this junction anymore. Instead, the typological movement is experiencing a transformation where it now occurs between the emerging New Testament narrative and a Christological reading of the Hebrew Scriptures—with Greek myth serving a mediating or instrumental function between the two. This chapter has been faithful to this nuanced economy of Justin by establishing a *typological trajectory* based primarily upon Old Testament passages he corralled within §30–53 for the purpose of proving that the full-fledged Creed Sequence in §31.7 had indeed been fulfilled. Every myth in this chapter we explored for garbled Christological

---

81. Hacker, "Religions of the Gentiles as viewed by Fathers of the Church," 254–55.

details had to be first validated by this typological trajectory Justin established or it was not given any consideration no matter how enticing the
parallel.

4

Separation from Myth

MOVEMENT OF SEPARATION FROM TYPE MATERIAL

THE PREVIOUS CHAPTER EMPHASIZED how Justin exploited story elements within myth, both explicitly and implicitly, to validate select themes contained in the Pseudo-Creed Sequence (cf. *1 Apol.* 21.2) in the mind of his readers. These mythical allusions replete within the type material (§21–22) served as a sort of theological primer that eventually prepared Justin's readers to tackle his later full-fledged discussion (§30–53) emerging from the Creed Sequence (cf. *1 Apol.* 31.7). Justin would support this latter sequence by relying almost solely on biblical allusions.

While the previous chapter focused upon Justin's incorporation of myth, this present chapter will take the opposite approach by exploring the apologist's movement to encourage his audience's departure from the mythological tradition that they were long suspicious of, but paradoxically still revered. Even in the case of incorporation of myth in the type material, there was a perpetual movement on the part of Justin to demonstrate the supremacy of the Christological themes (*a fortiori*) as they stood in relation to their pagan analogues with the caveat that the latter were perpetrated by wicked demons (οἱ φαῦλοι δαίμονες ταῦτα ἔπραξαν) and hence needed to be handled with extreme caution (*1 Apol.* 21.6). In this chapter, I will demonstrate how Justin's instances of separation from myth outside the type material not only further widened the gap between Christological theme and its respective pagan analogue, but was ultimately utilized to shatter the resonance altogether.[1]

In the treatment of Justin's incorporation of myth in the previous chapter, I had to systematize the apologist's disordered mythical allusions in the type material according to the thematic progression of the Pseudo-Creed Sequence (*1 Apol.* 21.2). In contrast, no such manipulation needs to occur in this chapter as Justin's allusions supporting a movement of separation from myth virtually corresponds with the chronological flow of the Christological themes in the Pseudo-Creed Sequence: (1) virgin birth is dealt with in *1 Apol.* 25–26 (2) healing ministry in *1 Apol.* 54, (3) dying in *1 Apol.* 54–55, and (4) rising in *1 Apol.* 54.

Related to the Christological theme of virgin birth, there is a cluster of allusions Justin makes in *1 Apol.* 25 that recounts the acts of "shame" (αἶσχος) and "sexual frenzy" (οἰστρηθείσας) the pagan gods have committed against human beings: Dionysus (§25.1), Apollo (§25.1), Persephone (§25.1), Aphrodite (§25.1), and finally Zeus' dalliances with Antiope (§25.2) and Ganymede (§25.2). In exposing these divine improprieties, Justin would use them as a foil to accentuate the "passionless" (ἀπαθεῖ) manner by which the Christian God impregnated the Virgin Mary (§25.2). Justin then goes on to argue in *1 Apol.* 27 how these poetic accounts of the sexual violence of the gods towards humanity has, in turn, provided divine sanction for humans to sexually violate themselves (e.g., eunuch priests of Magna Mater), which is exemplified in the sacrificial practices of the mystery cult of Magna Mater (§27.4).[2] Justin makes a few sporadic allusions towards the end of *1 Apology* to expose the demonic aping of the Virgin Birth found in the mythical accounts relating to Zeus (§33.3), Perseus (§54.8), Persephone once again (§64.1–4), and Athena (§64.5).

Also related to the Christological theme of Virgin Birth, there is a cluster of allusions in *1 Apol.* 26 where the apologist argues that demons have continued their diabolical mythmaking long after the Son of God has arrived and ascended by perpetuating it within the miracle workers and

1. I use the analogy of the tentativeness a doctor should exercise when prescribing a drug with a "Black Box" warning to describe the guarded approach Justin utilized in his incorporation of pagan myth. While its usage posed a significant risk towards the health of its patient (i.e., reader) due to its toxicity, Justin diagnosed that this was the initial "medication" that needed to be administered to prepare the mind of his Gentile reader to engage his full-fledged Messianic argument later in *1 Apology*. Once the reader was able to make the crossover, the use of the potentially hazardous treatment was immediately discontinued.

2. Carena, "La critica della mitologia pagana," 8: "L'accusa è duplice: per un lato l'immoralità degli dèi ripugna sommamente al concetto della perfezione divina; per l'altro è fonte di gravi e di rovinose conseguenze nella vita morale."

heretics of Justin's time: Simon (§26.2–3 and later again in §56.1–2) and his partner, Helen (§26.3), Menander (§26.4 and later again in §56.1), and Marcion of Pontus (§26.5 and later in §58.1–3). Although it would seem that these allusions would be dealing with the Christological theme of a healing ministry, they actually have to do with the demonic mimicking of the preexistence of a Logos figure found within the teachings of these individuals—a concern that belongs to the realm of the Virgin Birth.

The mythical allusions affecting a movement of separation for the last three Christological themes of miracles, dying, and rising are fairly sparse when compared to the amount Justin utilized for Virgin birth (13 instances). With regards to the Christological theme of a healing ministry, Justin reverts back to traditional mythology towards the end of *1 Apology* by his categorical dismissal of the renowned acts of service reportedly performed by Heracles (§54.9) and Asclepius (§54.10) for the benefit of humanity. He contends that these two accounts were, in fact, demonic subterfuge meant to distract future generations from taking the ministry of the Son of God seriously when he finally arrived.

There are two allusions for death represented in Dionysus (§54.4–6) and the trio of the sons of Zeus who suffered and died (§55.1–8). There are also two allusions for ascension when Bellerophon (§54.7) and Perseus (§54.8) are mentioned. Despite the paucity of the total mythical allusions for these latter themes of the Pseudo-Creed Sequence (6) when compared to the theme of the Virgin Birth, these movements of separation from myth still offer excellent samples of Justin's clever detecting of demonic mimicry at work within these pagan narratives.

EXPOSING DEMONIC IMITATIONS OF "BEING BORN OF A VIRGIN"

An important background to bring up at this juncture that certainly informed Justin's claim of the gods having committed acts of shame and sexual frenzy against human beings was the Enochic tradition of the Watchers inherited from Hellenistic Judaism.[3] This ancient Jewish tradition of the

---

3. Justin was the first Christian author to explicitly render the "sons of God" (οἱ υἱοὶ τοῦ θεοῦ) in Gen. 6:1–4 as fallen angels, paving the way for a whole host of Christian thinkers such as Irenaeus, Tertullian, and Cyprian to follow his lead. The New Testament authors of *1 Peter* and *2 Peter*, as well as, *Jude* may have been alluding to story of fallen angels procreating with women in 1 Peter 3:19–20; 2 Peter 2:4; and Jude 6 respectively. But this interpretation can only be inferred from these texts while it is undeniably present within Justin's *Apologies* (q.v. Reed, "The Trickery of the Fallen Angels and the Demonic Mimesis of the Divine," 144).

Book of the Watchers, found in *1 Enoch* 1–36 written around 200 BC (at the latest),[4] provided a fanciful narrative behind why God brought forth the Great Flood in Genesis 6 purportedly told from the perspective of the prediluvian patriarch, Enoch, before being brought into heaven.

Here, the "Sons of God" (οἱ υἱοὶ τοῦ θεοῦ) described in Gen. 6:1–4 were understood to be impassioned angels who left their duties as "watchers" or guardians over humankind to have illicit relations with women. From there, giants (γίγαντες) were born from these unions who caused terror and evil upon the earth. Although this supernatural progeny seemed unstoppable, Enoch prophesied that God would send a Great Flood to destroy them. Despite the eventual destruction of the giants by way of the Noahic deluge, their disembodied spirits (i.e., demons) would continue to roam the earth spreading evil in the world.[5] In fact in *1 Apol.* 5.2, Justin would assert that the primary means by which these spirits of the γίγαντες were reigning terror upon humanity in his day and age was by fooling the masses into believing that they were the Greco-Roman gods for whom they ascribed worship.

> Since, in ancient times, wicked demons, in apparitions, committed adultery with women and seduced boys and made people see horrifying things, so those who did not rationally evaluate what the demons were doing were stunned with terror. Carried away with fear, they named them gods, not knowing that they were wicked demons. And they called each of them by name which each of the demons had given it.[6]

---

4. Bauckham, "The Fall of the Angels as the Source of Philosophy in Hermias and Clement of Alexandria," 314. Ferguson argues that the LXX was translated prior to the composition of 1 Enoch (*Demonology of the Early Christian World*, 70), while Newman favors the possibility that *1 Enoch* was composed prior to the emergence of the LXX ("The Ancient Exegesis of Genesis 6:2, 4," 16).

5. Bauckham provides an excellent summary of this very complex narrative: "The story of the Book of Watchers interprets the 'sons of God' (Gen. 6:2, 4) as angels. It tells how in the days of Jared, the father of Enoch, two hundred angels (of the class of angels called 'Watchers'), under the leadership of Aśa'el and Šemiazah, were attracted by the daughters of men and descended from heaven on Mount Hermon. They took human wives, who bore them children, the giants (Gen. 6:4). The fallen angels and the giants were responsible for the corruption of the world in the period before the Flood. Enoch had the task of conveying God's sentence on the Watchers, which was that they themselves were to be imprisoned until the Day of Judgment, while their sons the giants were condemned to destroy each other in battle. Their Flood was sent to cleanse the earth of the corruption caused by the Watchers, but the spirits of the dead giants remained on earth as the demons who are the cause of evil in the world until the Day of Judgment" ("The Fall of the Angels," 314).

6. Minns and Parvis, *Justin, Philosopher and Martyr*, 91.

Some scholars have mistakenly credited Justin as the innovator who first pegged pagan gods as the evil spirits of the γίγαντες (i.e., demons).[7] In actuality, this connection had already been established by the author of *1 Enoch* who stated in 19:1, "And Uriel said to me [Enoch]: The spirits of the angels who were promiscuous with the women will stand here; and they, assuming many forms, made men unclean and will lead men astray so that they sacrifice to demons as gods."[8]

This allusion to the "gods" by the author of *1 Enoch*, though, was probably in reference to Near Eastern mythological figures. With that qualification, Justin would then be considered to be somewhat of an innovator for adapting the Enochic tradition in order to fit his critique of the Greco-Roman worship of the gods.[9] It is also interesting to note that Justin deviates somewhat from the account of the Book of Watchers when he "ignores the [Enochic] tradition that the angels who sinned with women in the time of Noah were punished and permanently removed from contact with mankind."[10] For Justin, the parents of the demons (i.e., the fallen angels) were also active participants in the divine masquerade.[11] This inclusion may have been one of the adjustments Justin had to make in adapting the Enochic tradition to fit his critique of the Greco-Roman religion where Zeus as well as his sons (e.g., Dionysus, Apollo) were both notorious for sexual exploitation of earthly women, "Zeus . . . enslaved by love to evil and shameful pleasures . . . and that his own children did similar things" (*1 Apol.* 21.5). In this case, Justin would have identified Zeus as a fallen angel while his sons were the disembodied giants (i.e., demons) swept away by the flood.

Gerald McDermott also argues that Justin possessed such a bipartite scheme of fallen angels and their demonic offspring with the former posing as the Greco-Roman gods and their demonic offspring working behind the scenes to keep the divine subterfuge going, "[Justin] believed that while the

---

7. Droge, *Homer or Moses?*, 56; Bamberger, *Fallen Angels*, 74.

8. Sparks, "1 Enoch," 208; cf. Skarsaune, "Judaism and Hellenism in Justin Martyr," 592.

9. Bauckham, "The Fall of the Angels," 314.

10. Kelly, *The Devil*, 29. Bamberger is incorrect when he states that "sometimes Justin confuses the wicked angels and their demon children" (*Fallen Angels*, 74).

11. In *2 Apol.* 4.2–6, Justin also accuses the parents of the demons, the fallen angels, as falsely parading themselves as the pagan deities: "Hence it is that poets and storytellers, not knowing that the things which they have recorded were done to men and women and cities and nations by the angels and the demons they begot, attributed these things to the god himself, and to the sons who were begotten as if from him by the sowing of seed and from those who were called his brothers and their children as well. For they—that is, the poets and storytellers—called them by the names which each of the angels gave to himself and to his children."

national angels established themselves as the gods of pagan religions, they assigned the maintenance of their religions to their demonic offspring."[12] It appears that McDermott in making such an assessment is trying to demonstrate how Justin simply adapted a Platonic notion of either benevolent or malevolent *daemons* serving as mediators of the gods (cf. *Symposium* 202d-e) with all these *daemons* now viewed as evil in order to fit his Christian purposes.[13]

But from Justin's own testimony, it appears that the evil demons he mentions play a much more visible role in the masquerading process, "For they—that is, the poets and storytellers—called them by the names which each of the angels gave to himself and to his children" (2 *Apol.* 4.6). In Justin's own words, the evil demons do not simply hide behind the aliases of their angelic parents. Instead, both work in tandem with the fallen angels functioning under their manufactured aliases while their demonic offspring function under the unique identities assigned to them by their angelic parents. With this distinction in mind, the eternals (i.e., gods of Mt. Olympus) would have been the fallen angels for Justin while the immortals or sons of Zeus would have been understood by the apologist as their demonic offspring. This distinction will be important, especially when encountering the myth in regards to the dispute of Aphrodite (i.e., eternal) and Persephone (i.e., immortal) over the human Adonis later on in this chapter.

Another notable adaptation Justin made to the Enochic tradition was that the promiscuity of the fallen angels and demons no longer was limited to just women per se but was also extended to men claiming in 1 *Apol.* 5.2 that these supernatural beings also "seduced boys" (παῖδας διαφθείρω). Justin's decision to add the sexual exploitation of men in his reception of the Enochic tradition was so that he could account for not only the notorious bisexual palettes of the Greco-Roman gods (e.g., Dionysus, Apollo, Zeus) but also the amorous longings the goddesses (e.g., Aphrodite, Persephone) had towards mortal men as mentioned above. Furthermore, Justin's decision to add the sexual exploitation of men in reference to the male gods was another means for the apologist to widen the contrast between the passionless manner of the Christian God in his approach towards the Virgin Mary and the male pagan gods whose passions were so unbridled and unmitigated that they seized not only upon human women but men as well.

---

12. McDermott, *God's Rivals*, 90.

13. Osborn, *Justin Martyr*, 56.

Dionysus son on Semele (25.1)

In the previous allusion to Dionysus in the type material (§21.2), Justin referenced the Dionysus Zagreus myth (First Dionysus) in which both his parents were of divine pedigree (Zeus and Persephone). In this particular allusion to Dionysus in *1 Apol.* 25.1, Justin was referencing an entirely different mythical tradition where Dionysus is now an immortal with Zeus being his father and the human, Semele, his mother.[14] In this switching of traditions, Justin reveals a tendency amongst the apologists not to limit themselves to a particular mythical tradition but were willing to "choose their examples in all sources and in all ages" in order to serve their purposes.[15]

Dionysus, son of Semele, had a reputation for having an extensive list of sexual relations with human women besides Ariadne (whose story was treated extensively in the previous chapter): (1) Althaia, (2) Pallene, and (3) Physkoa. While little intrigue has been passed down to us regarding the circumstances of how the wine god acquired Physkoa,[16] the other two were taken advantage of by the deity in either one shape or fashion: Althaia's husband was bribed by the wine god to give up his wife[17] and Dionysus

---

14. *Homeric Hymn to Dionysus* 26: "I am loud-crying Dionysus whom Cadmus' daughter Semele bare of union with Zeus"; Pseudo-Apollodorus, *The Library* 3.26; Diodorus Siculus, *Library of History* 4.2.1; Hesiod, *Theogony* 940; *Homeric Hymn to Dionysus* 1 and 7; Hyginus, *Fabulae* 179; Pausanias, *Description of Greece* 3.24.4; Pindar, *Pythian Ode* 3.

15. Carena, "La critica della mitologia pagana," 15: "Un'ultima osservazione: il Puech, considerando nel suo complesso la scelta dei miti fatti segno ai colpi degli apologeti, nota che essi non hanno tenuto conto sufficientemente delle condizioni proprie dell'età loro, di modo che hanno scelto i loro esempi in tutte le fonti e in tutte le età e gli uni dopo gli altri hanno continuato ad attaccare credenze dei tempi di Numa e di Solone, accanto a credenze recenti."

16. Pausanias, *Description of Greece* 5.16.7: "Physkoa they say came [to Olympia] from Elis in the Hollow, and the name of the parish where she lived was Orthia. She mated they say with Dionysus, and bore him a son called Narcaeus. When he grew up he made war against the neighboring folk, and rose to great power, setting up moreover a sanctuary of Athena surnamed Narcaea. They say too that Narcaeus and Physkoa were the first to pay worship to Dionysus [in Elis]."

17. Pseudo-Hyginus, *Fabulae* 129: "When Liber [Dionysus] had come as a guest to Oeneus, son of Parthaon, he fell in love with Althaea, daughter of Thestius and wife of Oeneus. When Oeneus realized this, he voluntarily left the city and pretended to be performing sacred rites. But Liber [Dionysus] lay with Althaea, who became mother of Deianira. To Oeneus, because of his generous hospitality, he gave the vine as a gift, and showed him how to plant it, and decreed that its fruit should be called 'oinos' from the name of his host"; Pseudo-Apollodorus, *The Library* 1.64; Theophilus of Antioch, *To Autolycus* 2.7.

unfairly overpowered Pallene in a wrestling match through the use of his divine powers.[18]

Justin also mentions in *1 Apol.* 25.1 that Dionysus and Apollo, "because of love of males did things which is shameful even to mention." The men Dionysus was known for having sexual relations were Ampelos and Polymnos. While little has been passed down regarding the satyr Ampelos who either tragically fell to his death while picking grapes from a vine or from falling off of a bull,[19] the story of Polymnos is most likely the shameful (αἶσχος) account to which Justin would have been referring. According to the mythological tradition, Polymnos granted Dionysus passage to Hades on the condition that the god of wine would have sex with him upon the return. When Dionysus arrived back from the underworld to make due on his promise, he discovered that Polymnos had passed away while he was on his journey and had already been buried. In order to honor the agreement he made with the mortal, Dionysus shaped a tree branch in the form of a phallus and placed it upon the grave of his deceased lover.[20]

18. Nonnus, *Dionysiaca* 48.106: "[Dionysus wrestled Pallene in a contest for her hand in marriage:] Then Cypris [Aphrodite] presided over the ring. In the midst was Eros naked, holding out to Bacchos the bridal wreath. Wrestling was to win the bride: Peitho clad her delicate body in a silvery robe, foretelling victory for Lyaios's wooing ... After the victory in this contest, with the consent of Zeus, Eros crowned his brother with the cluster that heralds a wedding; for he had accomplished a delectable wedding-bout"; Nonnus, *Dionysiaca* 43.420.

19. It is the account of Ovid (*Fasti* 3.412) that describes Ampelos as a reckless youth who, "while picking gaudy grapes upon a branch, he tumbled down," while it is the lengthy account of Nonnus (*Dionysiaca* 10.175–430; 11; 12.1–117) that describes Ampelos death as a result of falling off of a bull.

20. Clement of Alexandria, *Exhortation to the Greeks* 2.30: "This is the origin of these phalloi. Dionysus was anxious to descend into Hades, but did not know the way. Thereupon a certain man, Polymnos [Polymnos] by name, promises to tell him; though not without reward. The rewards was not a seemly one, though to Dionysus it was seemly enough. It was a favour of lust, this reward which Dionysus was asked for. The god is willing to grant the request; and so he promises, in the event of his return, to fulfill the wish of Prosymnus [Polymnos], confirming the promise with an oath. Having learnt the way he set out, and came back again. He does not find Prosymnus [Polymnos] for he was dead. In fulfillment of the vow to his lover Dionysus hastens to the tomb and indulges his unnatural lust. Cutting off a branch from a fig-tree which was at hand, he shaped it into the likeness of a phallus, and then made a show of fulfilling his promise to the dead man. As a mystic memorial of this passion *phalloi* are set up to Dionysus in cities"; Pausanias, *Description of Greece* 2.37.6; Pseudo-Hyginus, *Astronomica* 2.5.

Apollo the child of Leto (25.1)

According to the mythological tradition, the virility of the god of music, poetry, prophecy, medicine, and protector of herds and flocks was unsurpassed amongst his divine peers. All told, he was known as having twenty-five sexual encounters with mortal woman yielding offspring with every one of them.[21] It is this prolific number alone of reputed instances attributed to Apollo that probably led to Justin's selection of him as a prime example of the gods' inability to contain their passions. For Apollo, his romantic overtures also extended towards several mortal men for whom he was linked: (1) Adonis, (2) Cyparissus, (3) Hyacinth, and (4) Hymeneaus. Three of the four male lovers have colorful stories regarding their affairs with Apollo: Cyparissus was turned into a tree by Apollo when he was overcome by grief for accidently slaying his own pet deer,[22] Hyacinth was transformed into a flower after Apollo accidently killed him with a discus,[23] and Hymeneaus'

---

21. Below is a list of the mortal women who bore children from their sexual relationships with Apollo: Acalle (Apollonius Rhodius, *Argonautica* 4.1490); Amphissa (Pausanias, *Description of Greece.* 10.38.4); Aria (Pseudo-Apollodorus, *Library* 3.1.2); Arsinoe (Scholium on Pindar's *Pythians* 3.14); Celaeno (Pausanias, *Description of Greece* 10.6.3); Chione (Pseudo-Hyginus, *Fabulae* 200); Chrysorthe (Pausanias, *Description of Greece* 2.5.8); Coronis (Pseudo-Hyginus, *Fabulae* 202); Corycia (Pausanias, *Description of Greece* 10.6.3); Creusa (Eurpides, *Ion*); Dryope (Antoninus Liberalis, *Metamorphoses* 32); Erginos (Pausanias, *Description of Greece* 9.37.5); Euadne (Pindar, *Olympian Ode* 6.28–73); Hecuba (Pseudo-Apollodorus, *Library* 3.12.5); Hypermnestra (Pseudo-Hyginus, *Fabulae* 70); Hyria (Antoninus Liberalis, *Metamorphoses* 12); wife of Leucippus (Pausanias, *Description of Greece* 3.16.1); Manto (Strabo, *Geography* 14.5.16); Parthenope (Pausanias, *Description of Greece* 7.4.1); Phthia (Pseudo-Apollodorus, *The Library* 1.56); Prokleia (Pseudo-Apollodorus, *The Library* 3.23); Psamathe (Pausanias, *Description of Greece* 2.19.8); Rhoeo (Diodorus Siculus, *Library of History* 5.62.1); Thero (Pausanias, *Description of Greece* 9.40.5–6); Thyia (Pausanias, *Description of Greece* 10.6.4).

22. Ovid, *Metamorphoses* 10.106: "Him, all unwittingly, the boy, Cyparissus, pierced with a sharp javelin, and when he saw him dying of the cruel wound, he resolved on death himself . . . he became a stiff tree with a slender top and pointed up to the starry heavens. The god [Apollo] groaned with sorrow, said; 'You shall be mourned by me, shall mourn for others, and your place shall always be where others grieve'"; Nonnus, *Dionysiaca* 11.362.

23. Pausanias, *Description of Greece* 3.19.3–4: "Nikias, son of Nikomedes, has painted him [Hyakinthos, in the shrine at Amyklai] in the very prime of youthful beauty, hinting at the love of Apollon for Hyakinthos of which legend tells . . . As for Zephyros, how Apollon unintentionally killed Hyakinthos, and the story of the flower, we must be content with the legends, although perhaps they are not true history"; Clement of Alexandria, *Exhortation to the Greeks* 2, and *Recognitions* 10.26; Hesiod, *Catalogues of Women Fragment* 102; Lucian, *Dialogues of the Gods* 16 and 17; Ovid, *Metamorphoses* 10.162; Philostratus the Elder, *Imagines* 1.24; Philostratus the Younger, *Imagines* 14; Pseudo-Apollodorus, *The Library* 1.16 and 3.116; Pseudo-Hyginus, *Fabulae* 271.

handsomeness so captivated Apollo that the mischievous, infant god Hermes was able to steal the prized cattle of his distracted, fellow deity.[24]

Yet it is the male consort of Apollo least attested within the mythological tradition, Adonis, whose sexual relationship with the god of wisdom and the arts Justin most likely had in view here. This is because immediately after Justin finishes his allusions to Dionysus and Apollo (in that respective order) in *1 Apol.* 25.1 regarding their "love of males did things which it is shameful even to mention" he makes what seems to be an abrupt shift in his discussion. At the latter part of the same verse (§25.1), he concludes by ridiculing the adolescent behavior of two goddesses (i.e., Aphrodite and Persephone) pitted against each other over who would win the affection of the mortal Adonis.

But assuming that Justin's audience already identified Adonis as the man whom Apollo loved (ἔρωτας ἀρσένων) earlier in the passage, the transition to Aphrodite and Persephone immaturely clamoring over who would win over this ancient paragon of male beauty no longer seems so random. In this case, the ancient reader's awareness of Adonis as the male lover of Apollo acts as a segue for Justin to then go on to expose the shameful acts of the female goddesses pertaining to the same exact human subject (i.e., Adonis). It is interesting to note that the lone extant passage (from the late 1st century) establishing an explicit romantic connection between Apollo and Adonis also reveals Aphrodite's involvement with the mortal in what ends up becoming a sordid love-triangle, "Adonis, having become androgynous, behaved as a man for Aphrodite and as a woman for Apollo."[25] It is very possible that in transitioning from Apollo to Aphrodite, Justin may have been capitalizing upon a contemporary understanding of how the goddess of love as well as the god of wisdom were somehow inextricably linked in the minds of the ancient reader by virtue of the man they both lusted after.

Also according to the testimony of the same mythographer, Apollo was not only the lover of Adonis but also his eventual murderer. Instead of

24. Antoninus Liberalis, *Metamorphoses* 23: "He had a son, Hymenaeus., admired by all around for his appearance. Apollo saw the lad and fell in love with him and would not leave the house of Magnes. Because of this Hermes plotted to get the herd of cattle belonging to Apollo that pastured with those of Admetus"; Hesiod, *The Great Eoiae Fragment* 16.

25. Ptolemy Hephaestion, *New History Book* 5: "Ὡς Ἄδωνις ἀνδρόγυνος γενόμενος τὰ μὲν ἀνδρεῖα πρὸς Ἀφροδίτην πράσσειν ἐλέγετο, τὰ θηλυκὰ δὲ πρὸς Ἀπόλλωνα." The fragments of Ptolemy Hephaestion's *New History Book* reside within the massive compilation of the 9th century patriarch of Constantinople, Photius, known as the *Bibliotheca*. For reference sake, *New History Book* is codex 190 in Photius's *Bibliotheca* (trans. Henry, 51–72).

following the more conventional ascriptions that the goddess of hunting (i.e., Artemis) or the god of war (i.e., Ares) had transformed into a wild boar in order to kill Adonis,[26] Ptolemy Hephaestion identified Apollo as the deity responsible for his death. Upon finding out that Aphrodite punished his son Erymanthos with blindness for peeping on her and Adonis while they were making love, this mythographer states that Apollo in anger changed himself into the wild boar killing Adonis as payback for what the goddess of love did to his son.[27] If Justin's audience understood Apollo as the one responsible for the slaughtering of his innocent lover as his reaction against Aphrodite for justifiably punishing his guilty son (i.e., the blinding of Erymanthos), the reader would conclude that this irrational, vengeful act to be unbefitting for a god whose divine attribute was wisdom.[28] This fit of rage meted out disproportionately upon his own innocent lover would also certainly fit Justin's description of an unnamed passionate act of Apollo too shameful even to mention.

Aphrodite and Persephone [on account of Adonis] (25.1 and 64.4)

While the goddess of love was known for having affairs with a total of five different mortal men, Justin focused his allusion solely upon Aphrodite's dispute with Persephone regarding who was rightful owner over Adonis.[29]

26. Pseudo-Apollodorus, *The Library* 3.14.4: "And Adonis, while still a boy, was wounded and killed in hunting by a boar through the anger of Artemis"; Nonnus, *Dionysiaca* 42.1: "[O]nly the boars she would not watch in their pleasures, for being a prophet she knew, that in the shape of a wild boar, Ares with jagged tusk and spitting deadly poison was destined to weave fate for Adonis in jealous madness"; cf. Servius, *Commentary on the Eclogues of Vergil* 10.18.

27. Ptolemy Hephaestion, *New History Book* 1: "Ὅτι Ἐρύμανθος ὁ παῖς Ἀπόλλωνος ἐτυφλώθη διότι ἴδοι λουμένην Ἀφροδίτην ἀπό τῆς Ἀδώνιδος μίξεως εἰς, καὶ Ἀπόλλων μηνίσας ἑαυτὸν εἰς σύαγρον μετεμόρφωσε καὶ τοῖς ὀδοῦσι πλήξας ἀνεῖλε τὸν Ἀδωνιν."

28. Wartelle also points out that the Delphic religion was understood during the times of Justin as being one of the highest forms of Greek religion because of the heightened reasoning capabilities of its god: "Apollon, fils de Zeus et de Léto, est le dieu oraculaire de Delphes (supra, 18, §4), qui symbolise une des formes les plus élevées de la religion grecque" (*Apologies*, 263).

29. The list of mortal men Aphrodite was involved with sexually besides Adonis were: Achises (Hesiod, *Theogony* 1008; Homer, *Iliad* 2.820; *Homeric Hymn 5 to Aphrodite* 45), Boutes (Pseudo-Apollodorus, *The Library* 1.13; Pseudo-Hyginus, *Fabulae* 14), Phaon (Aelian, *Historical Miscellany* 12.18; Athenaeus, *Deipnosophistae* 2.69d), and Phaeton (Hesiod, *Theogony* 986; Pausanias, *Description of Greece* 1.3.1; Pseudo-Apollodorus, *The Library* 3.181). Achises is the most notable of the four listed above as he ends up being the father of the founder of Rome, Aeneas. She bore children with all the men she consorted with except Phaon.

The background of this episode summarized by Pseudo-Apollodorus was that Persephone having been entrusted by Aphrodite to guard Adonis from the sexual advances of other deities, eventually ended up advancing upon the one whom she was charged to protect.

> Because of his [the infant Adonis] beauty, Aphrodite secreted him away in a chest, keeping it from the gods, and left him with Persephone. But when Persephone got a glimpse of Adonis, she refused to return him. When the matter was brought to Zeus for arbitration, he divided the year into three parts and decreed that Adonis would spend one third of the year by himself, one third with Persephone, and the rest with Aphrodite. But Adonis added his own portion to Aphrodite's.[30]

Although this mythological tradition portrays Aphrodite as completely satisfied with Zeus' decision, another account has the god of thunder delegating the case to Calliope (goddess muse of epic poetry) who makes a fatal judgment that ends up tragically affecting her own child: "Calliope, the judge appointed by Jove [Zeus], decided that each should possess him half of the year. But Venus [Aphrodite], angry because she had not been granted what she thought was her right, stirred the women in Thrace by love, each to seek Orpheus for herself, so that they tore him limb from limb."[31] Aphrodite was also known to have used her divine powers as retribution against Calliope's sister, Cleio the muse of history, for criticizing her relationship with Adonis, "Aphrodite, furious with [the Muse] Cleio, who had chided her for loving Adonis, caused her to fall in love with [a mortal], Magnes' son Pieros."[32]

So while Apollo was depicted by Justin as committing unreasonable acts contrary to his nature as the divine ruler of wisdom (i.e., slaying of Adonis), Aphrodite in like manner contradictorily utilized her ability to incite love in others as either a means of compelling them to do unlovely things (e.g., Thracian women tearing apart Orpheus) or as a means of directly punishing those whom she incited (e.g., Cleio's love for the mortal Magnes). So Justin's exposé of Aphrodite being overcome by the sting of love ("l'aiguillon de l'amou" as Wartelle puts it) to the point of vengeance ironically reveals that Aphrodite was no longer its ruler but rather in her acts of passion proved that she had become its slave.[33]

30. Pseudo-Apollodorus, *The Library* 1.184–185.

31. Pseudo-Hyginus, *Astronomica* 2.7.

32. Pseudo-Apollodorus, *The Library* 1.6.

33. Wartelle, *Apologies*, 263: "[C]elle du Dieu impassible avec Perséphone et Aphrodite toutes deux taraudées par l'aiguillon de l'amour. Impassible signifie ici non

Persephone's role in this dispute is of particular interest here as she was charged to protect the young Adonis from the sexual advances of other deities. But just like the legend of the watchers from the Enochic tradition, she likewise forsook her duties by exploiting the very subject she had been entrusted guardianship over. So did Justin have the fall of the watchers in view here when alluding to Persephone? Despite this fascinating correspondence between the two traditions, there is an immediate disparity of how the goddess Persephone would have translated into Justin's unique Enochic economy. The goddess of the underworld would have not been considered a fallen angel but rather the offspring of one because based upon the mythological tradition Persephone was a child of Zeus.[34]

The key perhaps to unlocking this conundrum lies in how the goddess Aphrodite translated into Justin's Enochic economy. The goddess of love was not an offspring of Zeus but in many ways his equal as she emerged from the foam (ἀφρός) that floated around the genitals of Uranus (i.e., Zeus' grandfather) having been severed and thrown into the sea when his son Chronos (i.e., Zeus' father) usurped him.[35] Given her origin, the goddess of love would have then held the status of a watcher (i.e., angel) who originally had guardianship responsibilities over Adonis. But according to Justin's system, Aphrodite inexplicably granted *in loco parentis* privileges of Adonis to an offspring (i.e., Persephone) of one of her fellow angels who had already fallen (i.e., Zeus). This trust would be misplaced as Persephone would succumb to the base example provided by her father who would have been one of the original angels who abdicated his role as a guardian for humanity, "Zeus . . . enslaved by love to evil and shameful pleasure [taught] his own children similar things" (*1 Apol.* 21.5).

---

seulement qui ne souffre pas, mais qui n'est soumis à aucune passion."

34. Hesiod, *Theogony* 912; *Homeric Hymn 2 to Demeter*; Ovid, *Fasti* 4.575, and *Metamorphoses* 5.501; Pseudo-Apollodorus, *The Library* 1.29; Nonnus, *Dionysiaca* 5.562.

35. Hesiod, *Theogony* 176: "And [Uranus] came, bringing on night and longing for love, and he lay about Earth spreading himself full upon her. Then the son [Cronos] from his ambush stretched forth his left hand and in his right took the great long sickle with jagged teeth, and swiftly lopped off his own father's members and cast them away to fall behind him"; Apuleius, *The Golden Ass* 4.28 and 6.6; Cicero, *De Natura Deorum* 3.21; Nonnus *Dionysiaca* 7.222. Justin makes reference to this legacy of parricide in Zeus' genealogy in *1 Apol.* 21.5: "Far let it be from the sensible mind to be schooled in such an idea concerning the gods—that even Zeus, according to them the leader and begetter of all, was both a parricide and the son of a father who was also such."

Zeus as a poor paternal deity (33.3); his relations with Ganymede (25.2) and Antiope (25.2)

At first glance it appears that Justin is being merely redundant in his critique of the sexual exploits of Zeus here in *1 Apol.* 25.2 (a discussion he had just four chapters prior) even going as far as alluding to the same exact male lover of Zeus (i.e., Ganymede) mentioned in §21.5. Yet, this repetition served a two-fold purpose: (1) it acts as a marker that li nks the entire discussion about the interloping behavior of the gods here in chapter 25 with the type material surrounding the Virgin Birth in chapter 21 and (2) it forces the reader to re-visit the Justinian contrast between the Greco-Roman father deity, Zeus (Διὸς) with "the God who is most true and the Father (πατήρ) of justice and temperance who is unalloyed with evil" (*1 Apol.* 6.2).[36]

In regards to the latter point, this desire by Justin to prove the radical difference between the father of the gods in paganism versus God the Father in Christianity is most clearly evident in *1 Apol.* 33.3–5. In verses 3–4, the apologist rebuffs pagan claims that the paternal divine figure of the Christians (i.e., God the Father) was guilty of the same lascivious behavior for which the paternal divine figure of Greco-Roman religion (i.e., Zeus) was infamous:[37]

> But lest some people, not understanding the prophecy we have
> pointed to, should charge against us the things we charge against
> the poets, who said that Zeus came to women for the sake of
> sexual gratification, let us try to elucidate the words. So the
> phrase 'Behold the virgin will conceive' [Isa 7.14] signifies that
> the virgin conceived without intercourse, for is she had inter-
> course with anyone, she would no longer be a virgin. But the
> power of God came upon the virgin and overshadowed her, and
> caused her, though a virgin, to be pregnant.

36. It is interesting that this assertion by Justin regarding the "justice and temperance" of God the Father in *1 Apol.*6 comes right after Justin goes through a lengthy diatribe against "the promiscuity of Zeus as well as his sons" (*1 Apol.* 4.9) in *1 Apol.* 4–5. One can pick up here early on in *1 Apology* that Justin is setting up the stage to contrast the integrity of the father of the Greco-Roman gods, Zeus, with that of the Christian God the Father.

37. According to *Dial. Trypho* 67.2, this appears to be a claim that was being made by Judaism against Christianity as Justin recorded his Jewish interlocutor Trypho as saying, "Besides in the so-called Greek myths there is a story of how Perseus was born of Danaë, while she was a virgin, when the one whom they call Zeus descended upon her in the form of a golden shower. You Christians should be ashamed of yourselves, therefore, to repeat the same kind of stories as these men."

The "passionless" (ἀπαθεῖ) manner by which the Virgin Mary was impregnated by God the Father is further accentuated by the following verse (§33.5) where Justin announces that it was not He that actually caused the Virgin Mary to be of child but rather the πνεύματος ἁγίου, "And further, the angel of God sent at that time to this virgin announced good news to her, saying: 'Behold, you will conceive in the womb from holy Spirit [πνεύματος ἁγίου] and you will bear a son and he shall be called Son of the Most High, and you will call his name Jesus.'"[38] While scholarship has had difficulty ascertaining the exact identity of this πνεύματος ἁγίου in this passage (whether the third person of the Trinity or the Logos itself), the point still stands that Justin was able to strengthen the attribute of ἀπαθεῖ for God the Father in the mind of his reader by asserting that He was not even directly involved in Mary's impregnation but rather it actually occurred through the agency of His "holy Spirit."[39]

Justin's argument for God the Father's "passionless" nature on the basis of his utilization of a divine intermediary (πνεύματος ἁγίου) in human conception aids us in understanding what the apologist sought to accomplish in his prior allusions to Zeus with regards to Ganymede and Antiope (*1 Apol.* 25.2). Both allusions (the first being a male lover while the second a female one) were utilized by the apologist to establish that a careful scan of the poets' writings proves time and time again that the passion of Zeus had "gone amok." This notion would, in turn, serve as a contrasting backdrop for Justin's overall portrait of God the Father as ἀπαθεῖ (*1 Apol.* 33.3–5).

Although Ganymede is the only male love that is linked to Zeus within the entire mythological tradition, Justin took full advantage of this story (repeats it twice) in order to portray the paternal god of Greco-Roman religion as completely given over to his passions.[40] This male love of Zeus

38. Justin is here quoting Luke 1.31–32 and Matt 1.20–21.

39. There is divided scholarship on how to identify what Justin meant by πνεύματος ἁγίου in *1 Apol.* 33.5 as it lacks a definite article. Some scholars argue that despite missing this definite article that a traditional ascription to the third person of the Trinity, the Holy Spirit, is in view here (q.v. Martín, *El Espíritu Santo en los orígenes del Cristianismo*, 185–86), while others argue that the πνεύματος ἁγίου is none other than the Logos itself proposing that Justin meant "a self-incarnation of the Word" (q.v. Aldama, "El Espíritu Santo y el Verbo en la exégesis de Lc 1, 35," 146). For a concise summary of the debate, see Bucur, "The Angelic Spirit in Early Christianity," 190–208.

40. *Homeric Hymn 5 to Aphrodite* 204: "Verily wise Zeus carried off golden-haired Ganymedes because of his beauty, to be amongst the Deathless Ones and pour drink for the gods in the house of Zeus, a wonder to see, honored by all the immortals as he draws the red nectar from the golden bowl . . . deathless and un-aging, even as the gods"; Statius, *Silvae* 3. 4.13: "Pine-clad Ida . . . pride herself on the cloud of a holy rape [of Ganymede]—for surely she gave the High Ones him at whom Juno [Hera] ever looks askance, recoiling from his hand and refusing the nectar"; Euripides, *Iphigenia at*

with Ganymede was understood as "one of the most perfect symbols of debauchery attributed to the Greeks" making this episode perhaps Justin's prime example of the fallen angels (i.e., the eternals) and their offspring's (i.e., immortals) involvement in the "corruption of young boys" mentioned back in *1 Apol.* 5.2.[41] It is important to note at this juncture that Justin's primary concern was not condemning the practice of Greco-Roman male love, but rather his emphasis was to expose the stark difference between the passioned-filled Zeus with the passionless Christian God the Father. In other words, Zeus and Ganymede's relationship was proof to Justin that the father of the gods had been so overtaken by passion that his libido not only extended to women but to men as well.

The extent of the debauchery of Zeus is further accented by Justin's recollection of this god's encounter with Antiope, "and [we] have dedicated ourselves to the unbegotten and passionless God, whom we do not believe had frenzied sex [οἶστρος] either with Antiope or the other women like her."[42] The term "frenzied sex" has direct linkage to the narrative of Zeus and Antiope with the father of the gods changing into the appearance of a satyr in order to seduce the princess of Hyria.[43] Satyrs were known within the

---

Aulis 1051; Homer, *Iliad* 20.232; Ovid, *Metamorphoses* 10. 152; Pindar, *Olympian Ode* 1.40; Pseudo-Apollodorus, *The Library* 3.141; Pseudo-Hyginus, *Astronomica* 2.16, 29; Theognis, *Fragment* 1.1345.

41. Wartelle, *Apologies*, 263: "Ganymède, jeune héros aimé de Zeus, enlevé dans l'Olympe par l'aigle du dieu, est l'un des plus parfaits symboles de la débauche attribuée aux Grecs."

42. Below is a list of the mortal women who bore children from their sexual relationships with Zeus: Alcmene (Pseudo-Apollodorus, *The Library* 2.4.8); Antiope (Homer, *Odyssey* 11. 260); Danae (Homer, *Iliad* 14.312); Dia (Pseudo-Hyginus, *Fabulae* 155); Elare (Pseudo-Apollodorus, *The Library* 1.4.1); Europa (Pseudo-Apollodorus, *The Library* 3.1.1); Eurymedousa (Clement of Alexandria, *Exhortations* 2); Callisto (Hesiod, *The Astronomy Fragment* 3); Calyke (Pausanias, *Description of Greece* 5.1.3); Kassiopeia (Pseudo-Apollodorus, *The Library* 3.1.2); Lamia (Pausanias, *Description of Greece* 10.12.1); Laodameia (Pseudo-Apollodorus, *The Library* 3.1.1); Leda (Pseudo-Apollodorus, *The Library* 3.10. 5–7); Lysithoe (Cicero *De Natura Deorum* 3.16.42); Niobe (Pseudo-Hyginus, *Fabulae* 155); Olympias (Nonnus, *Dionysiaca* 7.110); Pandora (*Hesiod, Catalogues of Women Fragment* 2); Protogeneia (Pseudo-Hyginus, *Fabulae* 155); Pyrrha (Pseudo-Hyginus, *Fabulae* 155); Phthia (Aelian, *Historical Miscellany* 1.15); Semele (Hesiod, *Theogony* 940); Thyia (Hesiod, *Catalogues of Women Fragment* 3). As prodigious as the god of thunder was in exploiting female subjects according to the mythological tradition (22 women), he was not quite on par with the god of wisdom, Apollo, who was known for having children with 25 different women.

43. Pseudo-Clement, *Recognitions* 10.22: "In short, [Zeus] seduced Antiope, the daughter of Nycteus, when turned into a satyr, and of her were born Amphion and Zethus"; Apollonius Rhodius 1.735; Homer, *Odyssey* 11.260, Ovid, *Metamorphoses* 6. 111; Pausanias, *Description of Greece* 2.6.4; Pseudo-Apollodorus, *The Library* 3.5.5 and 3.10.1; Pseudo-Hyginus, *Fabulae* 7 & 8.

mythological tradition as, "minor deities of the forest, depicted as having the bodies of unusually hairy men, the legs and feet of goats and short horns on their head. Representing the raw power of nature, they attended upon the god Dionysus and were notorious for their lustful ways."[44] So when Justin alluded to the "frenzied sex" [οἶστρος] of Zeus in respect to Antiope, he has in view here the active role the satyr played within the coterie of Dionysus (maenads included) to facilitate the frenzied sexual state of those participating in the erotic Bacchanals.

A comparison between Zeus' hiding behind the guise of a satyr to seduce Antiope and Justin's portrait of the Christian God distancing Himself in the Virgin Mary's impregnation by use of a divine intermediary is in order here. On the one hand, the father of the Greco-Roman gods had become so overcome with lust that he would change himself into all things these minor deities notorious for their lustful behavior. These satyrs were thus not only renowned for their base sexual behavior but their ability to induce this same depravity out of their human subjects (i.e., Antiope). So a pattern is established here: not only is Zeus given over to immorality but the humans involved with him have succumbed to it as well.

On the other hand, the divine and human encounter in Christianity where the Son of God is born demonstrates a converse moral movement where the sanctity of all parties involved is upheld. According to Justin, not only does God the Father's use of a divine agent radically differentiate His encounter with Mary with that of Zeus with Antiope but the moral integrity of both this sent πνεύματος ἁγίου as well as that of the human recipient is preserved also. Justin's argument is very simple here: he interprets the LXX version of Isa 7:14 in *1 Apol.* 33.4, "Behold the virgin (παρθένος) will conceive," as a prophetic proof text confirming Mary's virginity even after conception. The deduction is that the complete absence of sexual intercourse here proves that the manner in which the πνεύματος ἁγίου caused Mary to conceive was truly holy per se. Also while Antiope is manipulated by Zeus through seduction and trickery, Justin reminds his reader in contrast of the gentleness and consideration by which Mary was approached prior to the arrival of the πνεύματος ἁγίου to impregnate her, "And further, the angel of God sent at that time to this virgin announced good news to her, saying: 'Behold, you will conceive in the womb from holy Spirit.'" (§33.5)

---

44. Manser, *The Facts of File Dictionary of Classical and Biblical Allusions*, 325.

Magna Mater (27.4)

In the previous discussion, attention was placed upon Justin's depiction of the immoral story of Zeus and Antiope as just one of many narratives from Greco-Roman poetry that provide poor examples for humanity to follow. In Justin's allusion to Magna Mater (i.e., Cybele) in *1 Apol.* 27.4, the apologist would take this argument a step further by revealing how these decadent stories came to corrupt the actual behaviors of individuals his audience would have seen daily walking the streets of Rome. In the following passage Justin mentions the *Galli,* which were eunuch priests of the cult of Magna Mater whose bombastic and bizarre public expressions of worship were recognized by all, "some openly emasculate themselves to become catamites, and they present the mysteries to the mother of the gods [Magna Mater], and the viewing of the things you suppose to be divine is proclaimed before everyone as a great symbol and mystery."[45]

Classicist Hugh Bowden provides a concise summary of the geographical origin of this mystery cult and the underlying mythical narrative behind why the priests of this mystery cult were involved in the extreme religious practice of self-mutilation.

> It is generally stated that Magna Mater at Rome was served by eunuch priests, known as *Galli*. It is assumed that these eunuch priests arrived with the cult from Anatolia, and that eunuch priests were a usual feature of the cult of the Mother there. It is assumed too that the castration of priests of the Mother lies behind myths about Attis, who is supposed to have castrated himself out of devotion to Cybele, that is, the Mother.[46]

The myth of Attis was about a young shepherd whom the goddess Cybele (i.e., Magna Mater) fell in love. So captivated was she of this male's beauty (similar to Aphrodite of Adonis) that she offered to make him priest of her cult on the condition that he remained ever faithful to her. According to Ovid, Attis vowed his fidelity swearing, "If I lie, let the Venus [Aphrodite] I cheat with be my last."[47] Attis would eventually break his covenant with the goddess mother by having an affair with a nymph. When Cybele discovered that she had been cheated on by her boy lover, the mother of

---

45 Tripolitis, *Religions of the Hellenistic-Roman Age,* 33: "The extravagance in the ceremonies, the barbaric corybantic enthusiasm of the *galli,* or eunuch priests, their mad hypnotic dances accompanied by the loud shrill of the flute, and the sound of the tympanum that led to their self-mutilation were abhorrent to the Romans."

46. Bowden, *Mystery Cults of the Ancient World,* 96.

47. *Fasti,* 4.222.

the gods not only kills the nymph but strikes Attis with a violent madness that compels him to fulfill the demands of his prior oath. Ovid provides a colorful narration of what ensues and how the outcome came to influence the emasculating rites of the cult, "He even hacked his body with a jagged stone, and dragged his long hair in squalid dirt, shouting, 'I deserved it; my blood is the penalty. Ah, death to the parts which have ruined me!' 'Ah, death to them!' he said, and cropped his groin's weight. Suddenly no signs of manhood remained. His madness became a model: soft-skinned acolytes toss their hair and cut their worthless organs.'"[48]

In alluding to these extreme practices performed by the *Galli*, Justin would go on in the following verse to critique society in general for venerating the self-laceration and self-mutilation the devotees of this mystery cult performed upon themselves in order to reenact the madness of Attis, "[these] things which are openly done and honoured by you, as if the divine light were overturned and absent, you ascribe to us" (*1 Apol.* 27.5). Justin's castigation of the general Roman populace for embracing these bizarre acts of self-destructiveness provides a window into a time where this mystery cult had just become legitimized within the Roman Empire. In former times, this mystery cult with its violent rites had been eschewed by most Romans but suddenly fell into wide acceptance a generation or so leading up to Justin's century, "During the reign of Claudius [AD 41–54], the cult (i.e., Magna Mater) gained new vigor and was one of the most popular and most favored of the foreign cults. By the end of the 1st century C.E., its popularity had spread throughout the Western world and Asia Minor. The restrictions on Roman participation were removed."[49] It was well-known that the emperor Antoninus Pius (AD 138–161), who was reigning during Justin's composition of *1 Apology*, greatly favored the cult of Cybele and Attis and its attending rites—a fact that according to Minns and Parvis makes Justin's, "ridiculing of the cult . . . either very brave or very foolhardy."[50]

For Justin, the Galli and the attending followers of the cult of Cybele and Attis were commemorating and celebrating a story where its chief figure (viz., Attis) was both guilty of immorality and also worthy of the punishment that came his way making the cult's emulating rites seem "as if the divine light were overturned and absent" in them (§27.5). And yet the Christian faith boasted that its chief figure (i.e., Christ) was entirely innocent yet died for the guilt of all but its followers reap the persecution that should really be applied to the followers of the Cybele and Attis cult.

48. Ibid.; Pausanias, *Description of Greece* 7.17.8.

49. Tripolitis, *Religions of the Hellenistic-Roman Age*, 33.

50. Minns and Parvis, *Justin, Philosopher and Martyr*, 157n1.

Perseus (54.8)

As stated in previous chapters, by the time we get to chapter 54 the montage of mythical analogies to the life of Christ established in chapters 21 and 22 are virtually repeated by Justin but now he goes to great lengths in this latter part of *1 Apology* to expose the diabolical origin behind these Greco-Roman religious narratives.[51] So while the discussion in chapter two of how the allusion to Perseus and Danaë in *1 Apol.* 22.5 centered around how this myth resonated with the Virgin Birth, this allusion to Perseus and Danaë exposes it as demonic fabrication, "But when they heard it said through the prophet Isaiah [Isaiah 7:14] as well that he would be a born of a virgin and would go up to heaven by himself, they would throw Perseus into the discussion."[52]

The stark contrast that Justin's readers would have immediately noticed between the Virgin Birth with the story of Zeus and Danaë parallels the circumstances surrounding the god of thunder's seduction of Antiope.[53] That is, no such manipulation or coercion would occur in the Gospel accounts as the angel Gabriel came to announce God's favor on Mary encouraging both her and Joseph to be willing participants in this miraculous occurrence they would soon experience.

In relation to this, Justin was also critical of Zeus sexually gratifying himself with the virgin Danaë (*1 Apol.* 33.3) while the Christian God preserved both His honor and that of Mary by causing, "her to be pregnant not through intercourse but through power" (*1 Apol.* 33.6). It is important to note that while Zeus in the guise of a golden shower actually made contact with Danaë (pouring himself into her lap), no such indiscretion is reported of God the Father who as discussed previously performed this conception through the divine agency of His πνεύματος ἁγίου (*1 Apol.* 33.5). So while Danaë no longer was a virgin after her encounter with Zeus, Mary's chastity was in contrast completely preserved.[54]

In so doing, Justin's audience would have been able to detect the differentiating emphases between the poetic account of Zeus and Danaë with

51. Prigent, *Justin et l'Ancien Testamente*, 160.

52. The discussion surrounding Perseus going "to heaven by himself" will be treated later in this chapter when dealing with the Christological theme of ascension as it relates to Justin.

53. Pseudo-Apollodorus, *The Library* 2.4.1: "When Akrisios later learned that she had given birth to Perseus, not believing that Zeus seduced her, he cast his daughter out to sea with her son on an ark. The ark drifted ashore at Seriphos, where Diktys recovered the child and brought him up"; Homer, *Iliad* 14.319.

54. Machen, *The Virgin Birth of Christ*, 336: "Whether the mothers of pagan heroes were represented as virgins before their union with the gods is the question before, they ceased to be virgins because of that event."

that of God the Father and Mary in the Gospel narratives. While the former had the lusting of Zeus after Danaë as its focus with her pregnancy being an incidental outcome of that encounter, the latter has the miraculous virginal conception of the child as its central concern. J. Gresham Machen remarks, "Where in the New Testament story is there any hint of a love of God for the maid of Nazareth, which can be analogous to the love of a husband for his wife? [Yet], the love of the gods for mortal women is the very point of the pagan stories—the thing without which they could not possibly exist."[55] By exposing the radical difference in the tenor between the poets description of miraculous births with that of Christian Scripture, Justin was presenting yet another case for his audience to abandon their trust in the pagan sacred texts (e.g., Homer) they were weaned upon as children and place their trust in this latter one, which belonged to the faith they had just recently come to profess.

Kore [Persephone] (64.1–4)

This passage has been a troubling one for scholars to analyze due to a variety of reasons: (1) there is ambiguity with respect to what goddess Justin was referring, (2) and once there is a consensus regarding her identity (i.e., Persephone) then uncertainty arises on which theogony Justin assigned her. Finally, (3) the person of the Holy Spirit seems to be randomly inserted into the discussion. The entire text is provided below for §64.1–4:

> And you are able to understand from what was said before that, in imitation of what was said by Moses, the demons caused the stirring of the reflection of the one called Kore at springs of waters, saying that she was the daughter of Zeus. For Moses said, as we wrote before: 'In the beginning God made the heaven and the earth. But the earth was invisible and unorganized, and Spirit of God (πνεῦμα θεοῦ) was borne upon [or "moved over"] the waters.' Therefore, in imitation of the Spirit of God spoken of as being born upon [or "moving over"] the water, Kore.[56]

Κόρη literally means "maiden" and it was a title ascribed not only to Persephone but to Athena as well, "'The maiden' [is] a title sometimes applied to

55. Ibid., 338–39.

56. I have taken the liberty to provide in brackets the more popular translation given for ἐπιφέρω in *1 Apol.* 64.1–4 "to move, or to hover." On the other hand, the translation of "borne upon" for ἐπιφέρω was supplied by Minns and Parvis. The importance of this distinction will emerge when discussing which theogony Justin attributed to Persephone.

Persephone, the daughter of Demeter . . . However the Achaeans brought with them the young warrior goddess who bore the title Core, Parthenos, and Pallas, meaning 'maiden,' 'virgin,' and 'girl.'"[57] For instance, Athenagoras in *Embassy for the Christians* §20 warned his reader about the vagueness surrounding this ascription, "For this reason she is mystically called Athela, though more usually Persephone and Kore. She must not however be confused with Athena, who is named 'Kore' from her virginity."[58]

While most scholarship identifies Persephone as the Κόρη that Justin was referencing, Robert Grant suggests that the apologist instead had Athena in mind.[59] His rationale is that because the ensuing passage (§64.5) deals explicitly with the goddess of the arts as it pertains to her cosmic function in creation, the ambiguous Kore described in §64.1–4 should be understood as Athena given that the topic of the passage is also with regards to creation (i.e., how Κόρη is a demonic imitation of Genesis 1:1–2).[60]

The problem with Grant's "Athenian" take on Κόρη, though, is that he goes against a whole host of ancient attestations that describe the statues of Persephone alongside "springs of water" (τῶν ὑδάτων πηγαῖς) a significant detail mentioned here in §64.1 and a phenomenon not attributed to Athena throughout the mythological tradition.[61] Still, Grant's insight to couple §64.1–4 with §64.5 due to the cosmic dimensions attributed to the goddesses in both set of verses should not be dismissed. In fact, it serves as an important interpretive key for determining what theogony Justin assigned to Persephone as well as to whom Justin was referring with regards to the "Spirit of God" (i.e., the Logos).

The most popular myth regarding the origin of Persephone is that she was the offspring of Zeus and Demeter who was later abducted against her will by Hades god of the Underworld.[62] The issue with this theogony, though, is that it does not reveal any sort of cosmic dimension as it relates

---

57. Dixon-Kennedy, "Core," *Encyclopedia of Greco-Roman Mythology*, 91.

58. Richardson, *Early Christian Fathers*, 318.

59. For a sampling of majority scholarship in favor of Kore as Persephone, see Barnard, *The First and Second Apologies*, 177n393; Lampe, *From Paul to Valentinus*, 267; Minns and Parvis, *Justin, Philosopher and Martyr*, 251n2, 3.

60. Grant, *Gods and the One God*, 155.

61. Pausanias, *Description of Greece* 4.33.4: "There are statues of the gods Apollo Carneius [and Hagne], also Hermes carrying a ram. Hagne [the holy one] is a title of Kore the daughter of Demeter. Water rises from a spring close to the statue"; Pausanias, *Description of Greece* 9.8.1: "Across the Asopus, about ten stades distant from the city, are the ruins of Potniae, in which is a grove of Demeter and the Maid [Persephone]. The images at the river that flows past Potniae . . . they name the goddesses"; Pausanias, *Description of Greece* 1.14.1 and 1.38.1; Diodorus Siculus, *Library of History* 5.4.1.

62. Hesiod, *Theogony* 912, and *Homeric Hymn 2 to Demeter* 1.

to Persephone. In addition, I contend that this more popular rendition of her origin actually serves as an impediment to our understanding of what Justin tried to convey in his allusion to her (this same problem will occur in our treatment of Athena).

Minns and Parvis assert that the best way to understand Justin's allusion to Persephone is to read it from the background provided by Pseudo-Apollodorus in which he states that the, "[river] Styx bore him [Zeus] Persephone."[63] With this theogony in place, it implicitly conveys a cosmic dimension to Persephone because she is conceived by Zeus without a partner. It also provides definition and shape for some of the more puzzling elements in §64.1–4: (1) the "stirring of the reflection of the one called Kore at springs of waters" that Justin referenced here was probably a religious observance honoring Kore's birth from Styx while (2) the "the Spirit of God was borne upon the waters" pretty much becomes self-explanatory.

It also seems that if Justin had the Holy Spirit in mind here when mentioning the πνεῦμα θεοῦ "borne upon the waters," this insertion would be considerably random given that Justin's discussion has been about demonic imitations of the Logos. Blunt laments, "It is not easy, in our present state of knowledge, to see the resemblance between the position of Koré and that which is ascribed to the Spirit."[64] Rather, it makes more contextual sense to understand πνεῦμα θεοῦ as a reference to the Logos. As we have discussed earlier in this chapter, "holy Spirit" (see footnote 39) for Justin did not have the firm grasp of the third person of the Trinity as its concern and was often synonymous (or closely related) to the concept of the Logos for Justin. Also if we take into consideration Grant's instinct to bundle §64.1–4 and §64.5, with the latter serving as a comparison of Athena as Logos against Christ as Logos, then the πνεῦμα θεοῦ mentioned in the Persephone discourse should be considered to be about the Logos as well.

Athena (64.5)

In this passage, Justin argues that the demons manufactured the myth of Athena being birthed from the mind of Zeus as his "first thought" (πρώτην ἔννοια) to somehow make the Christian belief that God the Father created the world through the agency of His preexistent Son appear as a mere fable, "And in a similarly malicious way, since [the demons] knew that God made the world, of which he formed a notion through the Logos, they said that Athena, the daughter of Zeus, was born, not of sexual intercourse but as

63. *The Library*, 1.3.1.
64. Blunt, *The Apologies of Justin Martyr*, 96.

the first thought. Which we consider to be most laughable—to introduce a female-shaped representation of thought" (§64.5).

The most famous theogony of this goddess whose divine jurisdiction encompassed war, wisdom, and the arts was that she sprung from the head of Zeus fully clothed in battle armor.[65] This grand entrance was the result of her divine father, Zeus, devouring Athena's divine mother Metis while Athena was still in the womb. According to Pseudo-Apollodorus, Zeus did this out of fear that the embittered titaness (i.e., Metis) whom he had sexually imposed himself upon would go on to produce a future male offspring who would eventually overthrow him. While Zeus was successful in deposing his first wife through this grotesque measure, the *in utero* Athena actually thrived in this new internalized state within the deep recesses of her father culminating in her renowned emergence from Zeus' head.[66]

But this fanciful account of Athena's inception should be dismissed as the birth story for which Justin was alluding because this rendition states that she was a product of sexual intercourse—an attribute of the goddess the apologist eliminates outright in 1 *Apol.* 64.5 (οὐκ ἀπὸ μίξεως). Instead, Justin seems to be referencing back to an earlier mythological tradition where Athena was understood to be the sole product of her divine father's mind being his "first thought" (πρώτην ἔννοια) and lacking "any allusion to her mother or to the manner in which she was called into existence."[67] In fact, viewing Justin's allusion to Athena with the more popular rendition of her theogony with all its fanciful elements (e.g., Zeus' swallowing the pregnant Metis) in mind can actually serve as an impediment in apprehending how Justin came to perceive the Athena myth a product of demonic subterfuge. For instance, Minns and Parvis who perhaps approach Justin's allusion to Athena in 1 *Apol.* 64.5 with this story as its background have surmised that, "As it stands, the text does not show how, in the myths about Athena, the demons imitated what they knew about God's making of the world."[68]

On the other hand, Robert Grant has been careful to link Justin's allusion to Athena with that of the earlier mythological tradition portraying her

---

65. Hesiod, *Theogony* 886 and 929a.

66. *The Library* 1.20: "Zeus slept with Metis, although she turned herself into many forms in order to avoid having sex with him. When she was pregnant, Zeus took the precaution of swallowing her, because she had said that, after giving birth to the daughter presently in her womb, she would bear a son who would gain the lordship of the sky. In fear of this he swallowed her. When it came time for the birth, Prometheus (or Hephaistos, according to some) by the river Triton struck the head of Zeus with an axe, and from his crown Athena sprang up, clad in her armour."

67. Smith, "Athena," in *Dictionary of Greek and Roman Biography and Mythology*, 397.

68. *Justin, Philosopher and Martyr*, 251n5.

existence solely being derived from the mind of Zeus.[69] Grant states that Middle Platonists such as Aelius Aristides (2nd century) seized upon this unique form of generation formerly attributed to her assigning a cosmic dimension unto the goddess of wisdom and the arts.[70] This was done in order to substantiate the trademark Middle Platonic concept of a personal Logos or "Second God" partnering with the Supreme God in establishing Creation of whom Aristides identified as Athena, "When Zeus considered (*ennoethesis*) making the world through his reason (*logos*), his first thought (*ennoia*) was Athena."[71]

So close is the "Cosmic Athena" of Aristides to the Christian concept of the Son of God as Logos that Friedrich Lenz is convinced that the 2nd century Middle Platonist must have erected it as a pagan countermeasure meant to offset the emerging ὁμοούσιος model being utilized by the Apologists to argue for the divinity of Christ, "showing that the old religion must be understood in this new sense with the old gods understood as functions of the one God [i.e., Zeus] and that the claims of the new religion, Christianity, were unfounded."[72] Although this analysis by Lenz is somewhat

69. Grant, *Gods and the One God*, 116.

70. Athena was not the only god who was assigned a cosmic dimension within Middle Platonism. According to Grant, Apollo (*Corpus Hermeticum*, Tractate 16), Dionysus (Plutarch, *On the E at Delphi* 388E, 389A), Hermes (*Kore Kosmou* 23, 29–30), Asclepius (Papyrus Oxyrhynchus 11.1381), and Heracles (Cornutus 31) were all identified by different Middle Platonists as Logos candidates who partnered with Zeus in creating the world (Grant, *Gods and the One God*, 112–20).

71. Grant, *Gods and the One God*, 116. Grant provides several compelling passages from Aristides that supports his claim that Athena was viewed logocentrically by this Middle Platonist. In an oration *To Zeus*, Aristides states, "Zeus made everything and all things are works of Zeus; rivers and earth and sea and heaven and whatever is within these and whatever is beyond them, gods and men and whatever has life and whatever appears to sight and whatever one can think of . . . one cannot say when [Zeus] came to be, but his was from the beginning and will be forever, father of himself and greater than one coming to be from another. And as Athena derived her nature from his head and he needed no partner to produce her, thus even earlier he made himself from himself and needed no other for coming to be; on the contrary, everything began its existence from him" (*Orations* 43.7–9, quoted in ibid., 116). Also in Aristides's *Oration to Athena* he goes on to assert, "[Zeus] had nothing of the same rank from which to make her, but himself withdrawing into himself generated the goddess from himself and bore her, so that she alone is securely the genuine offspring of the Father, coming to be from a race equal to him and acknowledged. What is yet greater than this is that from the most excellent part of himself, that is, from his head, he produced her . . . therefore it is not right for her ever to abandon the Father, but she is always present with him and lives with him as being of the same origin; she breathes toward him and is present alone with him alone" (*Orations* 37.2–4, quoted in ibid., *Gods and the One God*, 117).

72. Lenz, "Der Athenahymnos des Aristides," 339–40: "[S]o ist diese Ausdrucksweise nur ein Bild für das, was in der Sprache der christlichen Kirche ὁμοούσιος genannt

anachronistic (Christian thinkers would not come to grapple fully with the notion of the Son of God as *homoousia* until around the Council of Nicea in 325), the striking similarities that Lenz observes between Cosmic Athena as rendered by Aristides and the Son of God as Logos as presented by Justin are remarkable, "The daughter is constantly on the right hand of the Father [i.e, Zeus] to take his word, and then received orders to leave. Does this not remind us of the Christian idea of the Son, who sits at the right hand of the Father, and of the 'Logos' that with God, and God was?"[73] While it is difficult to prove with any certainty interchange that might have been occurring between the two traditions as Lenz suggests, he does establish that the myth of Cosmic Athena was very much alive and well in the second century.[74] A reader familiar with the Christian claim regarding the Son of God's involvement in Creation would have perceived the striking similarity in the account of Cosmic Athena who according to Aristides was, "consubstantial with the highest being [i.e., Zeus] and acting as his mediator who makes sure that the other gods are functions of the one God."[75]

Justin signals his awareness of this parallel tradition in *1 Apol.* 64.5 by proclaiming the resemblance the result of demonic activity. But unlike the other deities the apologist was able to dismiss summarily based upon their purported immoral behavior (e.g., Dionysus, Apollo), Justin did not have such a luxury when it came to the goddess of wisdom and the arts who was understood to be a chaste goddess.[76] This should help to explain partly

---

wird, oder dasselbe von Zeus her gesehen anders ausgedrückt: der Vater braucht die Tochter, um seine δύναμις den anderen Göttern und den Menschen zu manifestieren. So erklärt sich das wohl nur auf den ersten Blick seltsame Paradoxon, daß sie als sein Wort ständig bei ihm und um ihn ist und doch in ständiger Verbindung mit den anderen Göttern und Menschen steht ... Er will zeigen, daß die alte Religion in neuem Sinne und die alten Götter als Funktionen eines Gottes verstanden werden müssen und daß darum die Ansprüche des Christentums, eine neue Religion sein zu wollen, unbegründet sind."

73. Ibid., 340: "Die Tochter sitzt ständig zur Rechten des Vaters, um seine Aufträge in Empfang zu nehmen und dann Wort werden zu lassen. Erinnert das nicht an die christliche Vorstellung von dem Sohne, der zur Rechten des Vaters sitzt, und an das 'Wort,' das bei Gott und selbst Gott war?"

74. Grant dismisses any interplay between Aristides and the later Christian doctrine of the *homoousia*: "It is wrong to treat Aristides as an imitator of Christian theology as it would be to suggest that Christians relied on Aristides. The two interpretations reflect similar mediations on similar bases" (*Gods and the One God*, 117).

75. Lenz, "Der Athenahymnos des Aristides," 339: "So ist sie gleichzeitig wesensgleich mit dem höchsten Wesen und Mittlerin, die dafur sorgt, daß die anderen Gotter Funktionen des einen Gottes werden."

76. *Homeric Hymn 5 to Aphrodite* 7: "Golden Aphrodite Kypria, who stirs up sweet passion [i.e., sexual desire] in the gods and subdues the tribes of mortal men ... Yet there are three hearts that she cannot bend nor yet ensnare. First is the daughter of

why Justin goes on to attack the femininity of Athena proclaiming, "we consider to be most laughable—to introduce a female-shaped representation of
thought." One should consider that the impulse behind Justin's comment
was not misogynistic per se, but rather attacking the femininity of Athena
was perhaps the only recourse available to him in contrasting his doctrine
of the Son of God as Logos and partner with the Father in Creation over
what he perceived to be a demonic imitation found in "Cosmic Athena" of
Middle Platonism.[77]

Simon and Helen (26.2–3, 56.1–2), Menander (26.4, 56.1), and Marcion (26.5, 58.1–3)

In both *1 Apol.* 26.1, Justin states that the diabolical beings responsible for
fashioning deceptive myths were even in his day still very much embroiled
in the project of counterfeiting the activity of the Logos, "because even after the ascension of Christ to heaven the demons were putting up certain
people who asserted that they were gods, who were not only not persecuted
by you, but were even deemed worthy of honours."[78] Although these two
wonderworkers (i.e., Simon, Menander) and heretic (i.e., Marcion) cannot
be categorized as myths per se, Justin viewed their arrival unto the scene in
the late first century and the early second the extended work of the same
demons responsible for manufacturing the ancient myths.[79]

Zeus who holds the aigis, bright-eyed Athene; for she has no pleasure in the deeds of
golden Aphrodite, but delights in wars and in the work of Ares, in strifes and battles
and in preparing famous crafts. She first taught earthly craftsmen to make chariots of
war and cars variously wrought with bronze, and she, too, teaches tender maidens in
the house and puts knowledge of goodly arts in each one's mind. Nor does laughter-
loving Aphrodite ever tame in love Artemis . . . Nor yet does the pure maiden Hestia
love Aphrodite's works . . . Of these three Aphrodite cannot bend or ensnare the hearts.
But of all others there is nothing among the blessed gods or among mortal men that has
escaped Aphrodite"; Ovid, *Metamorphoses* 5.375; Telestes, *Fragment* 805.

77. For instance, Wartelle labels Justin's statement here as "antifeminist," stating,
"[O]n peut ne pas partager l'indignation de Justin: le symbolisme a aussi ses droits.
Toutefois, on se tromperait à ne voir là qu'une réaction grincheuse d'antiféminisme
épidermique" (*Apologies*, 294).

78. Minns and Parvis, *Justin, Philosopher and Martyr*, 149n9.

79. Although his scholarship of Justin is somewhat outdated, Lamson makes an
apt observation of how the apologist perceived an indelible connection between the
ancient myths and the contemporary phenomena of magicians and heretics of his time
period. Lamson remarks that Justin "accounts of miraculous feats [Simon, Helen, and
Menander], the craft and malice, of demons, who appear perpetually to haunt his imagination, and whom he considers the authors of the Heathen mythology, and inspirers of
the poets; the abettors of heresy [Marcion], and instigators of all the calamities under

In their critical edition of *1 Apology*, Minns and Parvis comment on what they conclude to be an incongruity in Justin's threefold selection of Simon and Helen, Menander, and Marcion in this chapter. While the first two sets of individuals qualify as those who went about asserting their divinity (τινὰς λέγοντας ἑαυτοὺς εἶναι θεούς), Marcion was not known for making such a claim.[80] Rather, he was known for promoting a dualistic system of two opposing deities: the evil God of the Old Testament (i.e., Demiurge) and the loving God of the New who sent the savior Jesus Christ.[81]

> The section referring to Marcion seems out of place here, since Justin has undertaken to give examples of human beings who claim that they are gods (*1A* 26.1). Simon certainly fits the argument, and Menander as his disciple may be presumed to do so as well—and in any case, he offers immortality to his followers. Marcion, however, does not fit the argument at all, and the reference to him may have been triggered by the reference to the two other heretics.[82]

The "trigger" for which Minns and Parvis seem to be referring here is the argumentative strategy made popular by Irenaeus in his *Against the Heresies* where he mapped out a line of succession linking the principal teachers of Gnosticism back to the infamous wonderworker Simon Magus of Acts 8 labeled by the bishop of Lyons "from whom all heresies got their start."[83] Because these magicians by trade (i.e., Simon Magus and Menander) predate the emergence of Gnosticism by a generation or so, Everett Ferguson has

---

which Christians were groaning" (*The Church of the First Three Centuries*, 45–46). In *1 Apol.* 56.1, Justin would go to even greater lengths establishing this connection between ancient myths and the emerging magicians and heretical teachers of his day: "But to say, before the appearing of Christ, that Zeus had the sons they said he had, was not enough for the evil demons. But—after [Christ] had been made manifest and lived among human beings—since both learnt how he had been proclaimed beforehand by the prophets and recognized that he was believed in and expected in every race, they would again put forward others, as we made clear earlier, Simon, that is, and Menander from Samaria."

80. According to Irenaeus in *Against the Heresies* 1.23.1, Simon was "glorified by many as a god. He taught that he himself was the one who appeared among the Jews as the Son of God, while in Samaria he descended as the Father, and among the other nation he came as the Holy Spirit"; In regards to Menander, Irenaeus claims that this successor to Simon asserted himself as "the one who was sent as Savior by the invisible [regions] for the salvation of men . . . his disciples received the resurrection by being baptized into him and can no longer die, but will continue on without growing old; they are immortal" (1.23.5).

81. Ferguson, *Church History*, 86–89.

82. Minns and Parvis, *Justin, Philosopher and Martyr*, 149n9.

83. Irenaeus, *Against the Heresies* 1.23.2.

described this genealogy developed by Irenaeus to be somewhat contrived and "artificial."[84] In a similar vein, Minns and Parvis posit that Justin engaged in a similar *non sequitor* polemic in linking Marcion to Simon Magus and Menander.[85]

Yet when one takes a closer inspection of the distinctive theologies held by Simon, Menander, and Marcion, two particular commonalities emerge: (1) each promoted the concept of a supreme being who partnered with a Logos figure and (2) salvation for humanity was sought out either by the supreme being itself (i.e., Simon) or by virtue of sending the Logos figure into the world (i.e., Menander, the Jesus of Marcion). With all three sets of individuals sharing this common framework within their teaching, Justin perceived in them the demonic impulse to ape how God the Father sent his divine Son into the world in order to save it, a concern inextricably linked to the theme of the Virgin Birth.[86]

It is also noteworthy that Justin chose to identify three sets of individuals here, which was a distinctive pattern established earlier in *1 Apol.* 22.4. In that chapter, Justin critiqued the renowned deaths of the trio Heracles, Asclepius, and Dionysus as being, "not all of a kind, but various sufferings are recounted" and that the variations in which the sons of Zeus perished was proof to Justin that demonic activity was very much at work. Besides each version representing a failed attempt by the demons to guess the proper manner in which the Son of God was to die, their ultimate aim for circulating these diverse stories of the sons of Zeus' dying was to lessen the significance of Christ's own death as God's Son within the minds of potential converts.[87]

84. Ferguson states that, while "Irenaeus traced a line leading from Simon to Menander to Saturninus and Basilides," the "earliest surviving report . . . puts Cerinthus [first] in the Gnostic orbit" (*Church History*, 94–95), who chronologically emerged unto the scene shortly after Menander.

85. Amman offers an explanation that harmonizes the disconnect between the first-century wonderworkers of Simon and Menander and the later principal Gnostic teachers of the second century by proposing that a certain Gnostic school in the second century made the long-deceased Simon and Helen the primary objects of their mythical speculations. In other words, a system was built around their legend (i.e., Simon and Helen), which took up Simon's name even though he was not its originator ("Simon le Magicien," *Dictionnaire de théologie catholique*, 2137). Irenaeus also connects Marcion to Simon Magus by way of "a certain Cerdo [who] got his start from the disciples of Simon" (*Against the Heretics* 1.27.1) and in turn "Marcion of Pontus succeeded Cerdo and amplified his doctrine" (1.27.2).

86. Machen, *The Virgin Birth of Christ*, 318: "[There is for Justin] the close connection between the doctrine of the virgin birth and the doctrine of the preexistence of Christ. That connection unquestionably exists."

87. McDermott provides an excellent monetary analogy for how Justin viewed the

For Justin, the emergence of the trio Simon, Menander, and Marcion served the same pernicious function as the deaths of the three sons of Zeus the main difference being that they arrived after Christ's advent instead of before. So instead of offering knockoffs of how the Son of God could both suffer and die, the wonderworkers and heretics of Justin's time through demonic inspiration put forward different variations of the Supreme Being/Logos framework for the purpose of diluting the strength of the Christian message that God the Father sent his divine Son into the world in order to save it.

According to Irenaeus (*Against the Heresies* 1.23.1), Simon was identified as the Supreme Being with his female partner, Helen, the Logos figure acting as "the first Thought of his mind, the Mother of all things, through whom in the beginning he conceived in his mind to make the Angels and Archangels."[88] The bishop of Lyons even mentioned how both, "have a statue of Simon patterned after Zeus, and one of Helen patterned after Athena" (§1.23.4) a detail that lends further support to how the followers of Simon and Helen not only understood how the two were divinely related but also the cosmic function attributed to the latter. In this version of the Supreme Being/Logos framework, Helen as Logos was overtaken by the Angels and Powers whom she created and it is Simon, the Supreme Being, who assumed the role of savior first to, "free [Helen] from the bonds, then bring salvation to humankind by his own knowledge. The Angels governed the world badly, because each one desired to be sovereign. So he came, he said, to set matters right" (§1.23.2).

---

existence of what he held to be multiple imitative accounts of the Logos within the mythological tradition, "In other words, demons minted counterfeit religion in order to cheapen true religion. Like skilled printers of bogus money, they hoped to flood the market with so many ersatz bills that seekers would confuse the imitation for the divine original" (*God's Rivals*, 92).

88. Justin's testimony concurs with Irenaeus here with the main difference being that the latter provides more extensive detail: "And nearly all the Samaritans and a few from other nations even now still confess [Simon] to be the first god [τὸν πρῶτον θεὸν], and worship him. And a certain Helen, who went about with him at that time, and who had formerly been placed in a brothel in Tyre of Phoenicia, they call the first thought that came to be from him" (*1 Apol.* 26.3). Dillon asserts that Irenaeus, in fact, may have derived his knowledge of Simon primarily from Justin: "The first ecclesiastical writer on record to give us information on Simon, apart from Acts, is Justin, *1 Apol.* 26, 56 and *Dial.* 120. Irenaeus could have used Justin for this matter" (*Against the Heresies*, 227n1). Besides gleaning from *1 Apology* and *Dialogue with Trypho*, Irenaeus could have also had access to Justin's handbook on heresies no longer extant, *The Syntagma*, which would have provided not only more details surrounding Simon, but for Menander and Marcion as well: "There is another composition [σύνταγμα] by us, written against all the heresies that have arisen. If you want to read it we will give you a copy" (*1 Apol.* 26.8).

Although Menander was deemed the successor to Simon according to the testimony of Irenaeus, Menander reworked the Supreme Being/Logos framework inherited from his master. Instead of Simon playing the role of the Supreme Being in Menander's system, he argued that "the first Power is unknown to all" but that Menander supplanted Helen in the role of the Logos, "sent as Savior by the invisible [regions] for the salvation of men" (§1.23.5).

While Marcion neither ascribed to himself the role of Supreme Being (i.e., Simon) or that of the Logos (i.e., Menander) as his predecessors did, he did share a similar outlook with Menander by arguing that the Supreme Being ultimately "was unknown" (§1.27.1). It is this apophatic theology shared between Menander and Marcion regarding the unknowability of the Supreme Being or first God (τὸν πρῶτον θεὸν) that likely contributed to Justin bundling Marcion alongside Simon and Menander with the latter serving as the apologist's point of connection for the group.

In the estimation of Justin, which would be later echoed by Irenaeus, this last rendition of the Supreme Being/Logos framework as taught by Marcion was perhaps the most harmful amongst the three for Marcion identified the Logos figure not as a personage alien to Christianity as in the case of his predecessors (e.g., Helen or Menander), but as Jesus Christ himself. Yet, the content behind the Jesus Christ that Marcion proposed was of vastly different import than the Jesus Christ the apologist subscribed. Justin stated that this "wolf" (λύκος) falsely taught that, "the one announced beforehand through the prophets—Christ his Son—[is] to be renounced, but [Marcion] proclaimed . . . similarly another son" (*1 Apol.* 58.1–2). In other words, with the presence of two opposing deities in Marcion's system (i.e., the unknown redeemer God vs. the evil creator God) also came the notion of two different types of "sons" that each deity would send forth, "[Marcion] insisted that the Jews were correct in contending that Jesus did not correspond to the messianic prophecies of Scripture. One could count on the God of the Old Testament someday sending such a Messiah; but Jesus had nothing to do with the Old Testament, its God, or the messianic prophecies."[89]

In *Against the Heresies* 1.27.4, Irenaeus lamented how alluring Marcionism was in his day—a phenomenon he directly attributed to the seductive, aberrant Christology of its founder.

> For even though they do not acknowledge the name of their teacher in order to mislead others, yet it is his doctrine they teach. By proposing the name of Christ Jesus as a kind of incentive, they put many to death by wickedly disseminating their

---

89. Skarsaune, *Incarnation: Myth or Fact?*, 64.

> own teaching by means of the good name [Jesus], and by hand-
> ing them the bitter and wicked poison of the Serpent, the author
> of the apostasy, under the guise of the delight and beauty of this
> name (§1.27.4).

In sizing the adverse effect Marcionism had upon Christianity in the second
century, Timothy George maybe overstating his claim when he maintains
that Marcion, "gathered a following so large that, when he was excommuni-
cated in 144, he is said to have carried half the Church with him."[90] But in
Justin's opinion, the havoc Marcion wreaked upon people's souls through his
teaching far eclipsed that of his predecessors Simon and Menander whose
scope of influence was mainly relegated to the provinces of Samaria and
Antioch respectively.[91] Justin portrayed Marcion's teachings to possess a
far more universal appeal, "And with the help of the demons, [Marcion] has
persuaded many from every race of humankind [κατὰ πᾶν γένος ἀνθρώπων]
to utter blasphemies."[92]

DISMISSING MYTHICAL ALLUSIONS IMITATING "A HEALING MINISTRY"

In *1 Apol.* 54, Justin reverts back to a conventional identification of the well-
known achievements ascribed to the sons of Zeus as the handiwork of demons aimed at diminishing the impact of Christ's mighty deeds. According
to the apologist, the renowned accomplishments of Heracles and Asclepius
were propagated by demons in order to mimic Christ's earthly ministry
both in its anticipated reach (i.e., Heracles) as well as the basis on which it
was to operate (i.e., Asclepius). While Justin argued that the tale of the *12
Labors of Heracles* was created to counteract the christological prophecy in
Psalm 19:5 signaling the prodigious manner in which the Son of God would
move about, "Strong as a giant to run his course" (§54.9), the telling of the
miraculous exploits of Asclepius "to cure every illness and raise the dead"
(§54.10) was meant to devaluate the predicted acts of healing and miracles
that would come to define Christ's earthly ministry.

90. George, "The Pattern of Christian Truth," 22. Also George and Dockery, *The
Great Tradition of Christian Thinking*, 52.

91. It is *1 Apol.* 26.3, where Justin described the provincial nature of the teachings attributed to Simon: "And nearly all the Samaritans and a few from other nations
even now still confess him to be the first god, and worship him." In *1 Apol.* 26.4, Justin
mentions the location where Menander's teachings held sway as being, "worked on by
demons, and, when he was in Antioch beguiled many through magic art."

92. *1 Apol.* 26.5.

Heracles (54.9)

Justin states in *1 Apol.* 54.9 that when the demons, "knew it was said, as it was said before in the previously written prophecies, 'Strong as a giant to run his course,' they spoke of Heracles, the strong one who traversed the whole earth." According to Michel Fédou, this specific allusion was a reference to the "Twelve Labors of Heracles" consisting of diverse trials imposed upon this son of Zeus by the Mycenaean king, Eurytheus, as atonement for Heracles murdering his own wife, Megara, and children in a fit of madness sent by Hera.[93]

The "Twelve Labor of Heracles" encompassed his dealing with the (1) Nemean Lion, (2) Lernaean Hydra, (3) Cerynitian Hind, (4) Erymanthian Boar, (5) Stables of Augeas, (6) Stymphalian Birds, (7) Erymanthian Boar, (8) Mares of Diomedes, (9) Belt of Hippolyte, (10) Cattle of Geryon, (11) Apples of Hesperides, and (12) Cerberus.[94] The trials fell into two different categories: (a) the vanquishing of a beast(s) that had oppressed the inhabitants of a particular locale and/or (b) stupendous feats that were humanly impossible to achieve [e.g., capturing the elusive Cerynitian Hind, cleaning the massive Stables of Augeas]. Regardless of the type of challenge presented Heracles, the common denominator they shared was that each and every labor forced him to travel far and wide.

Yet it is those Herculean challenges belonging to the former category where Justin would have recognized the demonic impulse to imitate the earthly ministry of the Logos. For in conquering each beast, Heracles was not only bolstering his reputation amongst the masses but more importantly was serving humanity through the disposal of a creature that had long plagued a specific region. Hence, the universality of Heracles beneficence in his Twelve Labors made him a, "type of missionary . . . who goes up and down the world, saving men."[95]

At the same time, it could be argued that the manner in which Heracles went about his humanitarian tour hardly resembled that of Christ's. In challenging the novel thesis of Fredrich Pfister that the Gospel writers

93. Fédou, "La vision de la croix dans l'oeuvre de saint Justin," 64: "Sans doute Justin ne fait-il pas allusion aux 'douze travaux,' à ces grandes épreuves que le héros avait dû affronter et dont il était venu à bout . . . ne devait-elle pas attirer l'attention d'un chrétien pour qui le parfait Serviteur, en Palestine, avait porté le poids de la condition humaine?"

94. The texts in the mythological tradition that contain the story of the "Twelve Labor of Heracles" are the following: Diodorus Siculus, *Library of History* 4.10.6–18.3; Euripides, *Heracles Furens; Greek Anthology* 2.65; Pseudo-Apollodorus, *The Library* 2.4.12–5.12; and Seneca, *Heracles Furens* 1.

95. Knox, "The 'Divine Hero' Christology in the New Testament," 232.

patterned their portrait of Jesus according to the myth of Heracles,[96] Herbert Rose points out just how divergent both figures went about operating their respective ministries.

> [Christ] nowhere displays remarkable physical strength, is celibate and of moderate appetite, but never exaggeratedly ascetic and his travels are confined to his own country and the districts bordering on it. Heracles is a huge eater and drinker, a great lover of women, a traveler all over the known and unknown world, his wanderings being limited only by the geographical knowledge of his biographers, and either literally a killer of monsters, human and bestial.[97]

But Justin could have very well had this disparity accounted for by virtue of the Scripture verse (i.e., Psalm 19:5) he identified as the one that demons based the "Twelve Labors of Heracles" upon. For in this passage, the word γίγας or "giant" is employed here to describe the coming Son of God who would "run his course"; coincidentally, the same word is used in Genesis 6:4 in the plural describing the powerful offspring of the fallen angels and human women, "The Nephilim (οἱ γίγαντες) were on the earth in those days—and also afterward—when the sons of God went to the daughters of men and had children by them. They were the heroes of old, men of renown." (NIV)

As discussed earlier in the chapter, it is the Enochic tradition Justin inherited from Judaism that made the concept of the γίγαντες found in Gen. 6:1–4 interchangeable with his notion of "demons" (δαίμονες).[98] This is most clearly demonstrated in 2 Apol. 4.2–4:

> When he made the whole universe God made earthly things subject to human beings. He also set in order the heavenly bodies for the growth of crops and for the change of the seasons, and established for them a divine law. It is clear that these things too he did for the sake of human beings. But providential care over human beings and of things beneath the firmament he handed over to angels whom he had established over them. But the angels transgressed this appointed order, succumbed to intercourse with women, and begot children—who are called demons (δαίμονες). They then went on to enslave the human race to themselves, partly through magical changes, partly through

96. Pfister, "Heracles und Christ," 42–60.

97. Rose, "Herakles and the Gospels," 120–21

98. Reed, "The Trickery of the Fallen Angels and the Demonic Mimesis of the Divine," 146.

fear and through the punishments they inflicted, partly through instructions about sacrifices and incense and libations—things they have needed ever since they were enslaved by passions and desires. And they sowed amongst human beings murders, wars, adulteries, licentiousness, and every kind of evil.

With a γίγας being synonymous to a δαίμων in Justin's economy, his description in *2 Apol.* 4.2 of the demonic penchant in prediluvian times to be involved in, "murders, wars, adulteries, licentiousness, and every kind of evil" bears a resemblance to many of the actions Heracles was notorious. Hence, Justin perhaps saw within the characteristics of this Greco-Roman hero the handiwork of demons projecting unto Heracles what they themselves were prior to the flood (i.e., οἱ γίγαντες). They anticipated that the one who was to be sent from God according to Psalm 19:5 would be in the mold of a γίγας albeit a "giant" performing marvelous acts in behalf of humanities benefit (especially when Heracles sought to atone for the murder of his own family). In the apologist's estimation, the demons completely missed the mark here as the focus of this prophecy was to announce the prodigious nature of Christ's ministry through use of metaphor (i.e., "Strong as a giant to run his course") and not to be understood as his literal traversing throughout the world as depicted in the labors of Heracles.

Asclepius (54.10)

As discussed in the previous chapter, a major contrast that Justin's audience would have detected between Christ as a healer to that of Asclepius was that the latter was put to the death by Zeus on account for raising someone from the dead for monetary gain. While Justin did not explicitly raise this concern in establishing the superiority of Christ over Asclepius, Christian thinkers that emerged soon after Justin such as Clement of Alexandria (*Protrepticus* 2.30.1–2), Tertullian (*To the Nations* 2.14.12), and Arnobius (*Against the Nations* 4.24) took the liberty to expose this foible in the god of healing and medicine citing the likes of Euripides and Pindar to substantiate their claim.[99]

99. Dölger, "Christus und 'der Heiler' Asklepios bei Justinus," 244: "Klemens von Alexandrien spricht von Asklepios als dem ἰατρὸς φιλάργυρος, als dem 'geldgierigen Arzt,' und zieht zum Beleg dafür die Stelle bei Pindar an, dazu für den Blitztod noch zwei Verse aus Euripides. In der Zusammenstellung weist dies auf Plato, der ja neben Pindar noch τραγῳδοποιοί genannt und damit wahrscheinlich auch an Euripidee gedacht hatte. Unter Berufung auf den Pindartext spricht auch Tertullianus von Geldgier und Geiz des Asklepios und von der Pflichtverletzung einer Verkäuflichen medizinischen Kunst. Auch Arnobius spricht von einer cupido und avaritia des Asklepios, was wohl eine

Justin admits that the myth of Asclepius was able to mimic the healing ministry of Christ in almost every way stating, "And when again [the demons] learnt that he prophesied as going to cure every illness and to raise the dead, they introduced Asclepius" (*1 Apol.* 54.10). Yet, the one type of healing Justin asserted (albeit not in *1 Apology*) that the demons were unable to replicate from Christ was exorcism (ἐξορκισμός), "For numberless demoniacs throughout the whole world, and in your city—many of our Christian people exorcising them in the name of Jesus Christ . . . rendering helpless and driving the possessing demons out of men, though they could not be cured by all the older exorcists, and those who used incantations and drugs (φάρμακον)" (*2 Apol.*6.6).

Justin's allusion to φάρμακον is noteworthy here as both the Enochic tradition of the Watchers (which greatly influenced his demonology) as well as Christian thinkers in the second and third century (who, too, were influenced by this same tradition)[100]who argued that the art of concocting drugs was taught to humans by the demonic forces of prediluvian times (i.e., *1 Enoch*) and amongst Christian thinkers specifically the demon masquerading as the god Asclepius (i.e., Aristides, Tertullian, and Arnobius).[101]

So while Justin concedes in *1 Apology* that many of the miraculous deeds attributed to Asclepius such as "curing all illnesses and raising the dead" may rival that of Christ, the one type of healing that healers of Asclepius could not perform (or had difficulty performing) was exorcism.[102] The

---

Anlehnung an die Ausdrucksweise seines afrikanischen Landsmannes Tertullian sein dürfte, mit einer geringfügigen Umänderung des ersten Wortes"; Euripides, *Alcestis* 3: "For Jove [Zeus] was the cause, by slaying my son Aesculapius, hurling the lightning against his breast"; Pindar, *Pythian Odes* 3.54: "Gold appearing in his hands with its lordly wage prompted even him to bring back from death a man already carried off. But then, with a cast from his hands, Kronos' son [Zeus] took the breath from both men's breasts in an instant; the flash of lightning hurled down doom."

100. In the early third century, it was Julius Africanus in his *Chronicles* where we see the first Christian thinker to challenge the "fallen angels" interpretation established by the Enochic tradition by offering a Sethite one (q.v., Bamberger, Fallen Angels, 78, 80).

101. *1 Enoch* 7.1 identifies the fallen angels as the culprits responsible for teaching the women they impregnated, "charms and enchantments, and the cutting of roots (φάρμακον)," which is the equivalent to the art of drug making. The assertion that the art of drug making was within the realm of Asclepius in the three Christian thinker mentioned are: Aristides, *Apology* 10; Tertullian, *On the Crown* 8; Arnobius, *Against the Heathen* 1.38.

102. I make a qualification here that the pagan exorcists may have not performed exorcisms as well as the Christian exorcists that Justin describes. The reason why is that he calls these pagan healers ἐξορκιστής inferring that they were able to successfully perform some exorcisms if this is the name ascribed to them. What we may have in view here is that Justin is arguing that the cases where pagan exorcists have failed in casting demons from an individual, the Christian exorcists have proved successful.

key to identifying these pagan healers as devotees to Asclepius was their use of drugs in trying to exorcise demons from individuals without any success.

DISMISSING MYTHICAL ALLUSIONS OF "DYING"

From amongst Asclepius, Dionysus, and Heracles who according to Justin were sons of Zeus whose deaths resonated with that of the Son of God (*1 Apol.* 22.3), the one he chose to further deconstruct out of the grouping was Dionysus (*1 Apol.* 54.4–6). One of the reasons why Justin may have deepened his focus to employ separation from myth specifically upon this god and not the others was that despite Dionysus' reputed immorality, as the infant god Zagreus he suffered as an innocent victim (i.e., torn apart by the Titans)—a claim that could not be ascribed to Asclepius and Heracles. As mentioned in the previous chapter, Asclepius was executed by Zeus on account of his greed while Heracles' self-immolation was less impressive because he did it primarily as an escape from the excruciating pain caused by his noxious exposure to the blood of Nessus the Centaur.[103]

Besides the innocence that Dionysus and Christ shared in their deaths, it is made clear in *1 Apol.* 54.4–6 that Justin perceived further similar aspects between the cult of Dionysus and the Christian faith that needed to be dismissed as demonic imitation. Finally in chapter 55, Justin would go on to provide an explanation why the demons failed to anticipate the Son of God's death by crucifixion as seen in the variegated deaths of Asclepius, Dionysus, and Heracles. Although he does not mention their names explicitly in this chapter, it is certainly this trio to whom he is referring.

Dionysus (54.4–6)

Not only did Justin aver demonic involvement to account for the resemblance between the deaths of Dionysus and Christ, but he also identified peculiar elements each shared in their stories (i.e., the invaluable service of a donkey) as well as in their rites (e.g., the centrality of wine in their worship) that was for him additional proof of diabolical imitation at work.

> And that they also did not accurately understand the things they heard said through the prophets, but imitated in erring fashion

---

103. Carena, "La critica della mitologia pagana," 13: "Gli apologeti mettono in luce non solo il supplizio di Eracle e di Asclepio, ma ancora le cause di esso: Asclepio trovò la morte in conseguenza della sua cupidigia per la quale aveva accettato di risuscitare un morto contro le leggi di natura. Eracle si accese il rogo per il suo furore."

the things concerning our Christ, we shall make clear. Thus Moses the prophet, as we said before, was older than all writers, and it was prophesied through him, as we mentioned before, thus: "A ruler shall not fail from Judah and a leader from his thighs until he should come from whom it is laid up. And he shall be the expectation of the nations, binding his foal to the vine, washing his garment in the blood of the grape." [Gen. 49:10–11] Therefore, hearing these prophetic words, the demons said that Dionysus is the son of Zeus, and they handed down that he was the discoverer of the vine. And they taught that he was torn in pieces and that he has gone up to heaven (1 Apol. 54.4–6).[104]

In this combination of a foal or "young" (πῶλος) ass alongside the "blood of the grape" (ἐν αἵματι σταφυλῆς) in this Old Testament passage, Justin perceived a foreshadowing of two significant events leading up to Christ's passion: (1) his entry into Jerusalem by riding on such an animal and (2) his institution of wine in the Lord's Supper as the partaking of the blood he would later shed on the behalf of humanity.

According to Fédou, these two occurrences that significantly contribute in defining the Passion Week of Christ would have seemed eerily familiar to those conversant with the Dionysian myth. It, too, honored donkeys for providing assistance to its central figure and also partook of wine as a religious rite symbolizing its followers' participation in the violent death of its god.[105]

The aspect of the Dionysian myth where the god of wine received the help of asses was when Hera threw him into a state of madness that caused him to wander aimlessly throughout the earth.[106] In order to break this spell, the god of wine needed to consult with the oracle of Zeus but was impeded from doing so due to a body of water surrounding the temple.

104. The phenomenon of Dionysus being "torn in pieces" (διασπαραχθέντα) and that he has gone up to heaven" as an analogue to Christ's own death and rising has been treated in the previous chapter.

105. Fédou, "La vision de la croix," 68: "Surtout, elle manifeste que le récit orphique rappelle le prix de cette vie nouvelle, et que ce prix n'est autre que la passion douloureuse d'un dieu. Or quel mythe pouvait mieux correspondre à l'annonce, dans l'Ecriture, d'un prince qui serait 'l'attente des nations,' 'attacherait son poulain à la vigne,' 'laverait sa robe dans le sang de la grappe'? Quel mythe pouvait être plus près du récit qui se répandrait un jour depuis Jérusalem? On comprend que Justin—et d'autres après lui, tel Clément d'Alexandrie—aient été saisis par de tels rapprochements."

106. It is interesting to note that Hera induced Heracles into a similar madness, the main difference being that Dionysus aimlessly wandered throughout the earth as a direct result of Hera's spell while Heracles went about traversing the earth but purposefully doing so in order to complete his Twelve Labors as atonement for the violence committed upon his family while under Hera's spell of madness.

According to Pseudo-Hyginus, "two asses met him. He caught one of them and in this way was carried across, not touching the water at all. So when he came to the temple of Dodonaean Zeus, freed at once from his madness, he acknowledged his thanks to the asses and placed them among the constellations."[107] It is this story that would serve as the basis behind the honoring of the ass in the Dionysian worship service.[108]

But even in this parallel where these unique animals came to the aid of both Dionysus and Christ in granting them passage to their respective temples, the reader would have been able to pick up the vastly different circumstances surrounding why the god of wine and the Son of God came to employ their particular beasts of burden. While the emergence of the two asses in the story of Dionysus was an *ad hoc* solution granting him passage over the watery barrier in order for him to arrive at his desired destination, Justin could argue in contrast that Christ's riding on an ass into Jerusalem was of superior quality being an event that was foretold by the prophet Moses.[109] Also, Dionysus needed the help of the asses to deliver him to the temple of Zeus so that he might be saved from his accursed insanity. Christ, on the other hand, rode upon his beast of burden not for his own benefit but rather to initiate the process of procuring salvation on behalf of all humanity.

With regards to the worship of Dionysus and Christ, both did possess a rite where the consumption of wine signified its followers' mystical participation in their deity's self-sacrifice on their behalf.[110] No better passage demonstrates this uncanny resemblance than Euripides *Bacchae* lines 275–285:

---

107. *Astronomica* 2.23.

108. Fédou, "La vision de la croix," 64: "Il fait d'autre part allusion à l'âne qui, selon certains rites était associé à Dionysos lui-même."

109. *1 Apol.* 23.3: "But certain human beings, <his prophets, proclaimed these things> in advance, before he came to be among human beings. But what was foretold by these evil demons, myth-making through the poets, spoke of as having happened."

110. We also see this in the Persian myth of Mithras, which Justin mentions briefly in *1 Apol.* 66.4 as possessing a rite that mimics the Christian rite of communion: "The evil demons, imitating this in the mysteries of Mithras, handed down the same should be done, for you either know or are able to learn that bread and a cup of water are presented in the rites of initiation along with some accompanying words." Although no doubt an influential religion during the time of Justin and beyond, I have decided not to treat this myth as it is neither considered one of the traditional ancestral religions of Greece nor one of its mystery cults. In Tripolitis' *Religions of the Hellenistic-Roman Age* she does not categorize the cult of Mithras as a religion deriving from the Hellenistic-Roman World (chapter 1) but as a religion whose origins were quite foreign to Greco-Romanism (chapter 2).

> The goddess Demeter—she is the earth, but call her whatever
> name you wish; she nourishes mortals with dry food; but he who
> came afterwards, the offspring of Semele [Dionysus], discovered
> a match to it, the liquid drink of the grape, and introduced it
> to mortals. It releases wretched mortals from grief, whenever
> they are filled with the stream of the vine, and gives them sleep,
> a means of forgetting their daily troubles, nor is there another
> cure for hardships. He who is a god is poured out in offerings to
> the gods, so that by his means men may have good things.

Despite the perceived similarity in which Dionysian and Christian followers received wine in a setting of worship to signify the organic reception of
the deity himself for their benefit, Justin was quick to point out how vastly
different the prescribed moral response was between each set of followers
after this rite.

While the Dionysian followers were generally encouraged to, "drink
excessive amounts of wine . . . to shed their social inhibitions and become
liberated in a realm of divine abandonment," Christians as portrayed by
Justin in *1 Apol.* 65.1–3 administered their ritual with self-control and
sobriety:[111]

> And, after earnestly saying prayers for ourselves and the one
> who was enlightened and all others everywhere that, having
> learnt the truth, we might be judged worthy also to be found
> through our deeds people who live good lives and guardians of
> what has been commanded, so that we might be saved in eternal
> salvation, we cease from prayer and greet one another with a
> kiss. Then there is brought to the president of the brothers bread
> and a cup of wine mixed with water, and the president takes
> them and sends up praise and glory to the Father of all through
> the name of his Son and of the holy Spirit, and he makes thanks-
> giving at length for being considered worthy of these things by
> him. And when he has finished the prayers and the thanksgiving
> all the people present give their assent saying "Amen."

Ironically, it was the culturally accepted Dionysian style of drinking wine
to excess that forced the church to modify the administration of the cup of
wine in a fashion that was orderly (as depicted here by Justin). Paul Ciholas
points out how the Apostle Paul had to confront the debauch tendencies of
the Bacchanalia that had seeped into how the early Corinthian church in

111. Day, *100 Characters from Classical Mythology*, 71. Manser also points out that
"the five festivals in Athens each year in [Dionysus] honor were notorious for the frenzied and licentious behavior of the celebrants, who indulged freely in drink and sex"
(*Classical and Biblical Allusions*, 100).

AD 55 celebrated the Lord's Supper, "Much more obvious was the Diony-sian context in the conduct of the Christians at Corinth, a conduct which led Paul to despair and resignation."[112]

Deaths of the three sons of Zeus (55.1–8)

In this chapter, Justin provides further elaboration to an assertion he made in *1 Apol.* 22.3–4 that the variegated deaths of the trio Asclepius, Diony-sus, and Heracles is evidence to the multiple failed attempts of the demons to identify the manner in which the Son of God would die. According to Justin, the primary reason behind their inability stemmed from Moses and the Prophets not explicitly mentioning the Cross but rather conveying it by way of symbol (σύμβολον), "For it was not understood by them, as the things said concerning it were said symbolically, as was made clear earlier" (§55.1). Justin is referring here to the strand of biblical passages he selected back in §35.2–5 to demonstrate how the third Christological theme from his Creed Sequence (§31.7) regarding the Son of God's death by crucifixion was foreshadowed in Hebrew Scripture albeit in a murky fashion: Isaiah 9:5 ("a young man was given for us, whose rule is on the shoulders"), Isaiah 65:2 ("I stretched out my hands to a disobedient and gainsaying people"), and Psalm 22:16 ("They pierced my hands and feet").

Unfortunately for the demons, the only way they could properly inter-pret these texts of suffering would be after the fact; that is, when the "event of the Cross" actually occurred.[113] Also, Fédou points out that due to the scandalous nature of crucifixion (i.e., reserved for only the worst of crimi-nals) that this would have served as a "blind spot" for the demons, "Without a doubt, the demons imagined the passion of Dionysus. But never in their imitations, did they attribute any of the alleged sons of Zeus, the agony of the Cross."[114]

---

112. Ciholas, *The Omphalos and the Cross*, 41.

113. Fédou, "La vision de la croix," 69: "Seul l'événement de la Croix, donnant la clef du symbole, opposerait au mythe son démenti le plus radical."

114. Ibid.: "Sans doute les démons ont-ils imaginé la passion de Dionysos. Mais jamais, dans leurs imitations, ils n'ont attribué à aucun des prétendus fils de Zeus le supplice de la Croix."

DISMISSING MYTHICAL ALLUSIONS IMITATING "RISING"

There are two myths of Greek heroes rising into the heavens that Justin alludes to in order that he might dismiss them as demonic imitations of Christ's own foretold ascension: Bellerophon (§54.7) and Perseus (§54.8). The clustering of these two mythical figures on the part of Justin and the order in which he treats them are hardly incidental. Chronologically, we know that Perseus was a predecessor to Bellerophon by virtue of the latter capturing, Pegasus, the immortal winged horse that originally belonged to the former.[115] Yet Justin reversed their order in his ascension discourse in chapter 54 first mentioning Bellerophon "the human being born of human beings" (ἄνθρωπον ἐξ ἀνθρώπου γενόμενον) followed by concluding remarks about Perseus a θεῖος ἀνήρ.

Why the switch? By doing so, Justin was able to highlight the vastly different outcomes of Bellerophon and Perseus' ascent stories (i.e., failure vs. success). More important here is how the particular makeup of each Greek hero (i.e., mere human vs. divine man) played a major role in determining whether their ascent to the heavens was met with either failure or success. In manufacturing these divergent ascent myths, the demons demonstrated their awareness of the ontological dynamics that needed to occur in order for the Son of God to come in the flesh. Justin was arguing that while the demons anticipated that he would indeed be human, they also understood he would be something much more than that. Bellerophon's failed ascent to the heavens exposed the limitations of being a mere human, a failure that served as a foil accentuating the successful ascension of Perseus who was both human as well as divine.

Bellerophon (54.7), Pegasus (54.7), and Perseus (54.8)

At first glance, it appears that both allusions of Bellerophon and Perseus could stand independent of one another. But despite their contrasting makeup (i.e., human vs. divine man) and the contrasting outcomes of their respective ascent narratives (i.e., failure vs. success), the common denominator linking Bellerophon and Perseus together is Πήγασος. This distinction they both shared as former riders of Pegasus is important to keep in mind as it helps us comprehend the significance of Justin's assertion that Perseus

---

115. After Perseus slew Medusa, the gorgon's "spilt blood created the horse Pegasus which, later Bellerophon tried to ride to heaven, incurring the wrath of the gods" (Day, *100 Characters from Classical Mythology*, 108).

went "up to heaven by himself" (§54.8).[116] While Bellerophon attempted
to ascend to the heavens with the aid of the immortal winged horse, its
previous owner Perseus needed no such assistance being placed by Athena
as a constellation in the sky for having saved the princess Andromeda from
Cetus the Sea Monster.[117]

But besides serving as a segue between Bellerophon and Perseus,
Pegasus also acts as a clever transitioning point between Bellerophon and
the prior set of passages of §54.4–6 where Justin discusses how Dionysus
riding on an ass was a demonic imitation to Christ's own riding on a foal.[118]
Despite this passage involving a different species of equine than the one
told in the Bellerophon myth (i.e., an ass versus a colt), Justin proceeded to
argue in §54.7 that the story involving Bellerophon and Pegasus served as
yet another demonic variation of the aping of the prophecy of Christ riding a foal into Jerusalem, "And since it was not expressly signified through
the prophecy of Moses whether the one is to come is the son of God, and
whether riding on a foal will remain on the earth [i.e., hence the myth of
Dionysus with the ass] or will go up to heaven . . . they [also] said that Bellerophon, a human being born of human beings, has gone up to heaven, and
specifically on the horse Pegasus."

Justin further accounts for the confusion of equine species between the
respective Dionysius and Bellerophon discourses on linguistic grounds. The
demons who read the Old Testament prophecy in Gen. 49:10–11 that the
Son of God would ride in on "foal" had difficulty navigating the ambiguous
nature of this term, "since the word foal (πῶλος) was able to signify the foal
of an ass or of a horse . . . [as] the symbol of his appearing" (§54.7). Hence,
Justin saw in the differing renditions of πῶλος as seen in the Dionysus myth
of the ass and the Bellerophon myth of the horse the demonic propensity to

---

116. Minns and Parvis do not seem to perceive the progression of Justin's argument
to contrast how Perseus did not utilize Pegasus to attempt an ascent into heaven while
Bellerophon did: "That is, not by horse. Editors point to Isa 7:14, but the connection
between this text and the legend of Perseus is the virgin birth. Isa 7:14 furnishes no
testimony text in respect of ascending unaided to heaven, and this is not part of the
Perseus legend."

117. Pseudo-Hyginus, *Astronomica* 2.11: "They say [Andromeda] was put among
the constellations by the favor of Athena, on account of the valor of Perseus, who freed
her from danger when exposed to the sea-monster"; Pseudo-Hyginus, *Fabulae* 224:
"Mortals who were made immortal . . . Perseus, son of Jove and Danae, put among the
stars."

118. Prigent, *Justin et l'Ancien Testamente*, 161: "Le raisonnement de Justin au
paragraphe 7 l'implique forcément en appliquant à l'histoire de Bellérophon la meme
prophétie de *Gen.* 49 dont le πῶλος peut designer aussi bien un cheval qu'un âne."

"throw out guesses" regarding the manner in which the Son of God would reveal himself based on the vague details of these predictions.

In regards to the myth of Perseus' ascent, Justin does a curious thing in §54.8 linking the success of his ascent into the heavens on the basis of his extraordinary birth, "But when [the demons] heard it said through the prophet Isaiah as well that he would be born of a virgin and would go up to heaven by himself, they would throw Perseus into the discussion." Minns and Parvis criticize Justin here for making what they believe to be a tenuous connection between the Christological theme of the Virgin Birth and that of the Ascension, "Editors point to Isa 7:14, but the connection between this text and the legend of Perseus is the virgin birth. Isa 7:14 furnishes no testimony text in respect of ascending unaided to heaven, and this is not part of the Perseus legend."[119]

First off, Minns and Parvis are incorrect in stating that an ascent to the heavens was never ascribed to Perseus when in fact he was awarded a place amongst stars for his role in rescuing the princess Andromeda. Secondly, the link between extraordinary birth and the rising of the immortalized θεῖος ἀνήρ to the heavens is not as disparate as Minns and Parvis contend. In describing the reasons for Perseus being installed as a constellation in the sky, Pseudo-Hyginus asserted that both his valiant exploits as well as his divine pedigree both contributed to his eventual deified state, "[Perseus] is said to have come to the stars because of his nobility and the unusual nature of his conception."[120]

As discussed in the previous chapter, if Greco-Roman ascent to heaven was based solely on one's deeds then Bellerophon would have certainly been a "shoe-in." But the tragedy of this myth was that despite his impressive résumé, Bellerophon was a mere human and did not have the right to aspire to a state reserved only persons of extraordinary birth such as Perseus. In discussing Christ's virgin birth and his ascension in the same sentence, Justin is seeking to establish that he is no mere human (such as Bellerophon) but possesses both the marvelous works as well as the divine pedigree (in the likeness of Perseus) to ultimately be worthy of their worship.

CONCLUSION

When going through Justin's *incorporation of myth* in Chapter 2 as it related to the four Christological themes of the Pseudo-Creed Sequence, the

119. *Justin, Philosopher and Martyr*, 223n5.

120. Pseudo-Hyginus, *Astronomica* 2.12: "He is said to have come to the stars because of his nobility and the unusual nature of his conception."

apologist provided a fairly even treatment of each theme identifying mythical allusions that contain within them refracted details of Christ's birth,
miracles, dying, and rising. But in this chapter, one can immediately see that
the Christological theme Justin spent the majority of his efforts demonstrating *separation from myth* was the theme of the Virgin Birth.

Of the nearly fifty pages of this chapter, over thirty of them (60%) dealt
with treating Justin's project of exposing those myths he perceived to be demonic imitations of the extraordinary birth of Christ.[121] Such a skewing of
distribution amongst the four Christological themes certainly reveals how
important it was for Justin to dismiss the so-called extraordinary births of
the Greek heroes.

Perhaps an explanation for this intriguing phenomenon is that Justin
realized that the most effective way to undermine the gods of Olympus as
well as their semi-divine children in one fell swoop was through exploiting
this particular Christological theme. While demonstrating how the gods'
relations with human women disqualified them as deities worthy of worship, he could then dismiss their offspring as a true θεῖος ἀνήρ by placing
the speckle of doubt in the mind of his reader whether their births should
be deemed extraordinary. Without an extraordinary birth, one can achieve
a multitude of mighty deeds (such as in the case of Bellerophon) but would
never be able to rise to the level of deity.

121. Another way to look at Justin's unevenness in treating the christological
themes with respect to separation of myth is to observe that Justin employed thirteen
allusions to evoke this movement with themes related to Virgin Birth (e.g., holiness of
procreation, preexistence of the offspring, etc.); the allusions of the other three christological themes of the Pseudo-Creed Sequence combined do not even make up half
(only a total of six) of the amount Justin used to discount the extraordinary births of
the supposed "divine men."

5

Other Applications of Poetic Material in Justin

STRATEGIC USE OF POETIC MATERIAL OUTSIDE THE PSEUDO-CREED SEQUENCE

THE FOCAL POINT OF this work thus far has been investigating Justin's incorporation (Chapter 3) and separation from myth (Chapter 4) in relation to how these movements are linked to the four Christological themes of the Pseudo-Creed Sequence. But it would be remiss to overlook the notable exceptions in *1 Apology* where Justin worked outside this framework altogether, alluding to the poets (i.e., the human agents he deemed most responsible for the proliferation of myth) so that he could treat broader theological concerns besides Christ's virgin birth, healing ministry, death, or rising to the heavens.[1] Examples of these occurrences include his men-

---

1. *1 Apol.* 23.3 serves as an excellent proof text demonstrating the onus Justin placed upon the ποιηταὶ for their role in perpetuating demonically inspired myths meant to compete against the Christ who was to come: "But certain human beings, his prophets, proclaimed these things in advance, before [the Son of God] came to be among human beings. But what was foretold by these the evil demons, myth-making through the poets, spoke of as having happened." Carena insightfully remarks on the scope of culpability Justin placed upon the poets: "Che la poesia sia stata il veicolo della diffusione della mitologia, non si può non riconoscerlo. È vero che per gli apologeti responsabilità iniziale dell'inganno non è nei poeti, ma nei demoni che li ispirano; ciò tuttavia non li salva dal biasimo di avere subìto l'inganno e di non essersi ribellati invece all'idea di un Dio brutale, impuro, avaro" ("La critica della mitologia pagana," 34).

tioning of the popular Homeric account of Odysseus' descent into Hades (*Odyssey* 11) to support the Christian doctrine of eternal punishment (*1 Apol.* 8.4, 18.5) as well as Justin's citing of the comic poet, Menander, to strengthen his argument against idol worship (*1 Apol.* 20.5).[2]

To begin our analysis of these handful of instances where Justin did not have the Pseudo-Creed sequence in mind when alluding to poetic material, we must first revisit the three different ways (established back in the introductory chapter) the apologist understood how the Poets came to acquire revelation from the Logos: they were either (1) duped into receiving it in caricatured form when the demons imitated Old Testament Messianic prophecy through myth [i.e., demon theory], (2) borrowed theological concepts from Moses and the Prophets for which they somehow had access [i.e., loan theory], or (3) received revelation directly via "seeds" of Logos dispersed to all [i.e., *Logos Spermatikos*].[3]

It is quite obvious to this point that Justin's appropriation of myth has been explored in the preceding chapters solely in light of "demon theory." Again, it is fascinating to behold the paradoxical manner in which the apologist approached poetic material of this particular stripe. On the one hand, he declared them to be the most harmful amongst the three ways poets received revelation from the Logos; the express purpose of these myths was to "relativize" the Christian message in the mind of the Gentiles.[4] On the other hand,

---

2. Carena also makes the qualification that just because Justin held the ποιηταὶ responsible for proliferating demonically inspired myths through their poetry—does not mean that he viewed the whole of their poetry the property of the devil, "La poesia è dunque tutta opera diabolica, opera di errore? No, anche i poeti hanno intraveduto e detto qualche cosa di vero" (ibid). Minns and Parvis echo this sentiment in their word study of ποιηταὶ, which occurs fifteen times in the *Apologies*—and despite the fact that Minns and Parvis emphasize that the majority of Justin's allusions to the poets are negative (ten of the instances)—five of the fifteen instances are positive, "in three of which they are coupled with 'philosophers' (*1 Apol.* 20.3, 4; 44.9) and in other two which they are coupled with 'Stoics' (*2 Apol.* 7(8).1 and 13.2)" (*Justin, Philosopher and Martyr*, 131n4). It is on the basis of this high view that Justin occasionally bestowed upon the ποιηταὶ for which this chapter is dedicated.

3. For the full discussion of this framework as outlined by Günter Glockmann, please refer to pp. 21–22 in the introductory chapter. Also, a major impetus behind the writing of this chapter is to make accessible in the English language the ideas found in Glockmann's seminal text *Homer in der frühchristlichen Literatur bis Justinus*. It is the only monograph I am aware of that provides an extensive exploration of Justin's interaction with Greco-Roman myth with an emphasis on the poet Homer with respects to "loan theory" and *Logos Spermatikos*.

4. Glockmann, *Homer in der frühchristlichen Literatur bis Justinus*, 181: "[S]o zeigt diese Stelle, 1. daß es hier um die Erzählungen der Dichter von Söhnen des Zeus geht, 2. daß die Dämonen dabei die Absicht verfolgten, die Botschaft vom Gottessohn Christus von vornherein zu relativieren . . . und ihr somit jede Bedeutung zu nehmen."

the apologist actually perceived a two-fold benefit in mentioning them to his audience: (a) their very existence ironically provided proof to his readers that there was an ancient, pagan anticipation [albeit demonic] of the Son of God who was yet to come[5] and (b) despite their primary function to rival the person of Christ through imitation they were paradoxically the most fecund in revelation compared to that of "loan theory" and *Logos Spermatikos*.[6]

The visual below (Figure 5.1) highlights some of the noteworthy distinctives surrounding poetical materials based on the "Demon-Theory." While there are two levels of mediation between the Logos and the Poets in this arrangement (i.e., Moses and the Prophets followed by the demons aping the Christological prophecies contained therein), the content of that distorted divine disclosure is quite specialized having the Son of God as its focus. As we go through the visual charts for both "loan theory" and *Logos Spermatikos* throughout this chapter, one will be able to observe a correlation between levels of mediation with that of revelatory scope. The more levels of mediation between the Logos and the Poets (e.g., demon-theory) the more that the divine disclosure is considered something akin to *special* revelation. The less mediation that occurs between the two parties (e.g., *Logos Spermatikos*) the more the divine disclosure contained therein is considered something more along the lines of *general* revelation.[7]

5. It is important to point out that Justin did not believe pre-Christian pagans to have longed for Christ's coming. According to his testimony in *1 Apol.* 49.1 he stated, "And again, how it is said through the same Isaiah that the peoples of the nations who did not expect him will worship him, but that the Jews who always expect him will not recognize him once he comes." But in the mind of the apologist, the demons must have taken this Christological prophecy to heart (i.e., "the peoples of the nations who did not expect him will worship him") so much so that they preempted his arrival by crafting these imitations of him through myth. The irony, though, is that this preemptive countermeasure by the demons actually served Justin's purposes, availing to him an *argumentum ad antiquitatem* of Christ's coming without having to appeal directly to the Hebrew Scriptures right away.

6. This should not be a surprise that "demon theory" possesses the fullest revelation amongst the three avenues mentioned. As stated in the footnote above, Justin held that pre-Christian pagans did not anticipate Christ's coming—hence aspects of his person foreshadowed in Moses and the Prophets would have not appeared in pagan texts based upon their own initiative (i.e., without demonic influence). That is why demon-theory myth is so ironic; while its purpose is to undermine Christian belief—it is the only one amongst the three that provides any sort of sketch of the person of Christ in pre-Christian pagan literature (hence, Pseudo-Creed Sequence). McDermott echoes this sentiment: "Even the demons should be credited for their partial understanding. They too copied from the Jewish Bible. They misunderstood much of it [e.g., death on the Cross], but the parts they got right show up in pagan myths as dim reflections of biblical stories [e.g., extraordinary birth, miracles, and ascending into the heavens]" (McDermott, *God's Rivals*, 91).

7. Berkhof provides an excellent distinction between general and special revelation,

"Demon-Theory"

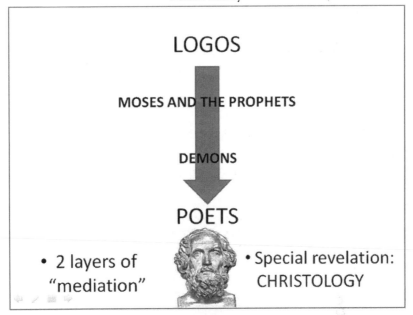

LOGOS

MOSES AND THE PROPHETS

DEMONS

POETS

• 2 layers of "mediation"

• Special revelation: CHRISTOLOGY

This chapter will be emphasizing the treatment of Justin's interaction with poetic material belonging to the last two categories of "loan theory" and *Logos Spermatikos*. With regards to divine truth the poets borrowed from Moses and the Prophets, all of Justin's allusions within this particular sphere (three instances) are eschatological in nature having to do with the theological topic of eternal punishment and reward: (1) judges of the underworld Rhadamanthus and Minos [§8.4], (2) Odysseus descent into Hades [§18.5], and (3) the Elysian fields [§20.4]. When the poet Menander remarked about the foolishness of idolatry (§20.5) or when Homer demonstrated an awareness of a supreme being he deemed as the "father of men and gods" (§22.1), this was sufficient evidence for Justin that the direct revelation from the Logos had become manifest even amongst the poets who were the reputed harbingers of myth.

While these last two categories can never support the notion that Justin believed that the Greek poets actually pined for the Son of God's appearance, these groupings do allow us to reconsider the position that the apologist viewed these human authors of myth as nothing more than lackeys

---

"General revelation is rooted in Creation, is addressed to man as man, and more particularly to human reason . . . Special revelation is rooted in the redemptive plan of God, is addressed to man as sinner, can be properly understood and appropriated only by faith" (*Systematic Theology*, 37).

of the demons.[8] Just as the apologist was known to possess a high regard for the philosophers, I will demonstrate through these select allusions that Justin found within the poets the capacity to assimilate revealed truth from God whether borrowed from the Old Testament or whether it came to be directly impressed upon them by virtue of the Logos.

POETS BORROWING FROM MOSES AND THE PROPHETS (I.E., "LOAN THEORY")

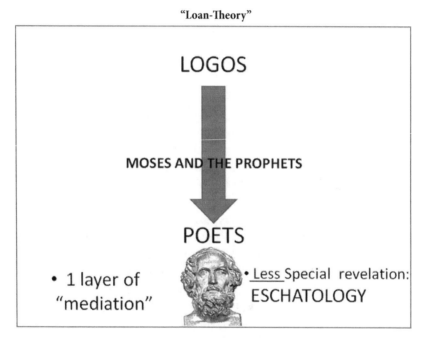

"Loan-Theory"

Justin argued that material from the poets affirming the Christian doctrine of life after death followed by eternal blessing or punishment were

8. A good representative of this school of thought who polarizes Justin's approach towards the philosophers over and against the poets is Droge: "On the one hand, Justin attributes the similarities between Christianity and the Greek *religion* to the activity of evil demons who tried to deceive humankind by imitating and caricaturing the true religion, Christianity. Similarities between Christianity and Greek *philosophy,* on the other hand, are explained either on the basis of the ancient writings of Moses, from which the Greeks acquired their wisdom, or through the inspiration of the *logos,* in which all men share" (*Homer or Moses?*, 53). For a full discussion of this tendency, please refer back to the introductory chapter to pp. 20–21 with special emphasis on footnote 57 to see who in scholarship share this sentiment.

theological ideas taken from Moses and the Prophets (Figure 5.2).[9] The key passage in *1 Apology* demonstrating the apologist's belief in such dependence is found in §44.8–9, "For Moses is older than even all the writers in Greek. And everything whatever both the philosophers (φιλόσοφοι) and the poets (ποιηταὶ) said concerning the immortality of the soul or punishments after death or contemplation of heavenly things or similar teachings they were enabled to understand and they explained because they took their starting-points from the prophets."

The apologist did not provide any sort of robust explanation of how the Greek philosophers or the poets came into contact with the Old Testament in the first place as his argument seems to be solely based upon the chronological priority of Moses and the Prophet.[10] But Arthur Droge asserts that there was no need for Justin to broach this discussion as he simply assumed his audience was acquainted with a prevalent legend held by both Jewish and Pagan thinkers containing these details.

> According to a widespread tradition Plato had at one time visited Egypt. The origin of this notion can be traced to Hecataeus of Abdera, the philosopher and historian whom Ptolemy I Soter commissioned to write a history of Egypt in the last decades of the fourth century B.C. In that work Hecataeus advanced what may be described as a pan-Egyptian theory of the history of culture and claimed that not only Plato but also Orpheus, Homer, Pythagoras, Solon, and other prominent Greeks had at one time visited Egypt and derived their wisdom and learning from the Egyptian priests. Justin's assertion that Plato had read Moses is really only a variant of this theory, for the implication is that while in Egypt Plato actually read a copy of the Pentateuch left behind by Moses. Admittedly, some ancient writers questioned the probability of such a theory, but no one in antiquity seems to have regarded it as preposterous.[11]

9. Glockmann, *Homer in der frühchristlichen Literatur bis Justinus*, 120: "Strafe zu empfinden, die den ungerechten unter ihnen zuteil wird. Der Apologet weiß sehr wohl, daß er als Christ seinen heidnischen Lesern damit nichts grundsätzlich Neues sagt."

10. Ibid., 160: "Er begnügt sich mit der generellen Behauptung der Priorität des Moses (Ap. 44, 8) und der Abhängigkeit jener griechischen Autoren vom Alten Testament, soweit es ihre Aussagen über das Leben nach dem Tode betrifft (Ap. 44, 9)."

11. *Homer or Moses*, 64–65. Droge also describes a late second-century pagan contemporary who leaned upon this very same tradition: "Numenius of Apamea in effect affirmed Justin's theory of dependence when asked, 'What is Plato but Moses in Attic Greek?'" (65). Barnard identifies the thinker from the Jewish community responsible for perpetuating the legend within that circle: "The belief that Plato and the Greek philosophers were dependent on Moses was first stated by Aristobulus, a Jewish peripatetic philosopher, who wrote a commentary on the Pentateuch addressed to Ptolemy

But after making the assertion that the philosophers and poets both borrowed eschatological concepts from the Hebrew Scriptures, Justin does a very curious thing. While he provided an example from the philosophers to demonstrate this dependence, it appears that he does not offer the same concession with respect to the poets. The passage he would supply in the immediate context on behalf of the philosophers is found in §44.8 where Justin cross-referenced *Republic* 10.617e with Deut. 30:15, 19, "So when Plato said 'blame belongs to the one who chooses; God is without blame' he spoke taking this from Moses the prophet."[12]

Is there a plausible explanation for this asymmetry? One possibility behind his unwillingness to furnish an example on behalf of the poets could have stemmed from the location of this passage (§44.8–9) towards the middle of the antitype material (§30–53)—a section where one of Justin's primary goals was to convince his reader to shift their trust from one sacred text (i.e., Homer) and place it onto another (i.e., Christian Scripture). Justin may have feared that citing a passage from a poet at this late stage of *1 Apology* would have been counterproductive to his cause.

Although not mutually exclusive to the explanation given above, it may have also been unnecessary for Justin to provide an example from the poets at this particular juncture as he had already supplied several examples earlier in *1 Apology*.[13] Glockmann identifies three such allusions to myth (§8.4, §18.5, and §20.4) each touching upon the eschatological concepts of "immortality of the soul or punishments after death or contemplation of heavenly things" outlined in §44.8–9. The first two allusions of (1) judges of the underworld Minos and Rhadamanthus [§8.4] and (2) Homer's Pit and Odysseus' subsequent descent into Hades [§18.5] highlight the concept of immortality of the soul and punishment laid up for the unrighteous while

Philometer c. 160–150 B.C.E" (*The First and Second Apologies*, 157n280).

12. The specific Old Testament passage Justin is arguing that Plato borrowed was a conflation of Deut. 30:15, 19 the gist of which the apologist produced in §44.1: "Behold, good and evil before your face. Choose the good." (Glockmann, *Homer in der frühchristlichen Literatur bis Justinus*, 159: "Ap. 44, 1 unterstreicht er seine eigenen Ausführungen durch ein alttestamentliches Zitat. Wie Moses bezeuge, habe Gott zu Adam gesagt: 'Siche, vor deinem Angesicht liegt das Gute und das Böse, wähle das Gute.' Im selben Sinne zitiert er kurz darauf, Ap. 44, 8, anerkennend das berühmte Wort Platos aus dem Mythos des Er, 'Die Schuld liegt beim Wählenden, Gott ist schuldlos.'")

13. Still, Justin's decision not to furnish a passage from one of the poets within the immediate vicinity of this important discussion is an unfortunate circumstance. Its absence has contributed no less to the polarized distinction often held in scholarship that Justin perceived the philosophers to be receptive to divine revelation while the poets not so much. This is despite the fact that Justin made it fairly clear in §44.8 that both the φιλόσοφοι καί ποιηταί had taken their turns borrowing concepts of eternal reward and punishment in the afterlife from Moses and the Prophets.

the last allusion regarding the (3) Elysian fields [§20.4] corresponds to the contemplation of heavenly things.[14]

Working off the paradigm that *1 Apology* was written with an internal audience in mind, the first twenty chapters (which contain all three afore-mentioned allusions) served two types of Christian readers: (1) those recent converts thinking about a return back to their ancestral religion due to the hazards of being a part of a *religio illicita* and (2) those students of Justin who needed arguments to bolster Christianity's standing in the court of public opinion. Interestingly enough, Justin rooted both of these concerns in eschatology. While believers have an eternal ruler whose final judgment trumps any judgment that any earthly ruler may pronounce upon them, these same earthly rulers will in turn be judged for how they conducted themselves in the treatment of Christians. Table 5.1 depicts where these eschatological emphases (chapters shaded in grey) emerge within the argu-mentative flow of the first twenty chapters of *1 Apology*.

Table 5.1
Eschatological Emphases in §1- 20 (in grey)[A]

ch.	Theme of Chapter
§1	*Formal address to the emperor (literary fiction)*
§2	*Bearing of emperor's piety and philosophy on what is to follow*
§3	*Obligation of rulers: their liability to divine punishment* (v. 4b-5), "but it is your task to let (as reason proves) to listen and to show yourself good judges. For there will be no excuse before God if, once you have learnt these things, you do not do what is right."
§4	*The name "Christian" cannot by itself be blameworthy*
§5	*Evil demons are responsible for the irrational punishment of blameless Christians, just as Socrates*
§6	*1st point re: complaint of atheism: We are not atheists*
§7	*2nd point re: complaint of atheism: Some of us may be malefactors, and if so, should be punished*
§8	*3rd point re: complaint of atheism: We cannot deny our faith or we risk eternal punishment* (v. 4), "In similar fashion, Plato said that Rhadaman-thus and Minos would punish the unrighteous who came into his pres-ence. We say that the same thing will happen, but that it will be done by Christ and to their bodies."
§9	*4th point regarding complaint of atheism: We do not worship idols*

14. Glockmann, *Homer in der frühchristlichen Literatur bis Justinus*, 160: "Der Pas-sus Ap. 44, 9 stellt nämlich geradezu eine Zusammenfassung und Weiterführung des-sen dar, was Justinus Ap. 18, 5 und besonders im dritten Punkt der Aufzählung Ap. 20, 4 ausgeführt hat."

§10	*5th point regarding complaint of atheism: We do not offer material oblations, but believe in a God who desires moral conduct on the part of men*
§11	*1st point regarding complaint of treason: The kingdom we look forward to is not one of this world. We are obedient to governmental authority*
§12	*2nd point regarding complaint of treason: We are really the best allies in the cause of peace and virtue throughout the empire*
§13	*The Christian faith is perfectly rational*
§14	*The Christian faith produces purity of life*
§15	*1st point regarding Christ's teaching: temperance and love of neighbor*
§16	*2nd point regarding Christ's teaching: meekness, oaths, truthfulness, worship of the one God*
§17	*3rd point regarding Christ's teaching: rulers will be punished by God for unjust governing* (v.17), "And if you will take no heed of our praying and putting everything in the open we will not be harmed at all; but rather we believe and have been convinced that each of you will pay penalties in eternal fire according to the worth of his actions; and in proportion to the capabilities which he received from God an account will be required, as Christ indicated, saying: 'To whom God gave more, more also will be required of him'"
§18	*Philosophers(Empedocles, Pythagoras, Plato, and Xenocrates) and a poet (Homer) who are universally revered believe in punishment after death* (v.5), "and the teachings of the writers, Empedocles and Pythagoras, Plato and Xenocrates, [and the pit of Homer and the descent of Odysseus to visit the dead, and those who say the same sort of things]. Receive us, at least like these, since we believe in God not less, but rather more, that they do: we who expect even to receive our own bodies again, after they have died and been put in the earth. "
§19	*The resurrection of the dead is not impossible*
§20	*Christian belief in the creation of the world by God, its destruction by fire, in reward and punishment after death, and that created things should not be worshipped is paralleled in pagan prophets, philosophers, and poets* (v. 4–5), "And in our saying that the souls of the wicked are punished after death, remaining in consciousness, and that the souls of the virtuous remain free from punishment and live happily, we will seem to say the same things as the poets and philosophers. And in saying that human beings should not worship inferior things, we announce the same as the comic poet Menander and those saying these things, for they declared the artisan to be greater than the thing crafted"

B. This chart is based on a conflation of two outlines for *1 Apology*. The first outline is from the introduction of Alfred Blunt's critical edition of *1 Apology* (*The Apologies of Justin Martyr* [Cambridge: The University Press, 1911], lv-lvii) and the second outline is from the respective critical edition of Minns and Parvis (*Justin, Philosopher and Martyr*, 46–54).

Chapter 8 would have struck fear in Christians who might be wavering in their faith while chapter 20 would have offered them the hope of eternal refreshment as long as they stayed the course. These same passages would have affected Justin's students in a different manner providing them the language to communicate to their opponents that their ultimate allegiance was to an eternal ruler and not a temporal one and that they were willing to forego peace in this life in order to obtain it in the next.[15]

Chapters 3, 5, 17, and 18 would have comforted discouraged believers by assuring them that eternal justice was due the persecuting emperor if he did not reform his ways. These eschatological assertions were also useful for Justin's "apologists in the making" who could argue to their pagan opponents that even the highest power in all the land was not above God's judgment. If anything, their level accountability is magnified due to the position of power bestowed upon them.[16]

Justin perceived how the three mythical allusions we will be treating in this section resonated with these bold eschatological claims. Glockmann points out that their selection by Justin was a product of not only how popular they were but also how widely accepted their description of the afterlife was amongst the populace.[17] So how would the wavering Christian benefit from Justin's allusions to myth here? By utilizing the pagan sacred text they

15. Regarding Justin's students, we only possess the identity of at least two, maybe three. Lampe supplies two of them for which we are certain: Tatian and Euelpistis who was one of the apologist's companions at his martyrdom (*From Paul to Valentinus*, 77) while Quasten offers Militiades as "most probably, also a pupil of Justin" (*Patrology*, 228).

16. I included *1 Apol.* 5 as having eschatological implications as the earthly rulers whose power have gone amuck during Justin's time will experience the same plight that befell the fallen angels and their prediluvian offspring (i.e., demons). Reed deems this as the "hermeneutic of inversion" based upon the Enochic tradition. Justin's argument here is undergirded by this tradition as through it he was able to vindicate the existence of Christians in the face of pagan oppressive rule (i.e., the emperor) whom he criticizes as being under the influence of these demonic forces. Just as the Watchers and their children (i.e., demons) once dominated the world only to be severely judged by God in the flood, so too, would the pagan rulers under the influence of these same evil forces experience a similar punishment (Reed, "The Trickery of the Fallen Angels and the Demonic Mimesis of the Divine," 153).

17. Glockmann, *Homer in der frühchristlichen Literatur bis Justinus*, 119–120: "In dieser Argumentation Justins ist die Lehre vom Weiterleben der Seel über den Tod hinaus von entscheidender Bedeutung. Dabei wird besonders betont, daß die Seelen auch wirklich in der Lage sind, den Schmerz der Strafe zu empfinden, die den ungerechten unter ihnen zuteil wird. Der Apologet weiß sehr wohl, daß er als Christ seinen heidnischen Lesern damit nichts grundsätzlich Neues sagt ... In dieser Hinsicht mußte nun freilich die Lehre vom Weiterleben der Seele über den Tod hinaus dem Apologeten als ein sich überaus günstig anbietender Ausgangspunkt willkommen sein."

still revered (i.e., with their temptation to revert back), Justin could provide additional weight to his eschatological claims by demonstrating how even Homer was in agreement with them. How would citing myth benefit Justin's students? He was modeling how they should exploit instances where Greek myth resonated with Christian belief for the ultimate advancement of the faith.

Rhadamanthus and Minos, judges of the Underworld (8.4)

In *1 Apol.* 8.4, Justin states that the myth of Rhadamanthus and Minos as judges of the underworld belonged to Plato.[18] But Glockmann is quick to point out that Plato was not the actual originator of this myth—rather he adapted it from Homer's *Odyssey* 11.568–571 where King Minos is described as the lone judge of the underworld, "There, you must know, I saw Minos, the glorious son of Zeus, golden scepter in hand, giving judgment to the dead from his seat, while they sat and stood about the king in the wide-gated house of Hades and asked him for judgment."[19] In Plato's adaptation, Minos is not the sole judge but rather he is part of a trio consisting of Rhadamanthus responsible for judging souls from Asia, Aeacus performing the same function over the departed from Europe, and Minos himself possessing the role as chief judge over both as he held the power to make the final decision whether a soul went to a place of bliss (i.e., Isle of the Blest) or that of punishment (i.e., Tartarus).[20]

This begs the question of why Justin opted for Plato's adaptation of Homer instead of going straight to the source itself (i.e., *Odyssey* 11.568–571). One possibility is that Justin felt more comfortable working with this mediated version of the Minos myth especially with Plato as its handler. As discussed previously in chapter one, Plato approached myth in a dichotomous fashion—eschewing these pagan narratives openly and yet referencing them on a constant basis due to their value as a form of religious discourse (e.g., "Homer as the unavoidable reference"). It is interesting to note that §8.4 was Justin's very first instance of incorporation of myth in *1 Apology*

18. *Gorgias* 523a–526d

19. Glockmann, *Homer in der frühchristlichen Literatur bis Justinus*, 132: "Der Verfasser dieser Verse ist für Plato selbstverständlich noch Homer."

20. *Gorgias* 523e–524a: "These, when their life is ended, shall give judgment in the meadow at the dividing of the road, whence are the two ways leading, one to the Isles of the Blest, and the other to Tartarus. And those who come from Asia shall Rhadamanthus try, and those from Europe, Aeacus; and to Minos I will give the privilege of the final decision, if the other two be in any doubt; that the judgment upon this journey of mankind may be supremely just."

(Table 2.1) so the very act of toting Plato alongside the allusion could have been Justin's way of hinting to his reader the sort of philosophic approach he would take regarding these pagan narratives.

The context of chapter 8 is that Justin is providing his third and last argument against the accusation that Christians were atheists (ἄθεοι) a charge he began dealing with back in chapter 6 (Table 5.1). Justin admits that, "it is in our power to deny we are Christians when examined. But we do not wish to avoid death by telling lies, for we desire the eternal, pure life, and we seek communion with God the Father and maker of all" (§8.1–2). It is opportune at this point to recall that Christians were branded atheists by the government not because they did not believe in a divine being, but rather for their unwillingness to participate in the worship of the ancestral gods.[21] Although stating this fact may seem axiomatic, it helps bring to our attention the fascinating approach Justin took here in order to cinch his third and last argument: appealing to a myth steeped in the very religious culture he was accused of abandoning!

Just as the judges of the underworld, Rhadamanthus and Minos, would expose every hidden falsehood a person embraced during their lifetime and sending such souls, "away in dishonor straight to the place of custody, where on its arrival it is to endure the sufferings that are fitting" (*Gorgias* 525a), Justin argued that in a similar manner Christians who denied their faith in order to avoid the wrath of a temporal judge will not be able to escape that of the eternal judge.

In addition, the punishment that the eternal judge would dole out upon the dishonest believer far surpassed that of what Rhadamanthus and Minos allegedly did to the deceitful soul. This is perhaps the primary reason why Justin chose Plato's rendition of the Minos myth over the Homeric original as it afforded him the opportunity to demonstrate not only how Christian eschatological claims were similar to that of the Minos myth (*ad similia*), but in the end how they were greater (*ad fortiori*), "In similar fashion, Plato said that Rhadamanthus and Minos would punish the unrighteous who came into his presence [*Gorgias* 525a-e]. We say that the same thing will happen, but that it will be done by Christ and to their bodies, and they will be punished everlasting, not just for a period of a thousand years, as he said [*Phaedrus* 249a]" (*1 Apol.* 8.4).

While the Minos myth in Homer's *Odyssey* does mention the punishment of the soul, it does not get into the nuance of the *Gorgias* account

---

21. Richardson, *Early Christian Fathers*, 293: "To deny the traditional gods, to stand in opposition to the syncretic temper of the age, and above all to claim to practice a religion which dispensed with the most essential mark of ancient religion, viz., sacrifice, could not but have provoked the accusation of atheism."

where Plato discusses the permanent separation of body and soul at death of which the soul is singled out before Rhadamanthus and Minos for judgment.[22] Also in *Phaedrus* 249a, Plato commented regarding the finite sentence Rhadamanthus and Minos assigned upon a soul found reprobate, "when they have finished their first life, receive judgment, and after the judgment some go to the places of correction under the earth and pay their penalty . . . But in the thousandth year . . . [they] come to draw lots and choose their second life." So while Justin perceived that Plato's account of the Minos myth resonated somewhat with Christianity's eschatological claims, in comparison the pagan narrative fell short in its severity by not passing judgment on the body whatsoever, (i.e., no resurrection) as well as limiting the length of perdition to that of a thousand years.[23]

Homer's Pit and Odysseus descent into Hades (§18.5)

The background behind Homer's pit (Ομήρω βόθρος) and Odysseus descent into Hades (κάθοδος Ὀδυσσέως εἰς τὴν τούτων ἐπίσκεψιν) was that Odysseus had been instructed by Circe the Witch towards the end of *Odyssey* 10 that if he wanted to find his way back to Ithaca, Odysseus would first have to travel to Hades to consult the spirit of the seer Tiresias for direction. At the beginning of *Odyssey* 11, he arrives on the shore of Hades and digs a pit (βόθρος) filling it with the sacrificial blood of a ram in order to conjure up the spirits of the dead.

While the spirit of Tiresias emerges from the Underworld to consult with Odysseus, other departed souls in Hades come up to the βόθρος to converse with Odysseus. This included his former crewman Elpenor, his fallen

---

22. *Gorgias* 524b–524d: "[D]eath, as it seems to me, is actually nothing but the disconnection of two things, the soul and the body, from each other. And so when they are disconnected from one another, each of them keeps its own condition very much as it was when the man was alive, the body having its own nature, with its treatments and experiences all manifest upon it . . . In a word, whatever sort of bodily appearance a man had acquired in life, that is manifest also after his death either wholly or in the main for some time. And so it seems to me that the same is the case with the soul too, Callicles: when a man's soul is stripped bare of the body, all its natural gifts, and the experiences added to that soul as the result of his various pursuits, are manifest in it. So when they have arrived."

23. Minns and Parvis also notice Justin's impulse here to expose how Plato's eschatological claims are inferior that of Christianity, "In the myth of Rhadamanthus and Minos at *Gorgias* 523c-e it is expressly said that it is naked souls, stripped of their bodies, that are judged. It is possible that Justin wished to correct Plato on this point, just as corrected him with respect to the agency of the punishment, and its duration" (*Justin, Philosopher and Martyr*, 95n7).

brothers in arms Achilles and Ajax, and even his mother Anticleia. It is important to note at this particular time that all the encounters listed above occurred at the site of "Homer's Pit" (*Od.* 11.23–567) while Odysseus' descent into Hades is considered a separate episode altogether (*Od.* 11.568–640). In the latter, he perilously decides to follow some of the spirits that visited him at the βόθρος back to Hades to observe how the Underworld operated for himself.[24] This is where he sees Minos passing judgment upon souls (*Od.* 11.568–571) with special emphasis placed upon the immense suffering this former king of Crete had imposed upon three other former kings/rulers consisting of Tityus (*Od.* 11.576–581), Tantalus (*Od.* 11.582–592), and Sisyphus (*Od.* 593–600). According to the account, they were experiencing these severe forms of punishment as payment for the reckless abuse of their power while they were living.[25]

> Others are suffering penance for the sins they committed when they were alive, as Sisyphus, who rolls a great rock forever up a hill, for when he gets it nearly to the top it rolls down and he has to do his work all over again . . . Near him, Tantalus is forever thirsty because the water that rises almost to his lips is siphoned out of his cup just before he is able to drink it . . . Tityus is tortured by an eagle, which comes every day to tear his liver out as fast as it grows again.[26]

For Justin to distinguish clearly between "Homer's pit" and "Odysseus' descent into Hades" is no small thing. While the former would aid him as a revered pagan testimony for the immortality of the soul, the latter affirmed the punishment of those immortal souls who lived badly (especially those in positions of high authority). Hence, "Homer's Pit" (i.e., supporting immortality of the soul) and "Odysseus' descent into Hades" (i.e., supporting eternal punishment with emphasis on rulers) served as colorful illustrations corresponding to what Justin announced at the beginning of *1 Apol.* 18,

---

24. Glockmann, *Homer in der frühchristlichen Literatur bis Justinus*, 129: "Diese Ebene wird jedoch mit den Versen Od. 11, 568–626 verlassen. Was hier berichtet wird setzt voraus, daß Odysseus seinen Posten neben dem βόθρος am Hadestor aufgegeben hat und selbst in den Erebos hinabgestiegen ist."

25. Tityus was a Titan whose crime was attempting to rape Apollo's mother, Leto (Pseudo-Apollodorus, *The Library* 1.22); Tantalus was a king who offended the gods by cutting his son Pelops into pieces of which he cooked and offered up to them as a meal (Pseudo-Hyginus, *Fabulae* 83); Sisyphus was the king of Corinth who throughout his reign was considered a bad character altogether (Homer, *Iliad* 6.153) who unmercifully killed innocent and defenseless travelers to take their possessions and was often known for defying the gods.

26. Hulst, *Homer and the Prophets*, 2.

"Consider what happened to each of the kings that have been. They died just like everybody else. Which, if death led to unconsciousness would have been a godsend to all the unjust. But, since consciousness endures for all those who have existed, and eternal punishment lies in store, take care to be persuaded to believe that these things are true."[27]

The allusion to "Odysseus' descent into Hades" is, therefore, a continuation of the Minos myth previously mentioned in §8.4 with the main difference being that Justin is no longer posing the eschatological warning towards Christians "on the fence" but now has adjusted the allusion to apply towards the emperor. Working under the assumption that *1 Apology* was written with an internal audience in mind, Justin did not intend for this admonition to reach the imperial court. Instead, the apologist was employing a rhetorical technique known as an *apostrophe* where the individual named in the formal address (i.e., the emperor) was not the target audience but rather the Christian reader suffering under his reign. Through this fictitious diatribe, those persecuted during the emperor's rule gained the comfort of knowing that he would have his day of reckoning as depicted in the vivid judgments placed upon Tityus, Tantalus, and Sisyphus.

---

27. It is because how well the separate episodes of "Homer's Pit" and "Odysseus' descent into Hades" correspond as illustrative material for Justin's eschatological principles of immortality of the soul and eternal punishment respectively (*1 Apol.* 18.1–2 and 44.8–9) that I disagree with Minns and Parvis editorial decision to omit the phrase, "and the pit in Homer and the descent of Odysseus to visit the dead" in §18.5 altogether. The rationale for their editorial decision was that the phrase "interrupts the genitival construction and hence must have been a latter edition" and that the phrase should be understood as a superfluous "gloss intended to provide an example of another writer saying 'things of that sort'" (*Justin, Philosopher and Martyr*, 125n3). The following is the entirety of §18.5 from the original manuscript with the italicized text the portion that Minns and Parvis decided to retain: καὶ τὰ τῶν συγγραφέων διδάγματα, Ἐμπεδοκλέους καὶ Πυθαγόρου, Πλάτωνός τε καὶ Ξενοκράτους, καὶ ὁ παρ' Ὁμήρῳ βόθρος καὶ ἡ κάθοδος Ὀδυσσέως εἰς τὴν τούτων ἐπίσκεψιν, καὶ τῶν τὰ αὐτὰ τούτοις εἰπόντων. I am in agreement with Glockmann who recognizes that the phrase is somewhat awkward where it stands but yet it is too important to omit altogether (Ashton, Schmid, and Marcovich also take this position). He suggests that the phrase be transferred toward the beginning of verse 5 so to be associated with the last phrase in verse 4, "other things of that sort," where it fits much better: "Anlaß. Ap. 18, 5 wird mit καὶ τῶν τὰ αὐτὰ τούτοις εἰπόντων ohne Zweifel an καὶ τὰ τῶν συγγραφέων διδάγματα, Ἐμπεδοκλέους χτλ. angekuüpft, so daß die Worte über Homer und die Hadesfahrt des Odysseus als Parenthese erscheinen, die indessen in sprachlicher wie sachlicher Hinsicht den Zusammenhang des Paragraphen 5 emplindlich stört . . . Ich schließe mich daher Schmid an, der einen Vorschlag von Davis und Ashton aufgreift und καὶ ὁ παρ' Ὁμήρῳ βόθρος καὶ ἡ κάθοδος Ὀδυσσέως εἰς τὴν τούτων ἐπίσκεψιν an den Anfang von Paragraph 5 stellt, so daß die Worte sich an καὶ ὅσα ἄλλα τοιαῦτά ἐστι anschließen" (*Homer in der frühchristlichen Literatur bis Justinus*, 123).

While Justin hoped that his audience would be able to recall these stark images of the three "incurable sinners" suffering in the afterlife (*Odyssey* 11.576–593), it was crucial that they understood that these former kings had been judged by a former earthly king himself who was also a son of Zeus (*Odyssey* 11.568).[28] The main lesson that is being conveyed by Justin is that even the seemingly all-powerful emperor will have a day of reckoning with one more powerful than he. As Justin's Christian gentile readers would have understood that tyrannical kings such as Tantalus and Sisyphus were eventually called into account by another king, King Minos, in even a greater sense will the emperor will experience retribution far superior that anything Minos could have doled out.[29] This is captured in the following verse where Justin proclaims, "Receive us, at least like these, since we believe in God not less, but rather more, than they do: we who expect even to receive our own bodies again, after they have died and been put in the earth" (*1 Apol.* 18.6). For Justin, the doctrine of the resurrection of the body amplifies the suffering the emperor will experience (if he did not amend his ways) because the punishment would be placed up both the soul and the body.

Elysian Fields (20.4)

Amongst the three aspects outlined in *1 Apol.* 44.8 regarding immortality of the soul, eternal punishment, and contemplation of heavenly things, it is the last one (i.e., contemplation of heavenly things) that receives the shortest treatment from Justin with respect to how the Poets interacted with this particular eschatological concern. While Justin alluded to Homer's Pit for the immortality of the soul (§18.5) and Odysseus' descent into Hades for eternal punishment (§8.4, §18.5), he did not produce a single explicit reference from the tradition of either the Poets or the Philosophers that served as a pagan analogue for the contemplation of heavenly things. Instead in *1 Apol.*20.4 he simply appends this final concept to the two previous

---

28. Ibid., 134: "Den Seelen, die heilbare begangen haben, gereichen die Strafen zur Besserung; die mit unheilbaren behafteten Seelen können selbst zwar auch durch die schwersten Strafen nicht mehr gebessert werden, ihre Strafen dienen aber allen übrigen als warnende παραδείγματα."

29. Ibid., 138: "Justins Verständnis dieser Verse ist zudem abhängig von ihrer Deutung durch Plato, wie sie namentlich im Schlußmythos des Gorgias vorliegt. Die richterliche Tätigkeit des Minos im Hades wird ihm so zum Totengericht, das über das letzte Schicksal der Seelen entscheidet, und in den Tityos-, Tantalos-, Sisyphosqualen sieht er ein Beispiel für die ewigen Strafen der Seelen, die mit schweren, unheilbaren Sünden behaftet sind, was vor allem von den Seelen ehemaliger Herrscher zu gelten hat Abschließend kann festgestellt warden."

eschatological concerns he treated earlier using myth, "And in saying that the souls of the wicked are punished after death, remaining in conscious-ness, and that the souls of the virtuous (σπουδαίων) remain free from pun-ishment and live happily (εὖ διάγειν), we will seem to say the same things as the as the poets and philosophers."

But despite Justin's lacuna here regarding an explicit reference from the poets supporting the notion of heaven, Glockmann argues that "it is im-possible to ignore here with respect to being free from punishment [living happily] . . . I mean *Odyssey* 4.563–568 in which Menelaus announces that he will not die because he was Helen's husband and also the son-in-law of Zeus."[30] Here is that passage provided below describing Menelaus' entrance into the Elysian fields:

> But for thyself, Menelaus, fostered of Zeus, it is not ordained that thou shouldst die and meet thy fate in horse-pasturing Argos, but to the Elysian plain and the bounds of the earth will the im-mortals convey thee, where dwells fair-haired Rhadamanthus, and where life is easiest for men. No snow is there, nor heavy storm, nor ever rain, but ever does Ocean send up blasts of the shrill-blowing West Wind that they may give cooling to men.

While Justin may have had this passage in mind when he proclaimed in §20.4 that "we will seem to say the same things as the poets," there is good reason why he would be hesitant in alluding to it explicitly. Given that his previous comparisons between mythical allusion and Christian belief with regards to immortality of the soul (§18.5) and eternal punishment (§8.4, §18.5) always ended with same *a fortiori* refrain that the Christian belief was greater due to the doctrine of the resurrection, this Homeric passage would sabotage that pattern. The reason being is that it appears Menelaus is translated into Elysian fields in bodily form according to Homer, "it is not ordained that thou shouldst die." Glockmann comments on this curious phrase, "in Homer only Menelaus as Zeus' son-in-law is raptured."[31]

Also, Justin may have anticipated that alluding to this particular Ho-meric passage could have caused confusion in his reader as it states that the "fair-haired Rhadamanthus" would be there in the Elysian fields to welcome

---

30. *Homer in der frühchristlichen Literatur bis Justinus*, 149: "Indessen bietet sich sogleich eine andere Odysseestelle an, die Justinus hier unmöglich außer acht lassen konnte, wo er in bezug auf das von Strafen freie εὖ διάγειν der Seelen der Gerechten auch ausdrücklich vermerkt: . . . ποιηταῖς καὶ φιλοσόφοις τὰ αὐτὰ λέγειν δόξομεν. Ich meine die Verse Od. 4, 563–568, in denen Proteus dem Menelaos verkündet, dieser werde nicht sterben . . . weil er Helenas Gatte und Eidaan des Zeus sei."

31. Ibid., 149: "[D]aß bei Homer lediglich Menelaos als des Zeus Eidam ins E. en-trückt wird."

Menelaus. This would seem to work against Justin's previous assertion established back in §8.4 that Rhadamanthus was one of judges in the Underworld. Still, Justin may have had this passage in mind as it undoubtedly was the most famous regarding the Elysian fields, "these verses are known to be the oldest and most famous literary testament to the popular belief of the Greeks prior to the Christian era of the vivid picture of blissful life after death."[32]

POETS ILLUMINATED DIRECTLY (LOGOS SPERMATIKOS)

In this last category Justin held that on the rarest occasions both the poets and philosophers came into direct contact with the Logos. This unmediated form of access to revelation, though, yielded theological notions considered vague and general at best, "limited to a few conceptions, i.e., certain ideas on God and on the falsity of idolatry and also certain basic moral conceptions"[33] (Figure 5.3). Glockmann also asserts that by analyzing Justin's understanding of Menander's insight regarding the divine that theme of "the sublimity of the Creator of all creation" belongs within the realm of *Logos Spermatikos*.[34] This is important as it allows us to assign Homer's famous phrase regarding Zeus as "the father of god and men" as an insight he received via *Logos Spermatikos*.

"Logos-Spermatikos Theory"

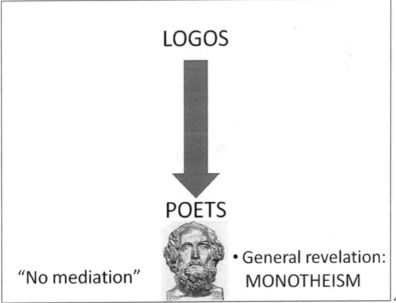

LOGOS

POETS

"No mediation"

• General revelation: MONOTHEISM

declared the artisan to be greater than the thing crafted" (§20.5).[35] It is from Justin's allusion to Menander that Rendell Harris has aptly described the comic poet "as a prophet of monotheism for the Greeks."[36]

So while Justin selected Socrates as his model philosopher who came to champion monotheism through the enlightening of the Logos (2 Apol. 10), the apologist made Menander his representative from amongst the poets to serve that same exact purpose.[37] The selection of Socrates and Menander as ancient, pagan spokespersons for the oneness of God is quite intriguing as the common denominator that both men shared was that their respective careers were not lauded until after their deaths. Out of the more than one-hundred plays that Menander composed, he was only recognized a handful of times by his generation, "Menander won the first prize at Athens only eight times, and later it became something of a commonplace that posterity appreciated him more than his contemporaries had done."[38]

Justin argues that Socrates unpopularity during his life was the result of the demons trying to prevent him from exposing their divine masquerade, "When Socrates attempted with true reason and judicious inquiry to bring these things in the open and to draw people away from the demons, the demons, using people who delight in evil, worked it that he too was killed" (1 Apol. 5.3). In fact, Justin linked the persecution of Christians in his day to the same diabolical stirrings that occurred during Socrates time—all on account of having been enlightened by the Logos with regards to God as One.[39] In the same vein, Justin could have also chalked up Menander's lack of success at the Athenian festivals of his day a direct result of the monotheistic impulse contained in his plays—a sight that was both displeasing to the demons and those Greek spectators under their influence.[40]

---

35. Harris conjectures two lost fragments from Menander that can be extrapolated from this allusion, where "Justin is actually quoting the poet, and not merely referring to him in a distant or obscure manner." The entire passage in the Greek for §20.4 is: τῷ δὲ καὶ μὴ δεῖν χειρῶν ἀνθρωπίνων ἔργοις προσκυνεῖν Μενάνδρῳ τῷ κωμικῷ καὶ τοῖς ταῦτα φήσασι ταὐτὰ φράζομεν· μείζονα γὰρ τὸν δημιουργὸν τοῦ σκευαζομένου ἀπε φήναντο. The first conjectured fragment Harris derives from Justin's verse is μὴ δεῖν χερῶν ἄνθρωπον ἔργα προσκυνεῖν, or "man should not worship the work of his hand," while the second conjectured fragment is μείζων γὰρ πάνυ ὁ δημιουργός ἐστι τοὺσκευασμένου, or "for the craftsman is far greater than the thing that he has wrought" (Justin Martyr and Menander, 5).

36. Ibid., 10.

37. Haddad, The Appropriateness of the Apologetical Arguments of Justin Martyr, 113).

38. Brown, The Plays and Fragments, 10.

39. Price, "Are There 'Holy Pagans' in Justin Martyr?," 170–71.

40. It is interesting to note that in 1 Apol. 4.9 Justin critiques these very same

"Father of men and gods" (§22.1) and Zeus and Thetis (§25.2)

Working off of the monotheistic insight Justin perceived in Menander's thought, one of the themes that specifically emerged from the comic poet's allusion against idolatry is the "sublimity of the Creator of all creation."[41] Menander found it absurd that a truly divine being could ever be considered the product of human hands for such an arrangement violated the notion of divine transcendence. In this arrangement, the deity in idolatry was subject to the whim and caprice of its human fashioner. Menander, instead, longed for a sublime divinity who was lord over his worshipers and not the other way around.

Menander was not the only poet who was an advocate for monotheism in the thought of Justin. According to Glockmann, Homer was also considered "a conscious or unconscious prophet of monotheism" for the apologist.[42] The clear Homeric wording in *1 Apology* that indicates this is found in §22.1b, "For all the writers call God (θεός) the father of men and gods (πατέρα ἀνδρῶν τε θεῶν τε)." This phrase was a well-known Homeric quip used to describe the sublimity of Zeus eulogized in *Iliad* 1.544, "Then made answer to her [Hera] the father of men and gods (πατὴρ ἀνδρῶν τε θεῶν τε)."[43]

Interestingly, Justin took this commonly known title "father of men and gods" belonging to Zeus (Διός) and in §22.2b applied it to the Christian God the Father (θεός). It is the latter that Justin definitely has in mind in attributing this phrase for in the previous line he states, "The Son of God who is called Jesus, even if he were only an ordinary human being, would be worthy to be called a son of God because of wisdom" (*1 Apol.* 22.1a). Then Justin proceeded to state later in that verse that this θεός who is the father of Jesus is the "father of men and gods."

How are we to understand Justin's adapting of a Homeric title his audience knew exclusively referred to Zeus now being used to describe God the Father of the Christians? I assert that the key to unlocking this in

---

festivals that are going on his day: "[A]nd those of them who were poets proclaimed the promiscuity of Zeus as well as of his sons, and you do not bar performers who take up their teaching. Rather, you give prizes and rewards for those who are in good voice when they offer insult to them."

41. Glockmann, *Homer in der frühchristlichen Literatur bis Justinus*, 164.

42. Ibid.: "Nun trifft man zwar in der frühohristlichen Literatur nach Justinus auf den ausdrücklichen Versuch, mit Hilfe einer mehr oder minder gewaltsamen Umdeutung von Ilias- und Odysseeversen sogar Homer zu einem bewußten oder unbewußten Künder des Monotheismus, ja des christlichen Gottesbegriffes zu machen."

43. Ibid., 114: "Diese Formel ist von den Griechen auch stets als von Homer stammend empfunden worden."

logos spermatikos. While Justin affirmed that Homer possessed a general awareness of a Supreme Being (as evidenced by the coining of this famous phrase), the way he went about attempting to portray this revelatory insight throughout his poetry fell short of that mark (as we will see in the account of Zeus and Thetis). For Justin, God the Father of the Christians was, in fact, the fulfillment of what Homer was vaguely aware with regards to the sublimity of the Supreme Being (via *logos spermatikos*) and hence was worthy of now officially taking over the title. In modifying a C.S. Lewis quote to illustrate the maneuver Justin employed here: God the Father "was myth made fact."[44]

Despite awarding the title of the "father of men and gods" to the Christian God the Father over and against its previous titleholder (i.e., Zeus), Justin was not satisfied with this mere replacement so he took additional steps in §25.2–3 to demonstrate that the paternal god of the Greek pantheon was no longer worthy of this ascription.

> nor do we believe that through Thetis he [Zeus] obtained the help of that hundred-handed one, and so was loosed from his bonds, nor do we believe that he was on that account concerned about Thetis' Achilles and so destroyed many of the Greeks, because of the concubine Briseis. And we pity those who do believe this, but we know that the demons are the cause of it.

The account for which Justin is referring is from *Iliad* 1.399–406 where Achilles prayed to his divine mother, Thetis, to convince Zeus to punish the Greeks on account of King Agamemnon wresting his concubine, Briseis, from him. His mother was able to get Zeus to comply with the request because he owed her a favor: she had previously obtained the help of the "One-Hundred Handed One" to assist Zeus in securing victory in his war against the Titans.

One can immediately see how any notion of Zeus' sublimity would be undercut in an account such as this.[45] First, the fact that Zeus was in the debt of any other being (i.e., Thetis) destroys any notion of transcendence. Second, that Zeus needed assistance (i.e., One Hundred Handed One) in the

---

44. Lewis, "Myth Became Fact," 66–67. The original quote is "Christ was myth made fact."

45. Glockmann, *Homer in der frühchristlichen Literatur bis Justinus*, 167: "Was Homer hier von Zeus berichtet, wird vom Apologeten mit dem christlichen Gottesbegriff konfrontiert. Daß Zeus der Hilfe der Thetis und des Ungetüms Briareos bedurft habe, um der Fesselung durch seine nächsten Anverwandten zu entgehen, ist mit jeder Vorstellung vom Wesen des höchsten Gottes unvereinbar. Völlig unmöglich sei es, meint Justinus, daß der Gott, an den die Christen glauben, jemals in eine derart unwürdige Situation hätte körnmen können."

first place to gain the victory over the Titans reveals lack of power. Third, that he would cause the demise of so many Greeks on account of Achilles personal vendetta with Agamemnon is also problematic.

Another additional slight to the sublimity of Zeus was that he was supposed to be objective in his dealings with humanity. In the Trojan War, the other deities of Pantheon took sides on whom they would support but Zeus was not to intervene. By conceding to Thetis request, this balance was compromised.

The Greeks are supported by Athena, Hera and Poseidon, and the Trojans by Apollo, Ares and Aphrodite. Zeus, who as President of the [Eternals] would otherwise maintain a dignified neutrality, becomes temporarily involved on the side of the Trojans through his undignified obligation to Thetis, the divine mother of Achilles. So much so that he asserts, but does not completely maintain, a monopoly of intervention from the beginning of Book VIII to the beginning of Book XX.[46]

CONCLUSION

In the previous chapters, we assumed that myths based off of demon-theory were pagan narratives *inspired by demons*. Although this assertion is obvious, it is an important point to bring up because an entire schema was developed (i.e., typology of myth) to understand how Justin was able to extract the original revelation behind the distortion. But with poetic material derived under the categories of "loan theory" and *logos spermatikos*, no such assumption abounds with regards to involvement of demonic activity. Yet mythical characters (even gods) were used to construct these narratives (e.g. "loan theory" [Minos] and *logos spermatikos* [Zeus]), so how do we not label poetical materials like this as being demonically inspired in nature if they utilize gods (i.e., demons in disguise for Justin) to tell their story?

A very helpful way to negotiate through this issue is using the framework supplied by Gerald McDermott.[47] As a quick review, McDermott distinguishes between when the demons and the fallen angels took on their names as gods (after the Great Flood) and when the myths about them were actually crafted. So as the demons pulled from this preset "cast of gods" to shape and develop their demonic narratives against Christ along the way, so to could the poets on their own volition pull from this demonically crafted preset "cast of gods" to construct stories regarding them that were not necessarily demon-inspired.

46. James, "The Limitation of the Gods in the *Iliad*," 218.

47. For review of this schema, see pg. 44 in chapter 2.

This would be the case in the example of "loan theory" and Minos as judge in the underworld; that name may have been demonically inspired (i.e., he is a son of Zeus) and yet Homer used the character to construct a colorful story about immortality of the soul and eternal punishment. This story according to Justin would have been based upon those eschatological concerns Homer picked up by reading Moses and the Prophets.

With respect to Homer's awareness of a Supreme Being as the "father of gods and men," Justin would argue that this initial awareness was the product of *logos spermatikos*. But in this case, this did not prevent the demons from eventually corrupting this *logos spermatikos* revelatory insight that Homer received as seen in his attributing the title to the much maligned paternal god of the Greek Pantheon, Zeus.

6

Conclusion

"MOVEABLE TYPE": THE KEY TO UNDERSTANDING JUSTIN'S DYNAMIC APPROPRIATION OF MYTH

AFTER READING THE PRECEDING five chapters culminating into this conclusion, one might be experiencing typological vertigo with respect to what exactly represents the *type* in this suggested framework. Does myth serve as the *type* for Justin (affirmed throughout the early portion of this work)?[1] Or did Justin perceive Moses and the Prophets as the *type*? In fact it is a statement towards the end of chapter three (p. 83) that could lend to some confusion by suggesting that Justin never seriously considered myth as a legitimate type in the first place:

> the typological movement for Justin is not really between the emerging New Testament narrative and that of Greek myth at this junction anymore. Instead, the typological movement is experiencing a transformation where it now occurs between the emerging New Testament narrative and a Christological reading of the Hebrew Scriptures—with Greek myth serving a mediating or instrumental function between the two.

So for clarification sake, I will dispel the ambiguity by answering the question whether in *1 Apology* myth served as a type for Justin or whether

---

1. Instances of where this claim is explicitly stated are pp. 2, 43, 45–47, 50, and 56–59.

Moses and the Prophet did; the appropriate answer would be "Yes." That is, it depends where one stands in *1 Apology* that determines whether myth or Moses and Prophets functioned as the type for Justin (hence the clever sub-heading of a "movable type"). From §1–22, myth was an *established* type; from §23–53, myth changes to a *provisional* type falling into obsolescence in favor of the OT Type Justin is introducing. From §54–66, I offer a third way of thinking how Justin approached myth towards the late stages of *1 Apology*: myth as *false antitype* (Figure 6.1).

Hence, the goal of this conclusion is to provide a concise overview of this study reviewing its salient elements within the framework of these three typological stages of myth in *1 Apology* (Figure 6.1). I will conclude by offering some final thoughts about how the findings of this work may impact other areas of Justin Martyr scholarship.

The flow of "Moveable Type" in *1 Apology*

Myth as an established type (§1–22)

In beginning this section, it is important to remember the premise established back in chapter two (pp.45–46) that Justin's interaction with myth at this initial stage of *1 Apology* was largely predicated by how his audience approached these pagan narratives (i.e., simultaneous reverence and suspicion) and not so much upon his own personal view of them (that will emerge later). So §1–22 should be understood as Justin strategically leveraging the assumed *reverence* his audience held regarding myth. It is important to point out that much of this sentiment was perhaps driven by the fact that these pagan narratives had been assimilated by Justin's readers from childhood as having historic import. Still, things are not entirely rosy for Justin with regards to myth in this section as towards the end of chapter 21 he states (verse 4), "these things are written to persuade to corruption those who are being educated. For all think that it is good to imitate the gods." But for the most part, the material between §1–22 is in the vein of incorporation of myth while the instances like the example of above were far and few between (i.e., partial separation of myth).

That is why in capturing the gist of §1–22, Figure 6.2 is entitled "poetical" type instead of "mythical" type (as will be the case for title of the next stage). This label is helpful in reinforcing that Justin is capitalizing upon the assumed reverence his audience held towards pagan narratives at this stage in *1 Apology* not having yet commenced his all-out barrage of full separation from myth.

"Poetical" Type and NT Antitype (§1–22)

It is here that Justin strategically leverages the concept of θεῖος ἀνήρ by comparing those aspects that make up an immortal in Greek mythology (i.e., extraordinary birth, having performed great service for humanity, dying, and ascending into the heavens) to that of Christ. There is a faint typological trajectory at work here as those believers acquainted with basic contours of the Christian story would be able to detect the similarities between the Son of God and the sons of Zeus that Justin identified. But it was nowhere as robust when he arrived at the next stage where the Old Testament Christological fulfillment passages provide brighter and richer colors for Justin to paint his portrait of Christ.

Still, this process of Justin demonstrating correspondence between the Son of God and the sons of Zeus using the characteristics of θεῖος ἀνήρ cannot be underestimated. This was a way Justin could make what was initially a very foreign concept to a Gentile audience (i.e., Christ as Messianic fulfillment of Jewish expectation) relevant to them. That is, Christ is the true "divine man" of which the sons of Zeus pale in comparison ("similar" but "greater").

149

Myth as a provisional type (§23–53)

As we move towards the next stage, we observe a shift in the title for the type material: from "poetic" to "mythical" (Figure 6.3). Here, Justin begins to chip away at both the credibility as well as the historicity of the pagan narratives from §23–30. He undermines their credibility by, of course, exposing the foibles of the gods throughout while attacking the historicity of their accounts, "But what was foretold by these evil demons, myth-making through the poets, spoke as having happened" (*1 Apol.* 23.3). While in the first stage Justin focused on his audience innate reverence of these narratives, in this section Justin exploits their paradoxical *suspicion* of them.

OT Type, "Mythical" Type, and NT Antitype (§23–53)

OT Type		"Poetical" "Mythical" Type		NT Antitype
		"Typological Trajectory"		• "Similar (ad similia) but greater(ad fortiori)
•Worthy of reverence		• Appeals to their suspicion of myth		
• Is historical		• Challenges historicity of stories		• Birth, healing, death, ascension
• Prophesies more than birth, heal-ing, death, & ascension		• Still taking advantage of framework...		•Plus 4 other themes

This is where we witness the emergence of a full-fledged Creed Sequence (§31.7) over and against a Pseudo-Creed Sequence (§21.1f). Justin in the full-fledged Creed Sequence produces nine Messianic themes that are prophesied in the Old Testament regarding the Christ. The Pseudo-Creed Sequence only contains about half of those, a significant deficiency that further proves that myths are of inferior quality when compared to that of Moses and the Prophets.

Because of this, there is impulse within Justin's biblical exposition with respect to the full Creed Sequence (§30–53) to have his reader migrate their trust from the religious pagan texts (e.g., Homer) and to begin placing it within the Christian Scriptures. Justin is incessant in demonstrating how the prophecies in Moses and the Prophets were fulfilled in Christ emphasizing a historical dimension to this faith. In chapter 2, I argued how Justin's typological framework was consistent with Northrop Frye's definition of typology: an antitype that is grounded in history is informed by a corresponding type also deemed as being historical (pp. 45–46). In the previous stage (i.e., myth as "poetical type"), Justin does not undermine the historicity of the myths right away and hence they function as a legitimate type for his reader. At this stage though, the historicity of myth is now brought into question (thereby undermining it as a legitimate type) and now is being applied to Moses and the Prophets.

Despite this conversion process that Justin is attempting to broker, the "mythical type" still possesses for him a beneficial function at this stage of *1 Apology*. This is because the details he supplies through the Old Testament fulfillment passages regarding Christ's extraordinary birth, prodigious service to humanity (i.e., healing ministry), death, and ascension to heaven can now be compared and contrasted with the narrative elements of the popular stories regarding the sons of Zeus. This interaction, in fact, is a form of subtle incorporation of myth still at work.

The typological trajectory that the Old Testament fulfillment passages generates allows us, as the modern reader, to mine legitimate resonances from these respective myths that the ancient reader may have picked up— even those narrative elements that Justin left silent when alluding to them. This is based on the phenomenon that although Justin briefly mentions a certain myth, the entire story would have emerged in the forefront of his reader's memory. Therefore, being mindful of this typological trajectory is important as it keeps the modern reader honest by selecting those silent narratival elements that reasonably conform to the typological trajectory.

Myth as a false antitype (§54–66)

At this stage of *1 Apology*, the goal of Justin is to have his reader dispense of any sort of dependency upon myth altogether. Justin commences a similar roll call of the sons of Zeus that he performed back in §21–22, but this time goes at great lengths to demonstrate the diabolical origin behind these pagan narratives. With a complete movement of separation of myth in mind, he no longer views myth as any sort of viable type. Instead, he exposes them now as "false antitypes" or Pseudo-Christian narratives meant to impede one from making the proper connection between Old Testament type and New Testament antitype. Thereby, he places a heavy emphasis on revealing the discontinuity between myth and the NT Antitype (Figure 6.4).

OT Type, False Antitype, and NT Antitype (§54–66)

OT Type	Bypass	"Poetical" "Mythical" False Type Antitype	"Typological Trajectory"	NT Antitype
•This sacred text should supplant the "Greek bible" (i.e., Homer)		• He exposes demonic origin and purpose • Considered a pernicious Pseudo-Creed…must be bypassed		• Emphasizes complete discontinuity with myth • Typological trajectory strictly between OT type and NT antitype

At first glance, it would be appear that Justin is beckoning his Gentile reader to abandon their revered ancient narratives of their ancestral religions (their myths) for this new emergent one in Christianity. But Justin would have not viewed it that way. Rather he was asking them actually take on the more ancient or original, (i.e., Moses and the Prophets) in place of the more recent or the imitation (i.e., Homer). This is where viewing myth as a false antitype can help us understand Justin's scheme here as he wants to show how myth acts as demonic "interference" between the OT type and NT antitype.

Justin, in fact, shared this sentiment as it related to the philosophers. J.C.M. Van Winden points out that the apologist did not view Christianity as a philosophy in continuity with previous Greek philosophical traditions. Rather, Justin understood his Christian philosophy as the re-emergence of a lost primordial philosophy that all the Greek schools based their existence and hence splintered off and fragmented from the original primordial philosophy.[2] So, too, do the myths fragment the Christian story by providing multiple ones that seek to dilute the significance of the original such as in the case with the deaths of the sons of Zeus (i.e., Heracles, Dionysus, and Asclepius) to compete with the story of Christ's Passion.

Therefore, Justin admonishes his reader to "bypass" (Figure 6.4) this false antitype altogether allowing the typological trajectory to flow freely between the Old Testament type and the New Testament antitype. This completes our overview of Justin's appropriation of myth through the three stages of poetic type, mythical type, and false antitype.

2. Van Winden, *An Early Christian Philosopher*, 43.

IMPACT THIS STUDY HAS ON OTHER AREAS OF JUSTIN MARTYR SCHOLARSHIP

One of the traditional criticisms of *1 Apology* is that Justin's arrangement of material is highly unorganized.[3] A good example of this critique can be found in Alfred Blunt's critical edition in which he opines, "In these [Apologies] Justin gives no formal or logical exposition, scarcely even an outline . . . his reasoning is sometimes rambling and fanciful, abounding in digressions, repetitions, and parentheses, which confuse the argument."[4] Minns and Parvis have sought to temper this universal censure by arguing that the text before us has been altered since the original, "It is highly probable that the text as we have it contains later glosses, and accidental transpositions of material."[5]

Before beginning this study myself, I was of the same opinion that *1 Apology* was difficult to traverse due to a lack of organization on the apologist's part. Even one of the main interlocutors I had to deal with right away regarding Justin's use of myth (i.e., Carlos Contreras) dismissed the apologists curious interaction with myth as nothing more than a result of his rambling prose. But as I began to track the flow of Justin's use of myth throughout *1 Apology*, a discernible pattern began to emerge.

Throughout the text there was an ebb and flow of incorporation of myth and separation of myth at work (Table 1.1). In §1–21, we observed a movement of mainly incorporation of myth with some partial separation of myth; in §22–29 a movement of separation of myth; in §30–53 back to a movement of incorporation of myth with partial separation of myth; and in §54–56 a decisive separation from myth altogether.

How is this weaving back and forth between incorporation of myth and separation of myth significant? One of the additional critiques provided by Blunt was that Justin "struggles to prove the claims of Christ, especially by the argument from the fulfillment of prophecy."[6] This would certainly be the case if one handled §30–53 in isolation, especially in light of the fact that the apologist was writing to a Gentile audience. But when one treats this section in light of §20–21 where Justin's exposition of the Pseudo-Creed sequence actually *prepared* his reader to handle §30–53 by introducing the first four themes of full Creed-Sequence in terms of the θεῖος ἀνήρ, what Justin was trying to do should not be considered overambitious.

3. Cf. Geffeken, *Zwei griechische Apologeten*, 97–98; Bousset, *Jüdisch-Christlicher Schulbetreib in Alexandrien und Rom*, 300–303.

4. Blunt, *The Apologies of Justin Martyr*, xi.

5. *Justin, Philosopher and Martyr*, 46.

6. Blunt, *The Apologies of Justin Martyr*, xi.

Justin was quick to point out how the demons crafted myth as subterfuge to confuse future generations from fully apprehending the message of Christ. It would be ironic if the apologist's own pattern of using myth in *1 Apology* ended up serving as the organizing principle that helped us grasp his message more fully.

Bibliography

PRIMARY SOURCES

Aelian. *Historical Miscellany*. Translated by Nigel G. Wilson. LCL 486. Cambridge, MA: Harvard University Press, 1997.

Antoninus Liberalis. *The Metamorphoses of Antoninus Liberalis: A Translation with Commentary*. Translated by Francis Celoria. New York: Routledge, 1992.

Apollodorus. *The Library*. Translated by James George Frazer. 2 vols. LCL 121–122. Cambridge, MA: Harvard University Press, 1921.

Callimachus. *Callimachus and Lycophron*. Translated by A. W. Mair and G. R. Mair. LCL 129. London: Heinemann, 1921.

Clement of Alexandria. *The Exhortation to the Greeks, The Rich Man's Salvation*, and *To the Newly Baptized (fragment)*. Translated by G. W. Butterworth. LCL 92. Cambridge, MA: Harvard University Press, 1953.

Diodorus Siculus. *Library of History*. Translated by C. H. Oldfather. 12 vols. LCL 279, 303, 340, 375, 384, 399, 389, 422, 377, 390, 409, and 423. Cambridge, MA: Harvard University Press, 1933.

Euripides, *The Tragedies of Euripides*. Translated and edited by T. A. Buckley. London: Bohn, 1874.

"1 Enoch." In *The Apocryphal Old Testament*, edited and translated by H. F. D. Sparks, 169–320. New York: Oxford University Press, 1984.

Hesiod. *The Homeric Hymns and Homerica*. Translated and edited by H. G. Evelyn-White. LCL 57. Cambridge, MA: Harvard University Press, 1982.

———. *Theogony, Works and Days, and Testimonia*. Translated by Glen W. Most. LCL 503. Cambridge, MA: Harvard University Press, 2006.

Homer. *Illiad*. Translated by A. T. Murray. 2 vols. LCL 170–171. Cambridge, MA: Harvard University Press, 1960.

———. *Odyssey*. Translated by A. T. Murray and rev. George E. Dimock. 2 vols. LCL 104–105. Cambridge, MA: Harvard University Press, 1995.

Hyginus. *The Myths of Hyginus*. Translated and edited by Mary Grant. University of Kansas Publications in Humanistic Studies 34. Lawrence: University of Kansas Press, 1960.

Irenaeus. *Against the Heresies*. Translated and edited by Dominic Unger and John Dillon. Vol. 1. New York: Paulist, 1992.

Bibliography

Justin Martyr. *Iustini Martyris Dialogus Cum Tryphone*. Edited by Miroslav Marcovich. New York: de Gruyter, 1997.

————. *Justin, Philosopher and Martyr: Apologies*. Translated and edited by Denis Minns and Paul Parvis. New York: Oxford University Press, 2009.

————. *The Martyrdom of the Holy Martyrs*. In *The Ante-Nicene Fathers: Translations of the Writings of the Father down to A.D. 325.*, translated by Marcus Dods and edited by Alexander Roberts and James Donaldson. 1:305–6. Edinburgh: T. & T. Clark, 1867.

Menander. *The Plays and Fragments*. Translated by Maurice Balme and intro. Peter Brown. New York: Oxford University Press, 2002.

Nonnus. *Dionysiaca*. Translated by W. H. D. Rouse. 3 vols. LCL 344, 354, and 356. Cambridge, MA: Harvard University Press, 1940

————. *Metamorphoses*. Translated by Frank Justus Miller. 2 vols. LCL 42–43. Cambridge, MA: Harvard University Press, 1984.

Pausanias. *Description of Greece*. Translated by W. H. S. Jones, and H. A. Omerod. 5 vols. LCL 93, 188, 272, 297, and 298. Cambridge, MA: Harvard University Press, 1954.

Philostratus. *Imagines*. Translated by Arthur Fairbanks. LCL 256. London: Heinemann, 1931.

Photius. *Bibliotheca: Tome III [Codices 186–222]*. Translated by René Henry. Paris: Société d'édition Les Belles lettres, 1962.

Pindar. *Selected Odes: Olympian One, Pythian Nine, Nemeans Two & Three, Isthmian One*. Translated and edited by Stephen Instone. Warminster: Aris & Phillips, 1996.

Pindar. *Olympic Odes and Pythian Odes*. Translated and edited by William H. Race. 2 vols. LCL 56 and 485. Cambridge, MA: Harvard University Press, 1997.

Plato. *Euthyphro, Apology, Crito, Phaedo, Phaedrus*. Translated by Harold North Fowler and introduced by W. R. M. Lamb. LCL 36. Cambridge, MA: Harvard University Press, 1990.

————. *Laws*. Translated by R. G. Bury. 2 vols. LCL 187 and 192. New York: Putnam,1926.

————. *Lysis, Symposium, Gorgias*. Translated by W. R. M. Lamb. LCL 166. Cambridge, MA: Harvard University Press, 1939.

Pseudo-Clement. *Recognitions*. In *The Ante-Nicene Fathers: Translations of the Writings of the Fathers down to A.D. 325*, translated by Thomas Smith and edited by Alexander Roberts and James Donaldson, 8:73–210. Edinburgh: T. & T. Clark, 1867.

Statius. *Silvae*. Edited and translated by D.R. Shackleton Bailey. LCL 206. Cambridge, MA.: Harvard University Press, 2003.

Strabo. *Geography*. Translated by Horace Leonard Jones and John Robert Sitlington Sterrett. 8 vols. LCL 49, 50, 182, 196, 211, 223, 241, and 267. Cambridge, MA: Harvard University Press, 1982.

Suetonius. *The Lives of the Caesars: Julius. Augustus, Tiberius, Gaius, Caligula*. Translated by J. C. Rolfe. LCL 31. Cambridge, MA: Harvard University Press, 1928.

SECONDARY SOURCES

Achtemeier, Paul J. "Gospel Miracle Tradition and the Divine Man." *Interpretation* 26 (1972) 174–97.

Aland, Kurt. *Über den Glaubenswechsel in der Geschichte des Christentums.* Berlin: Töpelmann, 1961.

Aldama, José Antonio de. "El Espíritu Santo y el Verbo en la exégesis de Lc 1, 35." In *María en la patrística de los siglos I y II.* Madrid: BAC, 1970.

Alexandre, Monique. "Apologétique judéo-hellénistique et premiéres apologies chrétiennes." In *Les apologistes chrétiens et la culture grecque,* edited by Bernard Pouderon and Joseph Doré, 1–40. Paris: Beauchesne, 1998.

Amann. Emile. "Simon le Magicien." In *Dictionnaire de théologie catholique,* edited by Alfred Vacant, Eugène Mangenot, and Emile Amann, 2130–39. Paris: Letouzey & Ané, 903–50.

Andresen, Carl. *Logos und Nomos: die Polemik des Kelsos wider das Christentum.* Berlin: de Gruyter, 1955.

Armstrong, Arthur. "Pagan and Christian Traditionalism in the First Three Centuries." *Studia Patristica* 15 (1975) 414–31.

Atsma, Aaron. *The Theoi Project: Greek Mythology.* Online: http://www.theoi.com.

Aubé, Benjamin. *Saint Justin, philosophe et martyr: etude critique sur l'apologétique chrétienne au IIe siècle.* Paris: Thorin, 1875.

Aune, David E. "Heracles and Christ: Heracles Imagery in the Christology of Early Christianity." In *Greeks, Romans, and Christians: Essays in Honor of Abraham J. Malherbe,* edited by David L. Balch, Everett Ferguson, and Wayne A. Meeks, 3–19. Minneapolis: Fortress, 1990.

———. "Justin Martyr's Use of the Old Testament." *Bulletin of the Evangelical Theological Society* 9 (1966) 179–97.

Baldwin, Barry. "Vergilius Graecus." *The American Journal of Philology* 97 (1976) 361–368.

Barnard, Leslie W. *The First and Second Apologies.* New York: Paulist, 1997.

———. *Justin Martyr: His Life and Thought.* Cambridge: Cambridge University Press, 1967.

———. "The Old Testament and Judaism in the Writings of Justin Martyr." *Vetus Testamentum* 14 (1964) 395–406.

Barthes, Roland. *Mythologies.* Translated by Annette Lavers. New York: Hill & Wang, 1972.

Bauckham, Richard. "The Fall of the Angels as the Source of Philosophy in Hermias and Clement of Alexandria." *Vigiliae Christianae* 39 (1985) 313–30.

Bergjan, Silke-Petra. "How to Speak about early Christian apologetic literature? Comments on the Recent Debate." *Studia Patristica* 36 (2001) 177–83.

Berkhof, Louis. *Systematic Theology.* Carlisle, PA: Banner of Truth Trust, 2003.

Bisbee, Gary. "The Acts of Justin Martyr: A Form-Critical Study." *Second Century* 3 (1983) 129–57.

Blunt, Alfred. *The Apologies of Justin Martyr.* Cambridge: Cambridge University Press, 1911.

Bonz, Marianne Palmer. *The Past as Legacy: Luke-Acts and Ancient Epic.* Minneapolis: Fortress, 2000.

Bibliography

Bourgeois, Daniel. *La sagesse des anciens dans le mystère du verbe: évangile et philosophie chez saint Justin, philosophe et martyr*. Paris: Téqui, 1981.

Bowden, Hugh. *Mystery Cults of the Ancient World*. Oxford: Princeton University Press, 2010.

Boys-Stones, George. *Post-Hellenistic Philosophy: A Study of its Development from the Stoics to Origen*. New York: Oxford University Press, 2001.

Bray, Gerald L. "Explaining Christianity to Pagans: The Second-Century Apologists." In *Trinity in a Pluralistic Age*, edited by Kevin Van Hoozer, 9–25. Grand Rapids: Eerdmans, 1997.

Brisson, Luc. *How Philosophers Saved Myths*. Chicago: University of Chicago Press, 2004.

Brown, David. *Tradition and Imagination: Revelation and Change*. New York: Oxford University Press, 1999.

Brown, Peter. "Aspects of the Christianization of the Roman Aristocracy." *Journal of Roman Studies* 51 (1961) 1–11.

Buck, Lorraine. "Athenagoras's Embassy: A Literary Fiction." *Harvard Theological Review* 89 (1996) 209–26.

———. "Justin Martyr's *Apologies*: Their Number, Destination, and Form." *Journal of Theological Studies*, NS 54 (2003) 45–59.

———. "Second Century Greek Christian Apologies Addressed to Emperors: Their Form and Function." PhD diss., University of Ottawa, 1998.

Bucur, Bogdan. "The Angelic Spirit in Early Christianity: Justin, the Martyr and Philosopher." *Journal of Religion* 88 (2008) 195–96.

Bullock, Karen. *The Writings of Justin Martyr*. Nashville: Broadman & Holman, 1998.

Campbell, Joseph. *The Masks of God: Creative Mythology*. New York: Viking, 1970.

Carena, Maria. "La critica della mitologia pagana negli Apologeti greci dei II secolo." *Didaskaleion* 1/2–3 (1923) 23–55.

Chadwick, Henry. *Early Christian Thought and the Classical Tradition: Studies in Justin, Clement, and Origen*. New York: Oxford University Press, 1966.

———. "The Gospel a Republication of Natural Religion in Justin Martyr." *Illinois Classical Studies* 18 (1993) 237–47.

———. "Justin Martyr's Defence of Christianity." *Bulletin of the John Rylands Library* 47 (1965) 275–97.

Ciholas, Paul. *The Omphalos and the Cross: Pagans and Christians in Search of a Divine Center*. Macon, GA: Mercer University Press, 2003.

Contreras, Carlos A. "Christian Views of Paganism." *Aufstieg und Niedergang der römischen Welt* 23 (1980) 974–1022.

Daniélou, Jean. *From Shadows to Reality: Studies in Biblical Typology of the Fathers*. Translated by Wulstan Hibberd. London: Burns & Oates, 1960.

———. *Gospel Message and Hellenistic Culture*. Translated and edited by John Austin Baker. Philadelphia: Westminster, 1973.

Davids, Adelbert. *Iustinus philosophus et martyr: Bibliographie 1923–1973*. Nijmegen: Katholieke Universiteit Nijmegen, Faculteit der Godgeleerdheid, 1983.

———. "Justin Martyr on Monotheism and Heresy." *Nederlands archief voor kerkgeschiednis* 56 (1975–1976) 210–234.

Day, Malcolm. *100 Characters from Classical Mythology*. Hauppauge, NY: Barron's Educational Series, 2007.

Dickerson, Matthew and David O'Hara. *From Homer to Harry Potter.* Grand Rapids: Brazos, 2006.

Dillon, John. "Ganymede as the Logos: Traces of a Forgotten Allegorization in Philo?" *Classical Quarterly* 31 (1983) 183–85.

Dillon, Matthew. *Girls and Women in Classical Greek Religion.* New York: Routledge, 2002.

Dixon-Kennedy, Mike. "Core." In *Encyclopedia of Greco-Roman Mythology*, edited by Mike Dixon-Kennedy, 91. Santa Barbara, CA: ABC-CLIO, 1998.

Dölger, F.J. "Christus und 'der Heiler' Asklepios bei Justinus." *Antike und Christentum* 6 (1956) 241–48.

Droge, Arthur J. *Homer or Moses? Early Christian Interpretations of the History of Culture.* Tübingen: Mohr, 1989.

Edsman, Carl-Martin. *Ignis Divinus; Le Feu Comme Moyen De Rajeunissement Et D'immortalité: Contes, Légendes, Mythes Et Rites.* Lund: Gleerup, 1949.

Edwards, Mark. "Introduction: Apologetics in the Roman World." In *Apologetics in the Roman Empire: Pagans, Jews, and Christians*, edited by Mark Edwards, Martin Goodman, and Simon Price, 1–14. New York: Oxford University Press, 1999.

———. "On the Platonic schooling of Justin Martyr." *Journal of Theological Studies* 42 (1991) 17–34.

Eliade, Mircea. *Patterns in Comparative Religion.* Translated by Rosemary Sheed. Lincoln: University of Nebraska Press, 1996.

Erhardt, A. "Justin Martyr's Two Apologies." *Journal of Ecclesiastical History* 4 (1953) 1–12.

Evslin, Bernard. *Heroes, Gods, and Monsters of the Greek Myths.* New York: Laurel Leaf, 2005.

Fédou, Michel. "La figure de Socrate selon Justin." In *Apologistes chrétiens et la culture grecque*, 51–66. Paris: Beauchesne, 1998.

———. "La vision de la croix dans l'oeuvre de saint Justin 'philosophe et martyr.'" *Recherches augustiniennes* 19 (1984) 29–110.

Fedrowicz, Michael. *Apologie Im Frühen Christentum: Die Kontroverse Um Den Christlichen Wahrheitsanspruch In Den Ersten* Jahrhunderten. Paderborn: Schöningh, 2000.

Feeney, Denis. *The Gods in Epic.* Oxford: Clarendon, 1991.

———. *Roman Literature and Its Contexts: Cultures, Contexts, and Beliefs.* Cambridge University Press, 1998.

Ferguson, Everett. *Backgrounds of Early Christianity.* 3rd ed. Grand Rapids: Eerdmans, 2003.

———. *Church History.* Grand Rapids: Zondervan, 2006.

———. *Demonology of the Early Christian World.* New York: Mellen, 1989.

———. *The Early Church and Greco-Roman Thought.* New York: Garland, 1993.

Finan, Thomas. "The Myth of the Innocent Sufferer: Some Greek Paradigms." *Proceedings of the Irish Biblical Association* 9 (1985) 121–35

Fishbane, Michael A. *Biblical Interpretation in Ancient Israel.* New York: Oxford University Press, 1985.

Flinterman, Jaap-Jan. "The Ubiquitous 'Divine Man.'" *Numen* 43 (1996) 82–98.

Fox, Robin Lane. *Pagans and Christians.* New York: Knopf, 1987.

Frend, W. H. C. *The Rise of Christianity.* Philadelphia: Fortress , 1984.

Bibliography

Frye, Northrop. *The Great Code: The Bible and Literature*. New York: Harcourt Brace Jovanovich, 1982.

Gamble, Harry. *Books and Readers in the Early Church: A History of Early Christian Texts*. New Haven: Yale University Press, 1995.

Garrison, Roman. *Why are You Silent, Lord?* Biblical Seminar 68. Sheffield: Sheffield Academic, 2000.

George, Timothy. "The Pattern of Christian Truth." *First Things* 154 (2005) 21–25.

George, Timothy, and David Dockery. *The Great Tradition of Christian Thinking: A Student's Guide*. Wheaton, IL: Crossway, 2012.

Gibbon, Edward. *History of the Fall and Decline of the Roman Empire*. Edited by William Smith. Vol 1. London: Murray, 1854.

Glockmann, Günter. "Homer in der christenlichen Apologetik des II. Jahrhunderte." *Orpheus* 14 (1967) 33–40.

———. *Homer in der frühchristlichen Literatur bis Justinus*. Berlin: Akademie, 1968.

Goodenough, Erwin R. *The Theology of Justin Martyr*. Amsterdam: Philo, 1968.

Goodspeed, Edgar J. *Index apologeticus sive Clavis Iustini Martyris operum aliorumque apologetarum pristinorum*. Leipzig: Hinrichs, 1912.

Gougel, Maurice. *The Eucharist: From the Beginning to the time of Justin Martyr*. Paris: Fischbacher, 1910.

Granados, José. *Los misterios de la vida de Cristo en Justino Mártir*. Roma: Pontificia Università gregoriana, 2005.

Grant, Robert M. "Forms and Occasions of the Greek Apologists." *Studi e materiali di storia delle religioni* 52 (1986) 213–226.

———. *Gods and the One God*. Philadelphia: Westminster, 1986.

———. *Greek Apologists of the Second Century*. Philadelphia: Westminster, 1988.

———. *The Letter and the Spirit*. Eugene, OR: Wipf & Stock, 2009.

Gruen, Erich S. *Rethinking the Other in Antiquity*. Princeton: Princeton University Press, 2011.

Guerra, Anthony J. "The Conversion of Marcus Aurelius and Justin Martyr: The Purpose, Genre, and Content of the First Apology." *Second Century* 9, no. 3 (1992) 171–87.

Guinot, Jean-Noël. "Muthos et récit bibliue chez Origène: Un danger d'ambiguïté?" In *Origeniana Nona*, edited by G. Heidl and R. Somos, 179–194. Leuven: Peeters, 2009.

Hacker, Paul. "Religions of the Gentiles as viewed by Fathers of the Church." *Zeitschrift für Missionswissenschaft und Religionswissenschaft* 54 (1970) 253–78.

Haddad, Robert Michael. "The Appropriateness of the Apologetical Arguments of Justin Martyr." Master's thesis, Australian Catholic University, 2008.

Hamman, Adalbert G. "Dialogue entre le christianisme et la culture grecque, de origines chrétiennes á Justin: genése et étapes." In *Les apologistes chrétiens et la culture grecque*, edited by Bernard Pouderon and Joseph Doré, 41–50. Paris: Beauchesne, 1998.

Harris, Rendel. *The Cult of the Heavenly Twins*. Cambridge: Cambridge University Press, 1906.

———. *Justin Martyr and Menander*. Cambridge: Heffer & Sons, 1932.

Hatch, Edwin. *The Influence of Greek Ideas on Christianity*. New York: Harper, 1957.

Hinds, Stephen. *Allusion and Intertext: Dynamics of Appropriation in Roman Poetry*. New York: Cambridge University Press, 1998.

Holfelder, Hans Hermann. "Eusebeia kai philosophia: literarische Einheit und politischer Kontext von Justins Apologie, 1." *Zeitschrift für die neutestamentliche Wissenschaft und die Kunde der älteren Kirche* 68 (1977) 48–66.

Holte, Ragnar. "Logos Spermatikos: Christianity and Ancient Philosophy according to St. Justin's Apologies." *Studia Theologica* 12 (1958) 109–68.

Hubbard, Moyer V. *Christianity in the Greco-Roman World*. Grand Rapids: Baker Academic, 2010.

Hulst, Cornelia. *Homer and the Prophets or Homer and Now*. Chicago: Open Court, 1925.

Jaeger, Werner Wilhelm. *Early Christianity and Greek Paideia*. Cambridge, MA: Belknap, 1961.

James, Alan. "The Limitation of the Gods in the *Iliad*." In *Religion in the Ancient World*, edited by Matthew Dillon, 217–227. Amsterdam: Hakkert, 1996.

Joly, Robert. "Parallèles païens pour Justin, *Apol.* I, 19." In *Hellenica et Judaica: Hommage à Valentin Nikiprowetzky*, edited by A. Caquot, M. Hadas-Lebel, and J. Riaud, 473–481. Leuven: Peeters, 1986.

Kannaday, Wayne. *Apologetic Discourse and the Scribal Tradition*. Atlanta: SBL, 2003.

Keith, Graham A. "Justin Martyr and Religious Exclusivism." *Tyndale Bulletin* 43 (1992) 57–80.

Kelly, Henry Ansgar. *The Devil, Demonology, and Witchcraft: The Development of Christian Beliefs in Evil Spirit*. Garden City, NY: Doubleday, 1974.

Keresztes, Paul. "The Literary Genre of Justin's First Apology." *Vigiliae Christianae* 19 (1965) 99–110.

King, Karen. *What is Gnosticism?* Cambridge, MA: Belknap, 2003.

Kinsig, Wolfram. "Der Sitz im Leben der Apologie in der Alten Kirche." *Zeitschrift für Kirchengeschichte* 100 (1989) 291–317.

Knox, Wilfred. "The 'Divine Hero' Christology in the New Testament." *Harvard Theological Review* 41 (1948) 229–49.

———. "The Divine Wisdom." *Journal of Theological Studies* 38 (1937) 230–237.

Labriolle, Pierre. *La Réaction Païenne; étude Sur La Polémique Antichrétienne Du Ier Au VIe Siècle*. Paris: L'Artisan du livre, 1948.

Lamberton, Robert. *Homer the Theologian: Neoplatonist Allegorical Reading and the Growth of the Epic Tradition*. Berkeley: University of California Press, 1986.

Lampe, G. W. H. "The Reasonableness of Typology." In *Essays on Typology*, 9–38. London: SCM, 1957.

Lampe, Peter. *From Paul to Valentinus: Christians at Rome in the First Two Centuries*. Translated by Michael Steinhauser. Minneapolis: Fortress, 2003.

Lamson, Alvan. *The Church of the First Three Centuries*. London: British and Foreign Unitarian Association, 1875.

Lanata, Giuliana. *Poetica Pre-Platonica: Testimonianze e Framementi*. Firenze: La Nuova Italia Editrice, 1963.

Leithart, Peter J. *Heroes of the City of Man: A Christian Guide to Select Ancient Literature*. Moscow, ID: Canon, 1999.

Lenz, Friedrich "Der Athenahymnos des Aristides." *Rivista di Cultura Classica e Mediaevale* 5 (1963) 329–47.

Lewis, C. S. "Myth Became Fact." In *God in the Dock*, edited by Walter Hooper, 63–67. Grand Rapids: Eerdmans, 1970.

Löhr, Winrich A. "The Theft of the Greeks: Christian Self Definition in the Age of the Schools." *Revue d'histoire ecclésiastique* 95, no. 3 (2000) 403–26.

Loos, Hendrik van der. *The Miracles of Jesus.* Translated by T. S. Preston. Leiden: Brill, 1965.

Luhumbu Shodu, Emmanuel. *La mémoire des origines chrétiennes selon Justin Martyr.* Fribourg: Academic, 2008.

MacDonald, Dennis R. *Does the New Testament Imitate Homer? Four Cases from the Acts of the Apostles.* New Haven: Yale University Press, 2003.

Machen, J. Gresham. *The Virgin Birth of Christ.* New York: Harper & Brothers, 1930.

MacMullen, Ramsay. *Changes in the Roman Empire: Essays in the Ordinary.* Princeton: Princeton University Press, 1990.

———. *Christianizing the Roman Empire.* New Haven: Yale University Press, 1984.

———. *Paganism in the Roman Empire.* New Haven: Yale University Press, 1981.

———. "Two Types of Conversion to Early Christianity." *Vigiliae Christianae* 37 (1983) 174–92.

Macpherson, Jay. *Four Ages of Man: The Classical Myths.* Toronto: Macmillan, 1962.

Malherbe, Abraham J. "Athenagoras on the Pagan Poets and Philosophers." In *Kyriakon: Festschrift Johannes Quasten,* edited by Patrick Granfield and Josef A. Jungmann, 214–225. Münster: Aschendorff, 1970.

———. "Towards Understanding the Apologists: A Review Article." *Restoration Quarterly* 11 (1968) 215–24.

Manguel, Alberto. *Homer's the Illiad and the Odyssey: A Biography.* New York: Atlantic Monthly, 2007.

Manser, Martin H. *The Facts of File Dictionary of Classical and Biblical Allusions.* New York: Facts On File, 2003.

Markos, Louis. *From Achilles to Christ: Why Christians Should Read the Pagan Classics.* Downers Grove, IL: IVP Academic, 2007.

Marshall, I.H. "Palestinian and Hellenistic Christianity: Some Critical Comments." *New Testament Studies* 19 (1972–73) 271–287.

Martens, Peter. "Revisiting the Allegory/Typology Distinction: The Case of Origen." *Journal of Early Christian Studies* 16 (2008) 283–317.

Martín, José Pablo. *El Espíritu Santo en los orígenes del Cristianismo: Estudio sobre I Clemente, Ignacio, II Clemente y Justino Martir.* Zurich: PAS, 1971.

Martindale, C.C. *St. Justin the Martyr.* London: Harding & More, 1921.

McDermott, Gerald *God's Rivals: Why Has God Allowed Different Religions?* Downer's Grove, IL: InterVarsity, 2007.

McKechnie, Paul. *The First Christian Centuries: Perspectives on the Early Church.* Downers Grove, IL: InterVarsity, 2001.

Meconi, David Vincent. "The Christian Cento and the Early Church's Appropriation of Prophet and Muse." Paper presented at the Medieval and Renaissance Conference, Villanova University, October 10, 2008.

———. "The Christian Cento and the Evangelization of Christian Culture." *Logos* 7 (2004) 109–132.

Millar, Fergus. *The Emperor in the Roman World.* London: Duckworth, 1977.

Miller, Brett A. *The Sacred Art of Verbal Self-Defense: Image Restoration Discourse in Christian Rhetoric.* PhD diss., University of Missouri-Columbia, 1999.

Munier, Charles. *Justin Martyr Apologie pour les chrétiens.* Paris: Cerf, 2006.

Newman, Robert C. "The Ancient Exegesis of Genesis 6:2, 4." *Grace Theological Journal* 5, no. 1 (1984) 13–36.

Nock, A. D. *Conversion: The Old and the New in Religion from Alexander the Great to Augustine of Hippo.* London: Oxford University Press, 1933.

Norris, Richard A. *God and World in Early Christian Theology.* New York: Seabury, 1965.

Osborn, Eric F. *Justin Martyr.* Tübingen: Mohr/Siebeck, 1973.

———. "Justin's Response to Second Century Challenges." *Australian Biblical Review* 14 (1966) 37–54.

Page, Denys. *Poetae melici Graeci.* Oxford: Clarendon, 1962.

Pagels, Elaine. "Christian Apologists and 'The Fall of the Angels': An Attack on Roman Imperial Power?" *Harvard Theological Review* 78 (1985) 301–25.

Parker, Robert. *Polytheism and Society at Athens.* New York: Oxford University Press, 2005.

Parvis, Sara and Paul Foster. *Justin Martyr and His Worlds.* Minneapolis: Fortress, 2007.

Patterson, L. G. *God and History in Early Christian Thought.* New York: Seabury, 1967.

Pépin, Jean. "Le 'challenge' Homère-Moïse aux premiers siècles chrétiens." *Revue des Sciences religieuses* 29 (1955) 105–22.

———. *Mythe et Allégorie: Les Origines Grecques et Les Contestations Judéo-Chrétiennes.* Paris: Aubier, 1958.

Peretti, Aurelio. "Sulla duplice stesura del libro d'Istaspe." *Wiener Studien* 69 (1956) 350–62.

Peterson, Erik. *Theologische Traktate.* Würzburg: Echter, 1994.

Pfister, Friedrich. "Heracles und Christ." *Archiv für Religionswissenschaft* 34 (1937) 42–60.

Pouderon, Bernard. *Les apologistes grecs du IIe siècle.* Paris: Cerf, 2005.

Price, Richard M. "Are There 'Holy Pagans' in Justin Martyr?" *Studia patristica* 31 (1997) 167–71.

———. "'Hellenization' and Logos Doctrine in Justin Martyr." *Vigiliae Christianae* 42 (1988) 18–23.

Prigent, Pierre. *Justin et l'Ancien Testamente.* Paris: Gabalda, 1964.

Pucci, Pietro. *Hesiod and the Language of Poetry.* Baltimore: John Hopkins University Press, 1977.

Purves, George T. *The Testimony of Justin Martyr to Early Christianity.* New York: Randolph, 1889.

Quasten, Johannes. *Patrology.* Vol. 1. Westminster, MD: Spectrum, 1960.

Rahner, Hugo. *Greek Myths and Christian Mystery.* Translated by Brian Battershaw. New York: Harper & Row, 1963.

Rance, Philip. "'Win but do not overwin'—The History of a Proverb from the *Sententiae Menandri*, and a Classical Allusion in St. Paul's Epistle to the Romans." *Philologus* 152 (2008) 191–204.

Reed, Annette Yoshiko. *Fallen Angels and the History of Judaism and Christianity.* New York: Cambridge University Press, 2005.

———. "The Trickery of the Fallen Angels and the Demonic Mimesis of the Divine: Aetiology, Demonology, and Polemics in the Writings of Justin Martyr." *Journal of Early Christian Studies* 12 (2004) 141–71.

Remus, Harold. "'Magic or Miracle'? Some Second Century Instances." *Second Century* 2 (1982) 127–56.

Bibliography

Rhee, Helen. *Early Christian Literature: Christ and Culture in the Second and Third Centuries.* New York: Routledge, 2005.

Richardson, Cyril. *Early Christian Fathers.* New York: Touchstone, 1996.

Ridings, Daniel. *The Attic Moses: The Dependency Theme in Some Early Christian Writers.* Göteborg, Sweden: Acta Universitatis Gothoburgensis, 1995.

Rivière, Jean. *Saint Justin et les apologistes du second siècle avec une introduction de Pierre Batiffol.* Paris: Librairie Bloud, 1907.

Rose, Herbert Jennings. "Herakles and the Gospels." *Harvard Theological Review* 31 (1938) 113–42.

Saldanha, Chrys. *Divine Pedagogy: A Patristic View of Non-Christian Religions.* Rome: LAS, 1984.

Samuel Samdel. "Parallelomania." *Journal of Bibical Studies* 81 (1962) 1–13.

Sanders, Louis. *L'hellénisme De Saint Clément De Rome Et Le Paulinisme.* Louvain: Studia Hellenistica in Bibliotheca Universitatis, 1943.

Sandnes, Karl Olav. *The Challenge of Homer: School, Pagan Poets and Early Christianity.* Library of New Testament Studies 400. New York: T. & T. Clark, 2009.

Schnusenberg, Christine. *The Mythological Traditions of Liturgical Drama: The Eucharist as Theater.* New York: Paulist, 2010.

Schoedel, William. "Apologetic Literature and Ambassadorial Activities." *Harvard Theological Review* 82 (1989) 55–78.

Shotwell, Willis A. *The Biblical Exegesis of Justin Martyr.* London: SPCK, 1965.

Skarsaune, Oskar. "Conversion of Justin Martyr." *Studia theologica* 30 (1976) 53–73.

———. *Incarnation: Myth or Fact?* Translated by Trygve R. Skarsten. St. Louis: Concordia, 1991.

———. "Judaism and Hellenism in Justin Martyr, elucidated from his portrait of Socrates." *Geschichte—Tradition—Reflexion: Festschriften für Martin Hengel zum 70,* edited by Hubert Cancik, Hermann Lichtenberger, and Peter Schäfer, 3:585–611. Tübingen: Mohr/Siebeck, 1996.

———. *The Proof from Prophecy: A Study in Justin Martyr's Proof-Text Tradition: Text-Type, Provenance, Theological Profile.* Leiden: Brill, 1987.

Slusser, Michael. *Dialogue with Trypho.* Washington, DC: Catholic University Press, 2003.

———. "Justin Scholarship: Trends and Trajectories." In *Justin Martyr and His Worlds,* edited by Sara Parvis and Paul Foster, 13–21. Minneapolis: Fortress, 2007.

Smith, William. *Dictionary of Greek and Roman Biography and Mythology.* Vol. 1. London: Paternoster Row, 1850.

Stander, Hendrik F. "Is Justin [Martyr] really a bad stylist?" *Second Century* 5 (1985–1986) 226–32.

Stehlikova, Eva. "Centones Christiani as a Means of Reception." *Listy filologicke* 110 (1987) 11–15.

Story, Cullen I. K. "The Cross as Ultimate in the Writings of Justin Martyr." *Ultimate Reality and Meaning* 21 (1998) 18–34.

Talbert, Charles H. "The Concept of Immortals in Mediterranean Antiquity." *Journal of Biblical Literature* 94 (1975) 419–36.

Taylor, John. *Classics and the Bible: Hospitality and Recognition.* London: Duckworth, 2007.

Tcherikover, Victor. "Jewish Apologetic Literature Reconsidered." *Eos* 48 (1956) 169–93.

Thalmann, William. *Conventions of Form and Thought in Early Greek Epic Poetry.* Baltimore: John Hopkins University Press, 1984.

Thompson, Geoff. "A Question of Posture: Engaging the World with Justin Martyr, George Lindbeck and Hans Frei." *Pacifica-Brunswick East* 13 (2000) 267–87.

Trakatellis, Demetrius C. *The Pre-Existence of Christ in Justin Martyr: An Exegetical Study with Reference to the Humiliation and Exaltation Christology.* Missoula, MT: Scholars, 1976.

Tripolitis, Antonia. *Religions of the Hellenistic-Roman Age.* Grand Rapids: Eerdmans, 2002.

Troxel, A. Craig. "All Things to All People: Justin Martyr's Apologetical Method." *Fides et historia* 27 (1995) 23–43.

Van Winden, J. C. M. *An Early Christian Philosopher: Justin Martyr's Dialogue with Trypho Chapters One to Nine.* Leiden: Brill, 1971.

VanderKam, James C. "1 Enoch, Enochic Motifs, and Enoch in Early Christian Literature." In *The Jewish Apocalyptic Heritage in Early Christianity,* edited by James C. VanderKam and William Adler, 33–101. Minneapolis: Fortress, 1996.

Veyne, Paul. *Did the Greeks believe in their Myths? An Essay on the Constitutive Imagination.* Translated by Paula Wissing. Chicago: University of Chicago Press, 1988.

Wagner, Walter. *Christianity in the Second Century—After the Apostles.* Minneapolis: Fortress, 1994.

Walsh, George. *The Varieties of Enchantment: Early Greek Views of the Nature and Function of Poetry.* Chapel Hill: University of North Carolina Press, 1984.

Wartelle, André. *Apologies.* Paris: Études augustiniennes, 1987.

————. *Bibliographie historique et critique de saint Justin, philosophe et martyr, et des apologistes grecs du IIe siècle, 1494–1994 (avec un supplément).* Paris: Lanore, 2001.

Weil, Simone. *Intimations of Christianity among the Ancient Greeks.* New York: Ark, 1987.

Wey, Heinrich. *Die Funktionen der bösen Geister bei den griechischen Apologeten des zweiten Jahrhunderts nach Christus.* Winterthur, Switzerland: Keller, 1957.

Wickham, Lionel R. "The Sons of God and the Daughters of Men: Genesis VI 2 in Early Christian Exegesis." *Oudtestamentische Studiën* 19 (1974) 135–47.

Widdicombe, Peter. "Justin Martyr, Allegorical Interpretation, and the Greek Myths." *Studia patristica* 31 (1997) 234–39.

Wilde, Wallace Stephen. "The Christian Attitude toward Rome during the Era of Justin, St., Martyr." Master's thesis, Washington University, 1948.

Wilken, Robert L. *The Christians as the Romans Saw Them.* New Haven: Yale, 1984.

————. "The Homeric Cento in Irenaeus, 'Adversus Haereses' I, 9,4." *Vigiliae Christianae* 21 (1967) 25–33.

————. "Toward a Social Interpretation of Early Christian Apologetics." *Church History* 39 (1970) 437–58.

Wolters, Albert M. "Christianity and the Classics: A Typology of Attitudes." In *Christianity and the Classics: The Acceptance of a Heritage,* edited by Wendy E. Helleman, 187–203. New York: University Press of America.

Woollcombe, K. J. "The Biblical Origins and Patristic Development of Typology." In *Essays on Typology,* 39–75. London: SCM, 1957.

Wright, David F. "Christian Faith in the Greek World: Justin Martyr's Testimony." *Evangelical Quarterly* 54 (1982) 77–87.

Young, Frances. *Biblical Exegesis and the Formation of Christian Culture*. New York: Cambridge University Press, 1997.

————. "Greek Apologists of the Second Century." In *Apologetics in the Roman Empire: Pagans, Jews, and Christians*, edited by Mark Edwards, Martin Goodman, and Simon Price, 81–104. New York: Oxford University Press, 1999.

————. "Two Roots of a Tangled Mass?" In *The Myth of God Incarnate*, edited by John Hick, 87–121. Philadelphia: Westminster, 1977.

Zeegers-vander Vorst, Nicole. *Les citations des poètes grecs chez les apologistes chrétiens du IIe siècle*. Louvain: Bibliothèque de l'Université, Bureau du Recueil, 1972.

Ziegler, Heinrich. *Irenaeus der Bischof von Lyon*. Berlin: Reimer, 1871.